ANNUAL recipes 2010

FOUR CHEESE
MAC & CHEESE
WITH BACON,
PAGE 246

Meredith® Consumer Marketing
Des Moines, Iowa

BLACK FOREST ICEBOX
PUDDING, PAGE 195

WELCOME TO A YEAR'S WORTH OF FABULOUS *FAMILY CIRCLE*® RECIPES!

Whatever the details of our daily lives—our family situations, work or community responsibilities—we all have in common the need to eat. Every day, we have to fuel up—and on special days, food is an integral part of celebrating. When you have a dinner party, it becomes the reason for getting together with friends. With all of the cooking and eating we do in a year, a little inspiration is certainly in order.

That's where *Family Circle Annual Recipes 2010* comes in. This book provides a wealth of fresh ideas and recipes—all of which appeared on the pages of *Family Circle* throughout 2010—so it's easy to find just the right recipe for the occasion. Whether it's a fast, family-friendly and healthy meal or an impressive sit-down dinner, you'll find it in this one volume.

When it's too hot to cook, sample some of the 25 fresh and hearty salad suppers that start on page 122. Bake a rich, decadent chocolate Blackout Cake for Valentine's Day (page 41) or pull a bubbling casserole from the oven to get everyone to the table in no time (see "The Family Dish" on page 54).

We know all too well that weeknights present the biggest cooking challenge. That's why we've focused on fast, simple and budget-minded ways to help you get delicious, nutritious food on your table any night of the week. In addition to the seasonally oriented food stories that appear each month, two regular features—Healthy Family Dinners and Slow Cooker Suppers—do just that.

We also know that cooking for family and friends isn't just about putting food on the table. It's about being together around the table. See you there!

Linda

Linda Fears, Editor in Chief
Family Circle® magazine

Family Circle® Annual Recipes 2010

Meredith® Corporation Consumer Marketing
Vice President, Consumer Marketing: David Ball
Consumer Product Marketing Director: Steve Swanson
Consumer Marketing Product Manager: Wendy Merical
Business Director: Ron Clingman
Associate Director, Production: Al Rodruck

Waterbury Publications, Inc.
Editorial Director: Lisa Kingsley
Associate Editor: Tricia Laning
Creative Director: Ken Carlson
Associate Design Director: Doug Samuelson
Contributing Copy Editors: Terri Fredrickson, Gretchen Kauffman, Peg Smith
Contributing Indexer: Elizabeth T. Parson

Family Circle® **Magazine**
Editor in Chief: Linda Fears
Creative Director: Karmen Lizzul
Food Director: Regina Ragone, M.S., R.D.
Senior Food Editor: Julie Miltenberger
Associate Food Editor: Michael Tyrrell
Assistant Food Editor: Cindy Heller
Editorial Assistant: Allison Baker

Meredith National Media Group
President: Tom Harty
Executive Vice President: Andy Sareyan
Vice President, Manufacturing: Bruce Heston

Meredith Corporation
Chairman and Chief Executive Officer: Stephen M. Lacy

In Memoriam: E.T. Meredith III (1933–2003)

TIME TO EAT! Sitting down at your own table at the end of the day to enjoy a fresh, flavorful home-cooked meal is satisfying in so many ways. This compilation of recipes from the 2010 issues of *Family Circle* Magazine makes it simpler than ever to serve up delicious food you cook yourself—whether it's a quick weeknight dinner or a special evening with friends. Recipes are organized by month to take advantage of what's in season and to make it easy to find just the right recipe for any occasion. In addition to the hundreds of healthful, great-tasting recipes, you'll find dozens of tips, cooking tutorials and tantalizing photographs that will tempt you into the kitchen again and again.

Angel Hair with Arugula Pesto & Salmon (shown below; recipe on page 80) is just one of the fresh and delicious dishes that is part of the Healthy Family Dinners series in *Family Circle*. The recipes in the Healthy Family Dinners feature—along with those in Slow Cooker Suppers—are lifesavers for busy cooks. Look to Food University to expand your cooking repertoire using step-by-step instructions to classic dishes.

**VANILLA CAKE
DOUGHNUTS AND
CHOCOLATE CAKE
DOUGHNUTS,
PAGE 67**

CONTENTS

AFTER ALL OF THE HOLIDAY FEASTING, INDULGE IN LIGHTENED-UP VERSIONS OF YOUR FAVORITE COMFORT FOODS. AND FOR DESSERT, A SUNNY SUGAR COOKIE WILL BRING A SMILE TO YOUR FACE.

BUTTERMILK "FRIED" CHICKEN WITH SOUR CREAM MASHED POTATOES, PAGE 17

JANUARY

11

15

19

On the longest days of winter, when the sun doesn't put in much of an appearance, bake a batch of these bright and happy treats. The dough can be made a day ahead and chilled in the refrigerator overnight. Let the dough sit at room temperature for 20 minutes or so before rolling it out.

SMILEY FACE COOKIES

MAKES ten 3½-inch cookies and twelve 2½-inch cookies **PREP** 10 minutes
REFRIGERATE 2 hours or overnight **BAKE** at 350° for 16 minutes

COOKIES
¾ cup (1½ sticks) unsalted butter, softened
¾ cup sugar
1 egg
1 teaspoon vanilla extract
2 cups all-purpose flour

ICING
1 box (1 pound) confectioners' sugar
3 tablespoons powdered egg whites
   Black and yellow food coloring

① **Cookies:** In a large bowl, beat together the butter and sugar until light and blended, about 2 minutes. Beat in egg and vanilla. On low speed, beat in flour until dough begins to come together. Gather dough into a ball, flatten into a disc and refrigerate 2 hours or overnight.

② Heat oven to 350°. Roll out dough on lightly floured surface to ³⁄₁₆-inch thickness. Cut out circles using 3½-inch and 2½-inch cutters. Transfer circles to ungreased cookie sheets. Reroll scraps and cut more circles. Bake cookies at 350° for 14 to 16 minutes, rotating halfway, until just browning at edges. Transfer cookies to a rack to cool.

③ **Icing:** Combine confectioners' sugar, powdered egg whites and **7 tablespoons water** in a large bowl. With electric mixer on low speed, beat until blended then increase speed to high and beat 6 minutes. Remove 1 cup icing and tint black with food coloring. Tint remaining icing with yellow food coloring. Mix until smooth. Spread yellow icing onto cookies using a small angled spatula. Let dry completely.

④ Transfer black icing to a resealable plastic bag or a piping bag fitted with a writing tip. Pipe eyes and a smiling mouth onto each cookie. Let dry completely at room temperature before stacking cookies.

PER LARGE COOKIE 231 calories; 7 g fat (4 g sat.); 3 g protein; 40 g carbohydrate; 0 g fiber; 17 mg sodium; 29 mg cholesterol

PER SMALL COOKIE 192 calories; 6 g fat (4 g sat.); 2 g protein; 33 g carbohydrate; 0 g fiber; 14 mg sodium; 24 mg cholesterol

Do the Light Thing

Healthier takes on your favorite comfort foods that still taste like the real deal.

BUTTERMILK "FRIED" CHICKEN
WITH SOUR CREAM MASHED
POTATOES, PAGE 17

This rich meat sauce is loaded with sausage, tomatoes and carrots but is still surprisingly low in calories.

SAUSAGE BOLOGNESE WITH LINGUINE, PAGE 17

This burger really delivers. It's juicy, with lots of flavor, a creamy sauce and 20 fewer fat grams than the classic cheeseburger.

THE ULTIMATE TURKEY BURGER WITH CARAMELIZED ONIONS & BLUE CHEESE

THE ULTIMATE TURKEY BURGER WITH CARAMELIZED ONIONS & BLUE CHEESE

MAKES 4 servings **PREP** 15 minutes
COOK 30 minutes

1   tablespoon unsalted butter
1   large Vidalia onion, thinly sliced
1   package (20.8 ounces) ground turkey
½   cup part-skim ricotta cheese
1¾   teaspoons Worcestershire sauce
1¾   teaspoons Dijon mustard
¼   teaspoon salt
¼   teaspoon black pepper
1   tablespoon vegetable oil
¼   cup crumbled blue cheese
2   tablespoons light mayonnaise
4   whole-grain white hamburger buns
4   romaine lettuce leaves

① Melt butter in a large skillet over medium-high heat. Add onion; cook for 15 minutes or until well browned; set aside.

② In a large bowl, combine turkey, ricotta, Worcestershire sauce, mustard, salt and pepper. Stir until well combined. Form into 4 equal-size patties and flatten.

③ Heat oil in a large nonstick skillet over medium heat. Cook burgers about 5 minutes per side, then partially cover, reduce heat to medium and cook another 5 minutes or until instant-read thermometer registers 160°.

④ While burgers are cooking, stir together blue cheese and mayonnaise in a small bowl. Place burgers on buns and top each with some of the onions, 1 tablespoon blue cheese sauce and a lettuce leaf.

PER SERVING 425 calories; 17 g fat (6 g sat.); 46 g protein; 28 g carbohydrate; 4 g fiber; 716 mg sodium; 85 mg cholesterol

PANKO-CRUSTED EGGPLANT PARMESAN

MAKES 4 servings **PREP** 10 minutes **BAKE** at 400° for 55 minutes **COOK** 13 minutes

EGGPLANT

¾   cup panko Japanese bread crumbs
¼   cup grated Parmesan cheese
1   teaspoon dried oregano
½   teaspoon salt
¼   teaspoon black pepper
3   egg whites
1   large eggplant, about 1½ pounds, cut into ½-inch slices (about 16 slices)

SAUCE AND PASTA

4   cloves garlic, peeled and sliced
2   cans (14½ ounces each) no-salt-added diced tomatoes
1½   teaspoons dried oregano
½   teaspoon salt
¼   teaspoon red pepper flakes
½   cup fresh basil
½   cup shredded part-skim mozzarella
½   pound angel hair pasta, cooked following package directions

① **Eggplant:** Heat oven to 400°. Place a large rack on a baking sheet and spray with nonstick cooking spray.

② In a pie plate, mix together panko, Parmesan cheese, oregano, salt and pepper. In a second pie plate, lightly whisk egg whites.

③ Dip each slice of eggplant into egg whites and then into panko mixture, coating both sides. Place eggplant on prepared baking rack. Bake at 400° for 45 minutes, until browned and tender.

④ **Sauce:** While eggplant is baking, make sauce. Coat a medium-size nonstick skillet with nonstick cooking spray and place over medium heat. Cook garlic until lightly browned, about 3 minutes, stirring occasionally. Add tomatoes, oregano, salt and red pepper flakes. Simmer, stirring occasionally, for 10 minutes. Tear basil into bite-size pieces and stir in.

⑤ Overlap eggplant slices slightly on the baking sheet, making 4 piles. Spoon sauce evenly over each portion (reserve a quarter of it for serving) and evenly sprinkle with mozzarella cheese. Bake an additional 10 minutes.

⑥ Serve eggplant with cooked pasta and reserved sauce.

PER SERVING 416 calories; 6 g fat (3 g sat.); 21 g protein; 72 g carbohydrate; 10 g fiber; 856 mg sodium; 12 mg cholesterol

LIGHTER BROWNIE SUNDAE

MAKES 9 servings **PREP** 10 minutes **BAKE** at 350° for 28 minutes

- ¾ **cup all-purpose flour**
- ⅓ **cup cocoa powder**
- ½ **teaspoon baking powder**
- ¼ **teaspoon salt**
- 2 **ounces semisweet chocolate, chopped**
- 2 **tablespoons unsalted butter**
- 2 **tablespoons low-fat sour cream**
- 1 **tablespoon low-calorie chocolate syrup, plus additional for drizzling**
- 1¾ **teaspoons vanilla extract**
- 1 **egg**
- 1 **egg white**
- 1 **cup sugar**
- 1 **quart vanilla frozen yogurt**
- ¼ **cup glazed walnuts, chopped (optional)**
- 9 **maraschino cherries (optional)**

① Heat oven to 350°. Line an 8-inch square baking dish with foil so it hangs over sides; coat foil with nonstick cooking spray and set aside.

② In a small bowl, blend flour, cocoa, baking powder and salt.

③ In a medium-size microwave-safe bowl, microwave chocolate and butter for 40 seconds until melted, stirring halfway through. Stir until smooth, heating in 15 second increments if needed. Cool 2 minutes, then whisk in sour cream, chocolate syrup, vanilla, egg, egg white and sugar. Stir in flour mixture.

④ Spread batter into prepared pan and bake at 350° for 25 to 28 minutes or until a toothpick inserted in the center comes out clean. Remove brownie from pan using foil handles. Cut into squares and top each with 1 scoop frozen yogurt, drizzle with chocolate sauce and finish with chopped nuts and cherry, if desired.

PER SERVING 330 calories; 10 g fat (6 g sat.); 6 g protein; 55 g carbohydrate; 2 g fiber; 146 mg sodium; 45 mg cholesterol

This luscious brownie sundae doesn't look—or taste—like a light dessert in the least.

SAUSAGE BOLOGNESE WITH LINGUINE

MAKES 8 servings **PREP** 15 minutes
COOK 57 minutes

3   medium-size carrots, peeled and coarsely chopped
2   ribs celery, coarsely chopped
1   large onion, coarsely chopped
1   tablespoon vegetable oil
1   package (20 ounces) sweet Italian turkey sausage, casings removed
¾   cup dry white wine
1   can (28 ounces) whole tomatoes
¾   cup milk
1   box (13.25 ounces) low-carb linguine (such as Dreamfields) Grated Parmesan cheese (optional)

① Pulse carrots, celery and onion in a food processor until finely chopped.

② Heat oil in a large nonstick skillet over medium-high heat. Add vegetable mixture and cook, stirring, 6 minutes. Rinse food processor bowl; set aside. Crumble sausage into skillet and cook for 3 minutes.

③ Add wine to skillet; bring to a simmer over medium-low heat. Simmer for 10 minutes.

④ Drain tomatoes and save the liquid. Add tomatoes to food processor bowl; pulse until finely chopped. Add tomatoes and their liquid to skillet; bring to a simmer. Reduce heat to medium; cook for 30 minutes or until most of the liquid has been absorbed. Stir in milk and cook another 8 minutes.

⑤ Meanwhile, cook pasta according to package directions in salted boiling water, about 12 minutes. Serve pasta with sauce, and Parmesan, if desired.

PER SERVING 289 calories; 6 g fat (1 g sat.); 17 g protein; 39 g carbohydrate; 3 g fiber; 536 mg sodium; 38 mg cholesterol

BUTTERMILK "FRIED" CHICKEN WITH SOUR CREAM MASHED POTATOES

MAKES 8 servings **PREP** 15 minutes
REFRIGERATE 1 hour **BAKE** at 400° for
55 minutes **COOK** 15 minutes

CHICKEN

1½   cups buttermilk
2   tablespoons Dijon mustard
1½   teaspoons salt
1   teaspoon garlic powder
1   teaspoon black pepper
¾   teaspoon hot pepper sauce (such as Tabasco)
1   package (4½ pounds) chicken pieces, breasts cut in half diagonally and skin removed
5   cups corn flakes, coarsely crushed
½   cup bread crumbs
½   teaspoon poultry seasoning
½   teaspoon paprika
    Pinch cayenne pepper
2   tablespoons vegetable oil

MASHED POTATOES

2   pounds russet potatoes, peeled and cut into 1-inch cubes
½   cup skim milk
6   tablespoons reduced-fat sour cream

① **Chicken:** In a large bowl, whisk together buttermilk, mustard, ¾ teaspoon of the salt, ½ teaspoon of the garlic powder, ½ teaspoon of the pepper and the hot sauce. Add chicken (save wings for another use) and turn to coat. Refrigerate 1 hour.

② Heat oven to 400°. Coat a baking rack with nonstick cooking spray and place inside rimmed baking sheet.

③ Stir together crushed corn flakes, bread crumbs, remaining ¾ teaspoon salt, ½ teaspoon garlic powder, ½ teaspoon black pepper, the poultry seasoning, paprika and cayenne. Stir in oil until blended. Remove chicken from marinade and dip in crumb mixture, pressing to adhere.

④ Place chicken on rack and bake at 400° for 55 minutes or until instant-read thermometer registers 160° when inserted in thickest part of breast.

⑤ **Mashed Potatoes:** Place potatoes in a large pot; cover with cold water. Bring to a boil. Reduce heat to medium; simmer 15 minutes or until tender. Drain and return to pan. Add milk and sour cream. Mash to desired consistency.

PER SERVING 535 calories; 13 g fat (3 g sat.); 56 g protein; 47 g carbohydrate; 2 g fiber; 963 mg sodium; 167 mg cholesterol

This crispy southern-style chicken is so satisfyingly crunchy no one will notice it hasn't been fried—especially when served with a side of creamy mash.

Slow Cooker Suppers

After a few hours in the slow cooker, even inexpensive beef can taste like a five-star meal.

HARVEST POT ROAST, PAGE 19

HARVEST POT ROAST

MAKES 8 servings **PREP** 10 minutes
COOK 13 minutes **SLOW-COOK** 6 hours on
HIGH or 8 hours on LOW

- 3 pounds boneless chuck roast, trimmed and blotted dry
- 1 teaspoon dried thyme
- ½ teaspoon salt
- ¼ teaspoon black pepper
- 1 tablespoon canola oil
- 1 medium-size onion, thinly sliced
- 1 tablespoon tomato paste
- 2 tablespoons all-purpose flour
- ½ cup red wine
- ½ cup low-sodium beef broth
- 4 medium-size carrots, peeled, quartered lengthwise and cut into 1-inch pieces
- 3 ribs celery, cut into 1-inch pieces
- 1½ pounds new potatoes, scrubbed and quartered

① Sprinkle roast with ¼ teaspoon each thyme, salt and black pepper. Heat oil in a large nonstick skillet over medium-high heat. Cook roast 1 to 2 minutes per side or until browned; transfer roast to slow cooker.

② Reduce heat to medium and add onion to skillet; cook 3 minutes or until softened. Stir in tomato paste and cook 1 minute, stirring constantly. Stir in flour and cook, stirring constantly, for 1 minute. Whisk in wine, broth and ½ cup water; bring to a boil. Pour liquid into slow cooker over beef and cook on HIGH for 6 hours or LOW for 8 hours.

③ When there is 3 hours of cook time remaining on HIGH or 4 hours on LOW, remove meat from slow cooker and stir in carrots, celery, potatoes and remaining ¾ teaspoon thyme. Return meat to slow cooker for remaining cook time.

④ Remove meat from slow cooker; slice. Stir remaining ¼ teaspoon salt into liquid. Serve roast with vegetables and sauce.

PER SERVING 354 calories; 10 g fat (3 g sat.); 38 g protein; 23 g carbohydrate; 3 g fiber; 251 mg sodium; 82 mg cholesterol

SAUERBRATEN

MAKES 10 servings **PREP** 10 minutes **CHILL** overnight
SLOW-COOK 6 hours on HIGH or 8 hours on LOW

- 1 cup cider vinegar
- ¾ cup red wine vinegar
- 2 teaspoons salt
- ½ teaspoon black pepper
- 6 whole cloves
- 2 bay leaves
- 1 tablespoon mustard seeds
- 3½ pounds boneless top round roast, tied
- 20 gingersnaps (about 5 ounces), crushed
  Prepared mashed potatoes (optional)
  Green salad (optional)

① Combine vinegars, salt, pepper, cloves, bay leaves and mustard seeds in a large bowl. Place roast in bowl; cover and refrigerate overnight, turning once.

② Place roast and marinade in slow cooker and cook on HIGH for 6 hours or LOW for 8 hours.

③ Remove roast to a platter and keep warm. Strain liquid from slow cooker. Stir in crushed gingersnaps until well blended. Slice roast and serve with mashed potatoes and salad, if desired.

PER SERVING 258 calories; 6 g fat (2 g sat.); 37 g protein; 10 g carbohydrate; 1 g fiber; 662 mg sodium; 85 mg cholesterol

BEER-BRAISED SHORT RIBS

MAKES 8 servings **PREP** 10 minutes **COOK** 7 minutes
SLOW-COOK 5 hours on HIGH or 7 hours on LOW

4   pounds bone-in short ribs, trimmed
½   teaspoon salt
½   teaspoon black pepper
1   tablespoon olive oil
1   medium-size onion, chopped
½   cup low-sodium beef broth
1¼   cups dark beer (such as Guinness Draught)
1   tablespoon light-brown sugar
½   teaspoon dried thyme
2   cups baby carrots
8   ounces white mushrooms, cleaned and quartered
2   tablespoons cornstarch
1   tablespoon spicy brown mustard
     Cooked egg noodles (optional)

① Blot dry ribs with paper towels. Sprinkle ribs with ¼ teaspoon each salt and black pepper. Heat oil in a large nonstick skillet over medium-high heat. Cook meat for 5 minutes, turning once halfway through, in batches if necessary. Remove meat to slow cooker.

② Add onion to skillet and cook, 2 minutes, stirring often. Add broth, 1 cup of the beer, the sugar and thyme to skillet. Bring to a boil, then pour over meat. Cover and cook on HIGH for 5 hours or LOW for 7 hours.

③ When there is 1½ hours of cook time remaining on HIGH or 2½ hours on LOW, stir carrots and mushrooms into slow cooker.

④ Whisk together remaining ¼ cup beer, ¼ teaspoon each salt and pepper, and the cornstarch and mustard. Whisk into slow cooker. Replace cover and cook 15 more minutes or until sauce has thickened. Serve over egg noodles, if desired.

PER SERVING 465 calories; 25 g fat (10 g sat.); 44 g protein; 10 g carbohydrate; 1 g fiber; 331 mg sodium; 134 mg cholesterol

SWEET & SAVORY STEW

MAKES 6 servings **PREP** 10 minutes
COOK 11 minutes **SLOW-COOK** 5 hours on HIGH or 7 hours on LOW

⅓   cup all-purpose flour
2   teaspoons paprika
2   pounds chuck steak, trimmed, cut into 1-inch pieces and blotted dry
1   tablespoon plus 1 teaspoon olive oil
1   large onion, chopped
½   teaspoon salt
½   teaspoon black pepper
½   teaspoon cinnamon
1   tablespoon tomato paste
1   can (14.5 ounces) diced tomatoes, drained
1¼   cups low-sodium chicken broth
1   pound parsnips, peeled and sliced into ½-inch coins
1   cup pitted prunes, chopped
1   tablespoon light-brown sugar
3   cups cooked white rice (optional)

① Combine flour and 1½ teaspoons paprika in a large resealable bag. Add beef to bag in 2 batches; shake to coat with flour, then remove from bag.

② Heat 1 tablespoon oil in a large nonstick skillet over medium-high heat. Cook beef in batches, if necessary, for 5 minutes, turning occasionally, or until browned. Place beef in slow cooker.

③ Reduce heat to medium; add 1 teaspoon olive oil. Add onion and sprinkle with ¼ teaspoon each paprika, salt, pepper and cinnamon. Cook 4 minutes. Stir in tomato paste; cook 2 minutes, stirring. Place in slow cooker.

④ Add tomatoes and broth to skillet; bring to a boil; pour into slow cooker. Cover; cook for 5 hours on HIGH or 7 hours on LOW. When there is 1½ hours of cook time remaining for both methods, add parsnips and prunes to slow cooker. Stir in remaining ¼ teaspoon each paprika, salt, pepper and cinnamon, and the brown sugar just before serving. Serve over rice, if desired.

PER SERVING 521 calories; 10 g fat (3 g sat.); 38 g protein; 67 g carbohydrate; 7 g fiber; 569 mg sodium; 90 mg cholesterol

SWEET & SAVORY STEW

CELEBRATE YOUR LOVE OF CHOCOLATE THIS MONTH WITH FUDGY BROWNIES, CAKES AND SHAKES—THEN BALANCE IT OUT WITH A BEVY OF HEART-HEALTHY WEEKNIGHT DINNERS.

FUDGE BROWNIES WITH MACADAMIA NUTS, PAGE 39

FEBRUARY

28

33

43

It may take a little time to make—and bake—but the gooey, delicious result is well worth the wait. This dish is always a hit at potlucks—and it's the perfect thing to putter with in a warm kitchen on a leisurely winter weekend afternoon.

CLASSIC MEAT LASAGNA

MAKES 12 servings **PREP** 30 minutes **COOK** 43 minutes **BAKE** at 350° for 60 minutes

1	tablespoon olive oil
1	large onion, chopped
4	cloves garlic, finely chopped
2¼	pounds ground meat loaf mix (beef, pork and veal)
1	can (28½ ounces) crushed tomatoes
1	can (15½ ounces) crushed tomatoes
2	tablespoons tomato paste
1	teaspoon dried Italian seasoning
1	teaspoon sugar
1	teaspoon salt
¼	teaspoon black pepper
5	tablespoons chopped fresh basil
12	traditional lasagna noodles (from a 16-ounce package)
1	container (15 ounces) ricotta cheese
2	eggs
⅓	cup shredded Parmesan cheese
3	cups shredded mozzarella cheese
2	cups shredded Italian cheese blend

① Heat oil in a large saucepan over medium heat. Add onion and garlic. Cook for 5 minutes, stirring occasionally.

② Crumble in ground meat and cook for an additional 8 minutes, breaking up with a wooden spoon. Add tomatoes, tomato paste, Italian seasoning, sugar, salt and black pepper. Simmer with cover slightly ajar for 15 minutes, stirring occasionally. Uncover and simmer for 15 additional minutes. Stir in 3 tablespoons of the basil.

③ Meanwhile, cook lasagna noodles following package directions. Drain and rinse briefly under cold water. Heat oven to 350°. Coat a 13 x 9 x 2-inch baking dish with cooking spray.

④ In a medium-size bowl, combine the ricotta cheese, eggs, Parmesan cheese and remaining 2 tablespoons of basil. Set aside.

⑤ Spread 1 cup of sauce over the bottom of the prepared baking dish. Place 3 cooked noodles over the sauce. Evenly spoon the ricotta mixture over the noodles. Top with 3 more noodles and 3 cups of the meat sauce. Layer 3 noodles over sauce, then sprinkle on shredded mozzarella. Top with the 3 remaining noodles and 2 cups of the meat sauce.

⑥ Sprinkle shredded Italian cheese blend evenly over the last meat sauce layer and loosely cover with foil. Bake at 350° for 30 minutes. Uncover and bake for 30 additional minutes, until bubbly.

⑦ Cool 10 minutes before serving. Reheat extra sauce and serve on the side.

PER SERVING 551 calories; 30 g fat (15 g sat.); 37 g protein; 26 g carbohydrate; 3 g fiber; 830 mg sodium; 142 mg cholesterol

We ♥ Healthy Suppers

These six delicious dinners will change your mind about low-salt, low-cal recipes.

MAPLE-GLAZED PORK WITH MASHED SWEET POTATOES & PARSNIPS, PAGE 31

TERIYAKI SALMON WITH
GLAZED BROCCOLI SALAD,
PAGE 31

SPICY VEGGIE STIR-FRY

MAKES 4 servings **PREP** 10 minutes **COOK** 29 minutes

- 3 tablespoons low-sodium soy sauce
- 2 tablespoons light-brown sugar
- 1½ teaspoons Asian chili-garlic paste (such as Sriracha)
- 1 tablespoon grated fresh ginger
- ½ cup cornstarch
- 1 block (14 ounces) firm tofu, drained and cut into 1-inch cubes
- 1 tablespoon vegetable oil
- 2 large sweet red peppers, seeded and chopped
- 1 cup baby carrots, cut diagonally into thirds
- 4 ounces snow peas, trimmed and halved diagonally
- 6 cups leaf spinach, stems removed
- 8 ounces soba noodles, prepared according to package directions

① Blend soy sauce, sugar, chili-garlic paste, ginger and 1 tablespoon of the cornstarch.

② Pat tofu dry. Place remaining 7 tablespoons cornstarch in a pie plate; coat tofu on all sides.

③ Heat oil in a large nonstick skillet over medium-high heat. Add tofu to skillet in 2 batches; cook each 10 minutes or until lightly browned. Remove from skillet.

④ Add red pepper, carrots, snow peas and 3 tablespoons water to skillet and cover; cook 6 minutes or until tender. Add spinach; cover. Cook 1 minute. Stir in soy sauce mixture; cook 2 minutes or until thickened. Stir in tofu; serve with noodles.

PER SERVING 482 calories; 9 g fat (0 g sat.); 20 g protein; 81 g carbohydrate; 8 g fiber; 404 mg sodium; 0 mg cholesterol

STUFFED CHICKEN BREASTS & CHERRY TOMATO SALAD

MAKES 4 servings **PREP** 15 minutes **BAKE** at 425° for 30 minutes **COOK** 13 minutes

CHICKEN
⅔ cup part-skim ricotta cheese
¼ cup chopped fresh basil
4 sun-dried tomatoes (not oil packed), finely chopped
1 clove garlic, finely chopped
4 chicken breasts, each trimmed to weigh about 6½ ounces
  Wooden toothpicks
¾ teaspoon salt-free Onion & Herb seasoning blend (such as Mrs. Dash)

SALAD
8 ounces sugar snap peas, trimmed
2 cups cherry tomatoes, halved
1 clove garlic, minced
¾ teaspoon sugar
½ teaspoon salt-free Onion & Herb seasoning blend (such as Mrs. Dash)
1 tablespoon lemon juice

① Heat oven to 425°. **Chicken:** In a small bowl, stir together ricotta, basil, sun-dried tomatoes and garlic until well combined; set aside.

② Using a paring knife, cut deep pockets in the thickest part of the breasts, about 2 inches wide. Spoon about 2 tablespoons of the cheese mixture into each pocket. Seal closed with 3 wooden toothpicks.

③ Place chicken in a 9 x 13 x 2-inch baking dish and sprinkle with the salt-free seasoning. Bake at 425° for 25 to 30 minutes or until chicken registers 160° on an instant-read thermometer.

④ **Salad:** Meanwhile, heat a large nonstick skillet over medium heat for 5 minutes. Add snap peas and 2 tablespoons water to skillet and cover; cook 3 minutes or until bright green and tender. Remove cover and cook until water has evaporated, about 2 minutes. Add tomatoes, garlic, sugar and salt-free seasoning to skillet and cook 3 minutes. Stir in lemon juice and serve with chicken.

PER SERVING 333 calories; 6 g fat (3 g sat.); 51 g protein; 16 g carbohydrate; 4 g fiber; 217 mg sodium; 120 mg cholesterol

WARM SWEET & SAVORY PASTA SALAD

MAKES 6 servings **PREP** 15 minutes
COOK 11 minutes

8 ounces multigrain rotini pasta (such as Barilla Plus)
1 small red onion, thinly sliced
3 tablespoons finely chopped fresh oregano
½ cup low-sodium chicken broth
3 tablespoons white balsamic vinegar
2 cups cooked, shredded chicken breast
1 can (15.5 ounces) black beans, drained and rinsed
¼ cup chopped green olives

① Bring a large pot of salted water to a boil. Cook pasta according to package directions, about 11 minutes. Drain, reserving ½ cup pasta water. Return pasta to pot.

② While pasta is cooking, heat a large nonstick skillet over medium heat. Add onion and oregano; coat generously with nonstick cooking spray. Cover and cook, stirring occasionally, for 3 minutes.

③ Stir broth and vinegar into skillet. Stir in chicken, beans and olives; cook for 2 minutes or until heated through. Toss with pasta and serve, adding reserved pasta water if too dry.

PER SERVING 304 calories; 5 g fat (0 g sat.); 25 g protein; 38 g carbohydrate; 7 g fiber; 496 mg sodium; 40 mg cholesterol

LEMONY FLOUNDER WITH ROASTED ZUCCHINI

MAKES 4 servings **PREP** 15 minutes **ROAST** at 450° for 20 minutes **COOK** 14 minutes

- **4** **small zucchini (about 1½ pounds), cut lengthwise into ¼-inch-thick slices**
  Zest and juice of 1 lemon
- **4** **tablespoons chopped fresh parsley**
- **1½** **teaspoons dried oregano**
- **1** **medium-size onion, chopped**
- **2** **cloves garlic, chopped**
- **½** **cup white wine or water**
- **1⅓** **cups low-sodium vegetable broth**
- **2** **flounder fillets (about 1 pound), cut in half**
- **1** **cup orzo, prepared according to package directions (optional)**

① Cover 2 large baking sheets with nonstick foil and place in oven. Heat oven to 450°.

② Carefully spread zucchini slices in a single layer on prepared baking sheets. Drizzle with 2 tablespoons lemon juice and sprinkle with 1 tablespoon of the parsley and ½ teaspoon of the oregano. Roast at 450° for 20 minutes or until tender, flipping slices halfway through.

③ Heat a large nonstick skillet over medium heat. Add onion, remaining 3 tablespoons parsley and remaining 1 teaspoon oregano to skillet and spritz with nonstick cooking spray. Cover and cook for 5 minutes or until softened. Uncover and add lemon zest and garlic to skillet; cook 1 minute.

④ Pour wine or water, vegetable broth and remaining lemon juice (2 tablespoons) into skillet. Bring to a simmer over medium heat. Add fish to skillet and cook, covered, for 5 to 8 minutes, until opaque, carefully flipping halfway through.

⑤ Remove fish from skillet and pour some of the poaching liquid over orzo (if using). Serve orzo with fish and zucchini.

PER SERVING 188 calories; 2 g fat (0 g sat.); 24 g protein; 14 g carbohydrate; 3 g fiber; 311 mg sodium; 54 mg cholesterol

④ Add broth, sweet potatoes and ¼ cup water to saucepan and cook, covered, for about 23 minutes, stirring occasionally, or until liquid has been absorbed. Gently mash. Stir in remaining 2 tablespoons maple syrup and ½ teaspoon black pepper blend and serve with pork.

PER SERVING 400 calories; 5 g fat (2 g sat.); 33 g protein; 55 g carbohydrate; 8 g fiber; 246 mg sodium; 93 mg cholesterol

TERIYAKI SALMON WITH GLAZED BROCCOLI SALAD

MAKES 4 servings **PREP** 15 minutes
COOK 18 minutes **BROIL** 8 minutes

2	tablespoons honey
2	tablespoons low-sodium teriyaki sauce
1	tablespoon rice wine vinegar
4	scallions, trimmed and thinly sliced
2	cloves garlic, minced
½	cup sliced almonds
1	bunch broccoli (1½ pounds), cut into florets; stalks peeled and cut in ¼-inch coins
4	salmon fillets, about 4 ounces each
2	teaspoons cornstarch

① In a small bowl, blend honey, teriyaki, vinegar, scallions and garlic; divide in half and set aside.

② Adjust top oven rack so that it is 6 inches from heating element and heat broiler. Line a rimmed baking sheet with aluminum foil.

③ Heat a large nonstick skillet over medium-high heat; toast almonds for 6 minutes. Remove almonds; carefully wipe out skillet.

④ Place ¼ cup water in skillet; reduce heat to medium-low. Add broccoli and cook, covered, for 7 to 8 minutes or until bright green and tender.

⑤ Place salmon on prepared baking sheet; brush with half of the reserved teriyaki mixture. Broil salmon 5 to 8 minutes or until top is browned and the interior temperature registers 120° on an instant-read thermometer.

⑥ Stir cornstarch into remaining reserved teriyaki mixture and pour into skillet. Bring to a simmer and cook, stirring, for 4 minutes or until sauce has reduced to a thick glaze. Stir in almonds and serve alongside salmon.

PER SERVING 332 calories; 14 g fat (2 g sat.); 30 g protein; 25 g carbohydrate; 6 g fiber; 239 mg sodium; 62 mg cholesterol

The more fresh, unprocessed ingredients you cook with, the better—veggies and fish prevent and even help reverse heart damage.

MAPLE-GLAZED PORK WITH MASHED SWEET POTATOES & PARSNIPS

MAKES 4 servings **PREP** 10 minutes
ROAST at 400° for 25 minutes **COOK** 41 minutes

1	pork tenderloin (about 1¼ pounds)
1¼	teaspoons smoked black pepper blend (such as McCormick Smokehouse black pepper)
3	tablespoons maple syrup
8	ounces parsnips, trimmed, peeled and cut into ¼-inch-thick half-moons
½	cup low-sodium chicken broth
1½	pounds sweet potatoes, peeled and cut into ¼-inch-thick half-moons

① Heat oven to 400°. Heat a large oven-safe nonstick skillet over medium-high heat.

② Pat pork dry with paper towels and rub with ¾ teaspoon of the black pepper blend. Place pork in skillet and cook for 2 minutes per side or until browned. Transfer pork to oven and roast at 400° for about 25 minutes or until internal temperature registers 155° on an instant-read thermometer. Brush pork with 1 tablespoon of the maple syrup twice during last 10 minutes of cook time.

③ While pork is cooking, heat a medium-size saucepan over medium heat. Add parsnips to saucepan; coat generously with nonstick cooking spray. Cover and cook, stirring occasionally, for 10 minutes or until browned.

All Juiced Up
Citrus-infused dishes with fresh-squeezed appeal.

ESCAROLE WITH ORANGE DRESSING, PAGE 35

GRILLED SHRIMP & MEYER LEMON RISOTTO, PAGE 35

LOIN OF PORK & CITRUS CHUTNEY

MAKES 8 servings **PREP** 20 minutes **ROAST** at 450° for 30 minutes; at 325° for 75 minutes **COOK** 5 minutes

ROAST

- 1 tablespoon olive oil
- 1 tablespoon chopped rosemary
  Zest and juice of 1 lemon
- 2 cloves garlic, peeled and chopped
- 1 center-cut pork loin roast with 6 ribs, about 4½ pounds
- ¾ teaspoon salt
- ¼ teaspoon black pepper

CHUTNEY

- 1 tablespoon olive oil
- ½ small red onion
- ½ medium sweet red pepper, cored, seeded and diced
- 1 jalapeño pepper, trimmed, seeds removed and finely chopped
- 2 cloves garlic, peeled and finely chopped
- 3 oranges, peel removed, sectioned and cut into thirds
- 1 pink grapefruit, peel removed, sectioned and cut into thirds
- 1 lemon, peel removed, sectioned and cut into thirds
- 1 lime, peel removed, sectioned and cut into thirds
- ½ teaspoon salt
- ⅛ teaspoon black pepper

① Heat oven to 450°. Set a rack into a large roasting pan.

② **Roast:** In a small bowl, mix together olive oil, rosemary, lemon zest, lemon juice and garlic. Spoon over pork. Season with salt and pepper. Place in prepared pan; roast at 450° for 30 minutes. Reduce oven temperature to 325°. Continue roasting for 65 to 75 minutes or until internal temperature registers 155° on an instant-read thermometer. Allow to rest 10 minutes.

③ **Chutney:** In skillet, heat oil over medium heat. Add onion, red pepper, jalapeño and garlic; cook 5 minutes, stirring. Spoon mixture into a bowl; let cool. Stir in oranges, grapefruit, lemon and lime. Season with salt and pepper. Cover and refrigerate until ready to serve.

PER SERVING 520 calories; 20 g fat (6 g sat.); 70 g protein; 14 g carbohydrate; 3 g fiber; 468 mg sodium; 177 mg cholesterol

GRAPEFRUIT-TANGERINE FOOL

MAKES 6 servings **PREP** 15 minutes **COOK** 1 minute **CHILL** 4 hours, 10 minutes

1½ cups orange-tangerine juice
1 envelope unflavored gelatin
1¼ cups heavy cream
¼ cup sugar
1 teaspoon vanilla extract
2 pink grapefruits, peel removed, sectioned and cut into thirds, about 1 cup
2 clementines, peeled, sectioned and cut into thirds
Mint, grapefruit and clementine sections, for garnish

① Place ½ cup orange-tangerine juice in saucepan; top with gelatin. Let stand 1 minute. Stir over low heat 1 minute until gelatin dissolves. Cool to room temperature. Stir in remaining 1 cup juice and pour into a large bowl. Refrigerate 10 minutes.

② Remove juice mixture from fridge. Beat 2 minutes until frothy.

③ In another large bowl, beat the cream, sugar and vanilla on medium-high until soft peaks form. Gently fold whipped cream into gelatin mixture. Fold in the grapefruit and clementine pieces.

④ Spoon whipped cream–fruit mixture into 6 dessert dishes or martini glasses. Cover each and refrigerate for at least 4 hours. To serve, garnish with mint, grapefruit and clementine sections.

PER SERVING 280 calories; 19 g fat (11 g sat.); 3 g protein; 27 g carbohydrate; 2 g fiber; 23 mg sodium; 68 mg cholesterol

GRILLED SHRIMP & MEYER LEMON RISOTTO

MAKES 6 servings **PREP** 20 minutes
COOK 36 minutes **REFRIGERATE** 20 minutes
GRILL 6 minutes

MARINADE

2 tablespoons olive oil
Juice and zest from 2 Meyer lemons
6 cloves garlic, peeled and chopped
¼ teaspoon salt
¼ teaspoon black pepper

RISOTTO

3 cups reduced-sodium chicken broth mixed with 1½ cups water
2 tablespoons olive oil
1 large shallot, peeled and finely chopped
1½ cups arborio rice
⅔ cup dry white wine
Zest from 2 Meyer lemons
3 tablespoons Meyer lemon juice
1 cup shredded Fontina cheese
½ teaspoon salt
¼ teaspoon black pepper
½ cup fresh basil, coarsely chopped
1½ pounds extra large shrimp, shelled and deveined

① **Marinade:** Add olive oil, lemon juice, zest, garlic, salt and pepper to a large resealable bag. Set aside.

② **Risotto:** Place broth and water in a medium-size saucepan; bring to a simmer. In a large saucepan, heat olive oil over medium heat. Add shallot and cook 3 minutes, stirring occasionally. Add rice and stir until rice is coated with oil. Cook for 2 minutes. Add wine and cook until wine is absorbed, about 1 minute.

③ Add ½ cup of the simmering broth to rice. Cook over medium-low heat, stirring, until absorbed. Add remaining broth mixture, ½ cup at a time, cooking in the same manner. This will take about 25 to 30 minutes.

④ Stir in the zest, juice, cheese, salt and pepper. Stir in the basil just before serving.

⑤ While risotto is cooking, add shrimp to marinade and refrigerate for 20 minutes. Heat indoor grill. Grill shrimp, about 2 to 3 minutes per side, until cooked through. Remove to a plate; keep warm while risotto continues to cook.

PER SERVING 474 calories; 16 g fat (5 g sat.); 31 g protein; 47 g carbohydrate; 3 g fiber; 964 mg sodium; 219 mg cholesterol

ESCAROLE WITH ORANGE DRESSING

MAKES 4 servings **PREP** 10 minutes
COOK 7 minutes

¼ cup orange juice
2 teaspoons plus 2 tablespoons olive oil
1 teaspoon mustard
½ teaspoon salt
¼ teaspoon black pepper
½ large red onion, peeled and sliced thin
1½ pounds escarole, trimmed and cut crosswise into 1½-inch slices
1 large orange, peeled and sectioned

① In small bowl, blend orange juice, 2 teaspoons of olive oil, the mustard, ¼ teaspoon of the salt and ⅛ teaspoon of the pepper. Set aside.

② Heat 1 tablespoon olive oil in a large skillet over medium-high heat. Add onion; sauté 4 minutes or until lightly browned. Remove from skillet and reserve.

③ Add remaining tablespoon oil and the escarole to skillet. Cook, covered, for 3 minutes, stirring occasionally. Season with the remaining ¼ teaspoon salt and ⅛ teaspoon pepper.

④ Spoon escarole onto platter and drizzle with orange juice mixture. Scatter onions and orange segments over escarole and serve.

PER SERVING 140 calories; 9 g fat (1 g sat.); 3 g protein; 13 g carbohydrate; 6 g fiber; 359 mg sodium; 0 mg cholesterol

Look for Meyer lemons in your store's produce aisle. A hybrid of oranges and traditional lemons, they have a smoother, more fragrant peel and sweeter juice.

Chocolate Deluxe

Cakes, shakes and brownies that are out of this world.

BLACKOUT CAKE, PAGE 41

CHOCOLATE SHAKE

MAKES 4 servings **PREP** 10 minutes

3½ cups vanilla ice cream
½ cup chocolate sorbet
½ cup whole milk
3 tablespoons hot fudge sauce, at room temperature

① Soften ice cream and sorbet at room temperature for 5 minutes, if necessary.

② Combine ice cream, sorbet, milk and hot fudge sauce in a blender and puree until smooth, scraping down sides as necessary. Serve immediately.

PER SERVING 325 calories; 16 g fat (9 g sat.); 6 g protein; 41 g carbohydrate; 1 g fiber; 192 mg sodium; 58 mg cholesterol

FUDGE BROWNIES WITH
MACADAMIA NUTS

FUDGE BROWNIES WITH MACADAMIA NUTS

MAKES 16 brownies **PREP** 10 minutes
MICROWAVE 1 minute **BAKE** at 350° for
31 minutes **CHILL** 1 hour

1   bag (12 ounces) semisweet
    chocolate chips
¼   cup (½ stick) unsalted butter
¾   cup sugar
2   eggs
1   cup all-purpose flour
¼   teaspoon salt
⅔   cup plus 3 tablespoons chopped
    macadamia nuts
1   teaspoon vanilla extract

① Heat oven to 350°. Line an 8-inch
square baking pan with nonstick
aluminum foil; set aside.

② Place 1 cup of the chocolate chips
and the butter in a large microwave-safe
bowl and microwave for 1 minute. Stir
until smooth. Microwave an additional
30 seconds, if needed.

③ Whisk in sugar, then eggs. Stir in flour
and salt until smooth. Fold in ⅔ cup of the
chopped macadamia nuts and the vanilla.
Transfer batter to prepared pan.

④ Bake at 350° for 25 to 29 minutes.

⑤ Sprinkle remaining 1 cup chocolate
chips over brownie and return to oven for
2 minutes. Remove from oven, and spread
melted chips until smooth, to form a
"frosting." Top with remaining 3 tablespoons
nuts. Refrigerate 1 hour to firm chocolate,
then cut into squares.

PER SERVING 250 calories; 15 g fat (6 g sat.);
3 g protein; 35 g carbohydrate; 2 g fiber;
45 mg sodium; 35 mg cholesterol

FLOURLESS CHOCOLATE CAKE

MAKES 12 servings **PREP** 10 minutes **MICROWAVE** 4 minutes **BAKE** at 325° for 47 minutes

8   eggs, cold
1   pound semisweet chocolate,
    chopped
1   cup (2 sticks) unsalted butter, cut
    into ½-inch pieces
    Confectioners' sugar

① Heat oven to 325°. Coat an 8½-inch
springform pan with nonstick cooking
spray. Wrap pan's bottom and side with
foil to prevent water bath from seeping
into pan. Put kettle of water on to boil.

② Beat eggs with hand mixer on high
speed for 5 minutes or until eggs double
in volume.

③ Combine chocolate and butter in a
large microwave-safe bowl and heat on

50% power for 4 minutes or until chocolate
has melted, stirring twice. Fold eggs into
chocolate in 3 additions until fully mixed in.

④ Pour batter into prepared pan. Place
cake pan in a large roasting pan in oven.
Pour boiling water into roasting pan to
come halfway up side of cake pan. Bake at
325° for 40 to 47 minutes or until wooden
pick inserted in center comes out
completely clean.

⑤ Remove cake to a wire rack and cool
completely. Dust with confectioners' sugar
before serving, if desired.

PER SERVING 360 calories; 30 g fat (17 g sat.);
6 g protein; 24 g carbohydrate; 2 g fiber; 55 mg
sodium; 180 mg cholesterol

MARBLE CHEESECAKE

MARBLE CHEESECAKE

MAKES 10 servings **PREP** 15 minutes
MICROWAVE 40 seconds **BAKE** at 325° for 1 hour
CHILL 6 hours or overnight

CRUST

1½ cups chocolate wafer cookie crumbs (such as Famous Chocolate Wafers), about 36 cookies
3 tablespoons sugar
¼ cup (½ stick) unsalted butter, melted

FILLING

1½ pounds cream cheese, at room temperature
¾ cup sugar
5 teaspoons cornstarch
¼ teaspoon salt
4 eggs, at room temperature
1 teaspoon vanilla extract
⅓ cup semisweet chocolate chips

① **Crust:** Wrap bottom and side of 9-inch springform pan with aluminum foil to prevent water bath from seeping into pan; set aside. In small bowl, mix together cookie crumbs, sugar and melted butter until crumbs are evenly moistened. Press into bottom and 1 inch up side of springform pan.

② **Filling:** In large bowl, beat together cream cheese, sugar, cornstarch and salt for 2 minutes or until smooth and creamy. Put kettle of water on to boil.

③ Add eggs, beating well after each. Add vanilla; beat 30 seconds. Pour all but 1 cup of filling into prepared pan.

④ Heat oven to 325°. Heat chocolate chips in microwave for 40 seconds or until melted.

⑤ Stir the melted chocolate into reserved 1 cup filling. Spoon in dollops, evenly spaced, over top of the filling. With the tip of a small knife, swirl chocolate dollops into white batter to marbleize. Place cake pan in large roasting pan on oven rack. Pour enough boiling water into the roasting pan to come halfway up the side of the springform pan.

⑥ Bake at 325° for 55 to 60 minutes or until sides are set and center shakes slightly. Place cake on a wire rack and discard aluminum foil. Run thin knife around edge

of cake. Cool completely in pan on rack. Cover and refrigerate for 6 hours or overnight. To serve, remove side of pan.

PER SERVING 490 calories; 35 g fat (21 g sat.); 9 g protein; 37 g carbohydrate; 1 g fiber; 410 mg sodium; 170 mg cholesterol

BLACKOUT CAKE

MAKES 16 servings **PREP** 30 minutes
COOK 3 minutes **CHILL** 4 hours
MICROWAVE 1 minute **BAKE** at 350° for 35 minutes

FROSTING

1¼ cups granulated sugar
3 tablespoons cornstarch
3 cups whole milk
6 ounces unsweetened chocolate, chopped
1 teaspoon vanilla extract

CAKE

4 ounces bittersweet chocolate, chopped
1 teaspoon vegetable oil
2 cups all-purpose flour
½ cup cocoa powder
2 teaspoons baking powder
½ teaspoon baking soda
½ teaspoon salt
½ cup (1 stick) unsalted butter, softened
1 cup granulated sugar
¾ cup light-brown sugar
2 eggs
1 teaspoon vanilla extract
1 cup buttermilk

① **Frosting:** In a medium-size heavy-bottomed saucepan, whisk granulated sugar and cornstarch. Gradually add milk, whisking constantly to keep mixture from getting lumpy.

② Transfer saucepan to stove and heat over medium heat, stirring constantly with wooden spoon. Bring to a simmer, then add chocolate. Cook 3 minutes or until chocolate is melted. Stir in vanilla. Pour into a bowl; cover surface with plastic wrap. Refrigerate until cold, about 4 hours or overnight.

③ **Cake:** Heat oven to 350°. Coat two 8 x 2-inch round baking pans with nonstick cooking spray. Line bottoms with wax paper; spray paper.

④ Microwave chocolate and oil for 1 minute; stir until smooth. If needed, heat an additional 15 seconds. Cool slightly.

⑤ In medium-size bowl, mix flour, cocoa powder, baking powder, baking soda and salt. In large bowl, beat with mixer on medium speed the butter and sugars until well combined. Add eggs, one at a time, beating well after each. Beat in melted chocolate and vanilla.

⑥ On low speed, beat flour mixture into butter mixture, alternating with buttermilk, beginning and ending with flour. Spread into pans.

⑦ Bake at 350° for 30 to 35 minutes or until toothpick inserted in centers tests clean. Cool cakes in pans on wire racks 15 minutes. Turn cakes out onto racks; cool layers completely.

⑧ Cut each cake layer in half horizontally for a total of 4 layers; crumble 1 cake layer into crumbs and set aside. Place 1 cake layer cut side down on a serving platter. Spread with 1 heaping cup frosting and top with another cake layer. Repeat with 1 heaping cup frosting and last cake layer. Spread remaining frosting over top and side of cake. Sprinkle cake crumbs over top and side of cake, pressing gently to adhere.

PER SERVING 370 calories; 17 g fat (10 g sat.); 7 g protein; 54 g carbohydrate; 3 g fiber; 210 mg sodium; 45 mg cholesterol

Easy-Bake Bread

This recipe is so simple—it really is the best thing since sliced bread.

Unlike most doughs, this one has a scant amount of yeast, lots of water and is barely kneaded. However, a very wet dough left to ferment for hours is the perfect environment for all those molecules to align and create gluten, which gives this loaf its crisp crust and large, well-structured crumb.

EASY-BAKE BREAD

MAKES one 1½-pound loaf (about 12 slices) **PREP** 15 minutes **RISE** 20 hours **BAKE** at 450° for 45 minutes

3   **cups white wheat flour (such as King Arthur Flour), plus additional for dusting**
½   **teaspoon active dry yeast**
2¾   **teaspoons salt**
1½   **teaspoons sugar**
1½   **cups water, at room temperature**
1   **tablespoon white vinegar**

① In a large bowl, whisk together flour, yeast, salt and sugar. Add water and vinegar and stir just until ball of dough forms (see step A). Cover bowl with plastic wrap and let sit at room temperature for 18 hours.

② Place a large piece of parchment paper on a baking sheet. Place dough on a lightly floured work surface; knead for 10 seconds (see step B). Form into ball by pulling edges into middle. Place dough, seam side down, on parchment paper; coat with nonstick spray and cover with plastic wrap. Let sit at room temperature for 2 hours or until it's doubled in size.

③ About 30 minutes before dough is ready, place a 6- to 8-quart Dutch oven with lid on oven rack and heat oven to 500°.

④ Lightly flour dough on parchment. Carefully remove pot from oven; uncover. Using parchment paper to lift dough, place both the parchment and dough into pot (see step C). Cover pot, return to oven and lower temperature to 450°.

⑤ Bake bread, covered, for 30 minutes, then remove lid and continue to bake another 15 minutes or until bread is browned. Carefully remove bread from pot to a wire rack and cool.

PER SLICE 120 calories; ½ g fat (0 g sat.); 4 g protein; 24 g carbohydrate; 4 g fiber; 530 mg sodium; 0 mg cholesterol

step by step

A

Stir the dough just until it comes together, making sure to pick up any loose flour on the bottom of the bowl.

B

This dough needs very little kneading—a long rise time does the same job here—so just give it a few quick turns.

C

The parchment paper acts as a sling to transfer the dough into the pot easily and center it on the bottom.

TRY FIVE FRESH TAKES ON AMERICA'S FAVORITE BIRD, PLUS HEALTHFUL AND FAMILY-FRIENDLY CASSEROLES—AND LEARN HOW TO MAKE A CLASSIC UPSIDE-DOWN PINEAPPLE CAKE.

SCALLOP & SHRIMP FETTUCCINE, PAGE 54

MARCH

53   61   63

With a chocolate-cookie crust, layers of vanilla and coffee ice cream, and a fudge sauce-and-whipped cream crown topped with crunchy toasted almonds, this frozen treat will delight grown-ups and kids alike.

MUD PIE

MAKES 16 servings **PREP** 10 minutes **BAKE** at 350° for 15 minutes **FREEZE** 2 hours + overnight

CRUST

24   chocolate sandwich cookies (such as Oreos), finely crushed

4   tablespoons unsalted butter, melted

FILLING

2   pints vanilla ice cream

2   pints coffee ice cream

12   chocolate sandwich cookies (such as Oreos), coarsely crushed

1   cup bottled fudge sauce, at room temperature

½   cup plus 2 tablespoons toasted sliced almonds

2   cups heavy cream

2   tablespoons sugar

½   teaspoon vanilla extract
    Chocolate sauce, for drizzling

① **Crust:** Finely crush cookies with food processor. Heat oven to 350°. In a medium-size bowl, stir melted butter into cookie crumbs until moistened. Press into the bottom and up the sides of a 9-inch deep-dish pie plate.

② Bake crust at 350° for 15 minutes. Transfer to a wire rack and let cool for at least 30 minutes.

③ **Filling:** Remove ice creams from freezer; soften for 5 minutes. Transfer vanilla ice cream to a bowl; stir until good spreading consistency. Repeat with coffee ice cream. Spread vanilla ice cream into cooled crust and spread level. Sprinkle with coarsely crushed cookie crumbs and spread coffee ice cream over top; spread level. Freeze for 2 hours.

④ Carefully spread top of pie with fudge sauce; sprinkle with ½ cup of the almonds. Cover with plastic wrap and freeze overnight.

⑤ Remove pie from freezer. Let stand at room temperature for about 20 minutes before serving.

⑥ Meanwhile, whip heavy cream, sugar and vanilla extract on high speed until medium peaks form. Spread whipped cream over pie. Sprinkle with remaining almonds and drizzle with chocolate sauce.

PER SERVING 534 calories; 36 g fat (18 g sat.); 7 g protein; 47 g carbohydrate; 1 g fiber; 276 mg sodium; 127 mg cholesterol

Spring Chicken

Here are five delicious new reasons to love an old favorite.

HERB-ROASTED CHICKEN, PAGE 53

CHICKEN NOODLE
SOUP, PAGE 53

BAKED GREEK CHICKEN

BAKED GREEK CHICKEN

MAKES 6 servings **PREP** 10 minutes
COOK 9 minutes **BAKE** at 425° for 40 minutes

1   whole broiler/fryer chicken, about 5 pounds (giblets removed), cut into 6 pieces
¾   teaspoon salt
2   lemons
3   cloves garlic, minced
1   tablespoon fresh oregano, chopped
⅛   teaspoon black pepper
1   tablespoon olive oil
1   fennel bulb (about 1¼ pounds), trimmed, cored and sliced
1   cup dry orzo
⅓   cup pitted kalamata olives, halved
⅓   cup crumbled feta cheese

① Heat oven to 425°. Pat chicken pieces dry. Loosen skin and sprinkle ¼ teaspoon of the salt under skin. Grate zest of one lemon, then cut lemon in half and juice. In small bowl, stir together 2 teaspoons of the zest, 2 tablespoons of the lemon juice, remaining ½ teaspoon salt, the garlic, oregano and pepper. Tuck half of this mixture under skin of chicken. Cut peel off second lemon; chop fruit into pieces.

② Add olive oil to remaining herb mixture in bowl. Toss with sliced fennel and chopped lemon. Transfer to a large baking dish. Top with chicken pieces and bake at 425° for 40 minutes or until instant-read thermometer inserted in thickest part of the breast registers 160°.

③ Meanwhile, cook orzo following package directions, about 9 minutes. Drain and transfer to a bowl. Transfer chicken to a platter and spoon fennel and 1 tablespoon of the pan drippings in with orzo. Add olives and feta to bowl and stir to combine. Serve warm.

PER SERVING 416 calories; 12 g fat (3 g sat.); 45 g protein; 32 g carbohydrate; 5 g fiber; 684 mg sodium; 134 mg cholesterol

CHICKEN CACCIATORE

MAKES 8 servings **PREP** 15 minutes **COOK** 35 minutes

1   broiler/fryer chicken, about 5 pounds (giblets removed), cut into 8 pieces (save wings for another use)
¼   teaspoon salt
2   tablespoons olive oil
1   package (10 ounces) white mushrooms, cleaned and quartered
2   small green bell peppers, seeded and diced
1   medium onion, chopped
2   cloves garlic, sliced
2   cans (14 ounces each) diced tomatoes with basil, garlic and oregano
½   cup red wine or water
1   teaspoon fresh rosemary, chopped
¼   teaspoon red pepper flakes
1   pound whole-wheat spaghetti, cooked

① Remove skin from chicken and discard. Season chicken with salt.

② Heat 1 tablespoon of the oil in a large, deep covered sauté pan over medium-high heat. Add chicken and brown, meaty side down, 3 minutes. Turn chicken over and continue to cook 1 minute. Remove to plate.

③ Reduce heat to medium. Add remaining tablespoon oil to pan and add mushrooms, green peppers and onion. Cook, stirring occasionally, 5 minutes until softened. Add garlic and cook 1 more minute. Stir in tomatoes, wine or water, rosemary and red pepper flakes. Bring to a simmer. Add chicken, cover and simmer 15 minutes. Uncover and continue to cook 10 minutes, until chicken is cooked through and tender. Serve over whole-wheat spaghetti.

PER SERVING 437 calories; 9 g fat (2 g sat.); 39 g protein; 50 g carbohydrate; 9 g fiber; 418 mg sodium; 95 mg cholesterol

ARROZ CON POLLO

MAKES 8 servings **PREP** 15 minutes **COOK** 35 minutes

1   broiler/fryer chicken, about 5 pounds (giblets removed), cut into 8 pieces (save wings for another use)
¾   teaspoon salt
¼   teaspoon black pepper
¼   cup all-purpose flour
3   tablespoons vegetable oil
1   small onion, diced
3   cloves garlic, sliced
1   cup white rice, uncooked
1   can (14.5 ounces) reduced-sodium chicken broth
1   packet (from 1.41-ounce box) Goya Sazon with Azafràn seasoning
1   box (10 ounces) frozen green peas, thawed

① Remove skin from chicken and discard. Season pieces with ¼ teaspoon of the salt and ⅛ teaspoon of the pepper. Toss in flour to coat.

② Heat 1 tablespoon of the oil in a large covered sauté pan over medium-high heat. Brown half of the chicken pieces, about 3 minutes. Transfer to a plate. Add another 1 tablespoon oil and repeat with remaining chicken.

③ Reduce heat to medium and add remaining 1 tablespoon oil and the onion to pan. Cook 3 minutes. Add garlic; cook 1 minute. Stir in rice. Add broth, seasoning packet, remaining ½ teaspoon salt and remaining ⅛ teaspoon pepper. Increase heat to high and bring to a boil.

④ Stir in peas and return chicken to pan along with any accumulated juices. Cover and reduce heat to medium-low. Cook 20 to 25 minutes or until rice is tender. Let stand 5 minutes, covered, before serving.

PER SERVING 351 calories; 10 g fat (2 g sat.); 34 g protein; 30 g carbohydrate; 2 g fiber; 576 mg sodium; 95 mg cholesterol

CHICKEN NOODLE SOUP

MAKES 2 batches, 6 servings each
PREP 25 minutes **COOK** 1 hour, 39 minutes

1   roaster chicken, about 6 pounds, giblets removed
6   carrots
4   celery ribs
2   medium onions
6   cloves garlic
1   tablespoon salt
1½   teaspoons dried dill
1   tablespoon olive oil
1   can (14 ounces) diced tomatoes, drained
½   teaspoon black pepper
1   bag (12 ounces) wide egg noodles

①   Place chicken in a large stockpot (8 quarts). Peel 3 of the carrots and cut into 3 pieces. Trim 2 of the celery ribs and cut into 3 pieces. Peel and quarter 1 of the onions. Peel garlic; cut 3 cloves in half. Add prepped carrots, celery, onion and garlic to pot with chicken. Add enough cold water to cover, about 2½ quarts. Stir in 1 teaspoon each of the salt and dill. Bring to a boil over high heat and then reduce heat to medium. Simmer for 1½ hours, occasionally skimming any foam from top.

②   Meanwhile, peel and slice remaining 3 carrots and slice 2 ribs celery. Chop remaining onion and slice remaining 3 cloves garlic.

③   Carefully remove chicken from pot to a large bowl and let rest until cool enough to handle. Strain broth into a large bowl; discard soggy vegetables. Remove fat from top of broth. Once chicken has cooled, remove meat from bones and discard skin and bones. Chop meat into bite-size pieces.

④   Heat olive oil in soup pot over medium heat. Add sliced carrots, celery and onion. Cook 3 minutes. Add sliced garlic; cook an additional minute. Stir in remaining 2 teaspoons salt, remaining ½ teaspoon dried dill, the tomatoes and pepper. Add defatted broth back to pot and bring to a simmer. Simmer 6 minutes, until vegetables are tender.

⑤   Meanwhile, bring a large pot of salted water to boiling. Add noodles to boiling water and cook 6 minutes.

⑥   Once vegetables are tender, add chicken back to pot. Remove half of soup (8 cups) and transfer to a freezer-safe container. Save for another meal. Drain and freeze half of noodles along with soup (in a separate container). Stir remaining noodles into soup in pot and serve immediately.

PER SERVING 274 calories; 6 g fat (1 g sat.); 28 g protein; 24 g carbohydrate; 1 g fiber; 787 mg sodium; 109 mg cholesterol

HERB-ROASTED CHICKEN

MAKES 6 servings **PREP** 15 minutes
ROAST at 450° for 30 minutes; then at 400° for 55 minutes

2   tablespoons fresh parsley, chopped
1   tablespoon fresh sage leaves (about 6), chopped, plus a few sprigs
2   cloves garlic, minced
2   teaspoons fresh thyme leaves, chopped, plus 1 sprig
1   roaster chicken, about 6½ pounds, giblets removed
½   teaspoon salt
2   medium red onions, trimmed
1½   pounds baby new potatoes
1   teaspoon olive oil
¼   teaspoon black pepper

①   Heat oven to 450°. In small bowl, combine parsley, chopped sage, garlic and chopped thyme. Pat chicken dry with paper towels and place in a large roasting pan. Loosen skin around breast, thighs and legs and tuck half the herb mixture (about 2 tablespoons) under the skin. Rub ¼ teaspoon of the salt under the skin.

②   Cut 1 of the onions in quarters. Place 2 quarters in the cavity of the bird, along with the sage and thyme sprigs. Tie legs together.

③   Transfer roasting pan to oven. Roast at 450° for 30 minutes. Meanwhile, halve or quarter potatoes. Quarter the second onion, then cut all onion pieces into 1-inch chunks. Combine potatoes, onion, remaining herb mixture, the oil, pepper and remaining ¼ teaspoon salt in a bowl. Toss to combine.

④   After 30 minutes, reduce oven temperature to 400° and add potato mixture to pan. Roast at 400° for 55 minutes or until instant-read thermometer inserted in thickest part of the thigh registers 180°. Let chicken rest 5 minutes before removing skin and carving.

PER SERVING 416 calories; 12 g fat (3 g sat.); 54 g protein; 19 g carbohydrate; 3 g fiber; 381 mg sodium; 169 mg cholesterol

The Family Dish

These hearty (and healthy!) casseroles will have them coming back for more.

SCALLOP & SHRIMP FETTUCCINE

MAKES 6 servings **PREP** 25 minutes **COOK** 5 minutes **BAKE** at 350° for 20 minutes

- 2 tablespoons olive oil
- ¾ pound scallops
- ¾ pound large shrimp, shelled and deveined
- ½ teaspoon salt
- ⅛ teaspoon black pepper
- 2 cups fat-free half-and-half
- 1 tablespoon cornstarch
- 1 can (6.5 ounces) chopped clams, undrained
- ½ cup plus 6 tablespoons shredded Swiss & Gruyère cheese blend
- 2 tablespoons chopped fresh tarragon
- ⅛ teaspoon cayenne pepper
- 1 box (12 ounces) spinach fettuccine, cooked following package directions

① Heat oven to 350°. Coat a 3½-quart oval dish with nonstick cooking spray.

② Heat oil in a large nonstick skillet over medium-high heat. Add scallops, shrimp, ¼ teaspoon of the salt and the pepper. Cook for 2 minutes per side. Remove to a plate.

③ Blend half-and-half and cornstarch. Bring to a simmer in the skillet. Simmer 1 minute. Take off heat and stir in clams and the juices, ½ cup of the cheese, the tarragon, cayenne and remaining ¼ teaspoon salt. Add cooked shellfish and toss with fettuccine.

④ Spoon into prepared dish. Sprinkle with remaining 6 tablespoons cheese. Bake at 350° for 20 minutes.

PER SERVING 467 calories; 12 g fat (4 g sat.); 35 g protein; 53 g carbohydrate; 2 g fiber; 736 mg sodium; 127 mg cholesterol

MOROCCAN BEEF,
PAGE 59

CHICKEN CURRY & BROWN BASMATI RICE, PAGE 59

Sweet and savory flavors blend perfectly in this anything-but-old-school chicken casserole.

ROASTED VEGETABLE PIE

MAKES 6 servings **PREP** 25 minutes **COOK** 1 minute **BAKE** at 450° for 45 minutes; at 425° for 30 minutes

1 small cauliflower, cut into florets, about 4 cups
1 small butternut squash, peeled and cut into 1-inch pieces
2 medium parsnips, peeled and cut into ½-inch pieces
1 cup baby carrots
1 sweet red pepper, cut into 1-inch pieces
2 tablespoons olive oil
½ teaspoon salt
½ teaspoon black pepper
1 cup vegetable broth
1 tablespoon cornstarch
¾ teaspoon dried thyme
¾ teaspoon dried oregano
2 tablespoons plain bread crumbs
1 package (15 ounces) refrigerated rolled piecrusts
2 tablespoons grated Parmesan cheese
1 egg beaten with 1 tablespoon water

① Heat oven to 450°. Coat a large baking pan with nonstick cooking spray.

② In a large bowl, add cauliflower, squash, parsnips, carrots and red pepper. Toss with olive oil and ¼ teaspoon each of the salt and pepper. Spread out on the baking pan in a single layer. Bake at 450° for 30 minutes, stirring halfway.

③ Meanwhile, place the broth in a medium-size saucepan and stir in the cornstarch. Bring to a boil, lower heat and simmer 1 minute until thickened. Stir in the thyme, oregano and remaining salt and pepper. In a large bowl, gently toss roasted vegetables, bread crumbs and sauce.

④ Fit one of the piecrusts into a deep-dish 9-inch pie plate. Sprinkle 1 tablespoon of the cheese over the bottom. Spoon in vegetable mixture and sprinkle with remaining 1 tablespoon cheese. Place the second piecrust on top and crimp crusts together. Pierce a few times with a paring knife to vent. Brush lightly with the egg-water mixture.

⑤ Bake at 450° for 15 minutes. Lower heat to 425° and bake for an additional 30 minutes. Remove from oven and allow to cool slightly before slicing.

PER SERVING 467 calories; 25 g fat (9 g sat.); 8 g protein; 56 g carbohydrate; 7 g fiber; 729 mg sodium; 50 mg cholesterol

**CHIPOTLE BEANS & PORK,
PAGE 59**

Chipotle chiles give this comforting
meal a smoky kick. For more heat,
switch to a spicy sausage.

MOROCCAN BEEF

MAKES 6 servings **PREP** 20 minutes
COOK 12 minutes **BAKE** at 350° for 2 hours

1¾ **pounds beef round, cut into
     1½-inch cubes**
¼   **teaspoon salt**
¼   **teaspoon black pepper**
2   **tablespoons vegetable oil**
1   **large onion, peeled and sliced**
¾   **teaspoon ground cumin**
¾   **teaspoon ground ginger**
2   **cinnamon sticks**
1   **can (14½ ounces) diced tomatoes**
1   **can (14½ ounces) reduced-sodium
     beef broth**
½   **pound green beans, cut into 1-inch
     pieces**
2   **cups shredded carrots**
3   **cups cooked whole-wheat couscous**

① Heat oven to 350°.

② Season beef with ⅛ teaspoon each of
the salt and pepper. Heat 1 tablespoon oil
in a large flame-proof covered casserole
over medium-high heat. Brown beef for
3 minutes, turn and brown for 3 additional
minutes. Remove to a plate and reserve.
Add remaining tablespoon oil and the onion
and cook for 3 minutes. Stir in cumin, ginger,
cinnamon, tomatoes, broth and remaining
⅛ teaspoon each salt and pepper. Bring to
a simmer over high heat and stir in the
beef and any accumulated juices. With a
wooden spoon, scrape up any browned bits
from the bottom of the casserole. Cover
and bake at 350° for 1½ hours.

③ Meanwhile, bring a medium-size pot of
water to a boil. Add green beans and cook
3 minutes, until crisp-tender. Drain and
rinse in cold water. Set aside.

④ After 1½ hours, stir the green beans
and shredded carrots into the casserole.
Cover and bake an additional 30 minutes.

⑤ Serve with couscous.

PER SERVING 516 calories; 23 g fat (7 g sat.); 35 g
protein; 43 g carbohydrate; 8 g fiber; 641 mg
sodium; 82 mg cholesterol

CHICKEN CURRY
& BROWN BASMATI RICE

MAKES 6 servings **PREP** 15 minutes
COOK 10 minutes **BAKE** at 350° for 45 minutes

1   **tablespoon vegetable oil**
1½ **pounds boneless, skinless chicken
      thighs, cut into 1-inch pieces**
¼   **teaspoon salt**
1   **medium onion, chopped**
1   **tablespoon chopped fresh ginger root**
2   **teaspoons curry powder**
1½ **cups reduced-sodium chicken broth**
1   **can (15 ounces) chickpeas, drained
      and rinsed**
½   **cup golden raisins**
3   **cups cooked brown basmati rice**
2   **small sweet red peppers, seeded
      and sliced**
¼   **cup sliced almonds**

① Heat oven to 350°. Coat a 13 x 9 x 2-inch
baking dish with nonstick cooking spray.

② Heat oil in a large nonstick skillet over
medium-high heat. Add chicken and sauté
for 5 minutes, turning after 3 minutes.
Season with ⅛ teaspoon of the salt. Remove
from skillet and keep warm.

③ Add onion and ginger to skillet and
cook for 3 minutes, stirring occasionally.
Add curry and cook 1 minute. Add broth
and remaining ⅛ teaspoon salt to skillet.
Bring to a simmer and add chickpeas,
raisins and chicken. Simmer for 1 minute.

④ Evenly spoon cooked rice into prepared
dish. Spoon chicken curry mixture over
top. Scatter peppers over curry. Cover with
foil. Bake, covered, at 350° for 30 minutes.
Uncover and scatter almonds over
peppers. Bake, uncovered, for 15 additional
minutes. Cool slightly before serving.

PER SERVING 297 calories; 7 g fat (1 g sat.); 10 g
protein; 51 g carbohydrate; 7 g fiber; 353 mg
sodium; 7 mg cholesterol

CHIPOTLE BEANS & PORK

MAKES 6 servings **PREP** 10 minutes
COOK 5 minutes **BAKE** at 350° for 70 minutes

1   **tablespoon vegetable oil**
1   **pound thick-cut boneless pork chops,
     cut into 1½-inch cubes**
2   **fully cooked roasted garlic-flavored
     chicken sausages (from a 12-ounce
     package), cut into ½-inch coins**
1   **can (15 ounces) small white beans,
     undrained**
1   **can (15 ounces) pinto beans,
     undrained**
1   **can (15 ounces) red kidney beans,
     undrained**
1   **can (8 ounces) no-salt-added
     tomato sauce**
2   **chipotle chiles in adobo sauce,
     chopped**
1   **cup loosely packed cilantro leaves,
     chopped**

① Heat oven to 350°. Coat a large covered
casserole with nonstick cooking spray.

② Heat oil in a large nonstick skillet over
medium-high heat. Add the pork and
sausage and cook 5 minutes, turning
halfway through cooking time.

③ In prepared casserole, stir together the
beans, tomato sauce, chipotle, half of the
cilantro, the pork and sausage. Bake, covered,
for 30 minutes. Uncover and bake for an
additional 30 to 40 minutes, until thickened.

④ Allow to cool slightly and garnish with
remaining cilantro.

PER SERVING 361 calories; 11 g fat (3 g sat.); 32 g
protein; 36 g carbohydrate; 12 g fiber; 930 mg
sodium; 74 mg cholesterol

Slow Cooker Suppers

Classic dishes with a vegetarian twist.

CHICKPEA STEW OVER COUSCOUS

MAKES 8 servings **SOAK** overnight **PREP** 10 minutes **SLOW-COOK** 5 hours on HIGH or 7 hours on LOW

- 1 **pound dried chickpeas, picked over and rinsed**
- 1 **medium onion, chopped**
- 2 **teaspoons dried oregano**
- 3 **small zucchini (6 ounces each), cut into ¾-inch pieces**
- 1 **can (14.5 ounces) diced tomatoes with basil, garlic and oregano**
- ½ **cup vegetable broth**
- 1 **teaspoon salt**
- ½ **teaspoon black pepper**

- 1 **box (7.6 ounces) whole-wheat couscous, cooked according to package directions**
- 1 **cup crumbled feta (optional)**

① Soak chickpeas overnight. Drain and place them in slow cooker with onion and 1 teaspoon oregano; add 4 cups water. Cover and cook for 3 hours on HIGH or 5 hours on LOW or until tender.

② Drain chickpea mixture and return to slow cooker. Stir zucchini, tomatoes and broth into slow cooker. Cover and cook an additional 2 hours. Stir in remaining 1 teaspoon oregano, salt and black pepper right before serving; spoon over couscous and sprinkle each serving with feta cheese, if desired.

PER SERVING 350 calories; 5 g fat (0 g sat.); 17 g protein; 62 g carbohydrate; 15 g fiber; 489 mg sodium; 0 mg cholesterol

INDIAN-SPICED YELLOW SPLIT PEA SOUP

MAKES 8 servings **PREP** 10 minutes
SLOW-COOK 5½ hours on HIGH or
7 hours on LOW **COOK** 2 minutes

- 2 cups yellow split peas, rinsed and picked over
- 5 whole cloves
- 1 cinnamon stick
- 1½ tablespoons unsalted butter
- 1¾ teaspoons ground cumin
- 1 teaspoon grated ginger
- ½ teaspoon ground turmeric
- ½ teaspoon mustard seeds
- ½ teaspoon ground coriander
- ⅛ teaspoon cayenne pepper
- ½ cup light cream
- 2 teaspoons salt
- 1 teaspoon black pepper
- 4 cups cooked basmati rice (optional)

① Combine 5 cups water, peas, cloves and cinnamon stick in slow cooker. Cover and cook on HIGH for 3 hours or LOW for 4 hours.

② Remove the cloves and cinnamon stick. In a medium-size nonstick skillet, melt the butter over medium heat. Add cumin, ½ teaspoon ginger, turmeric, mustard seeds, coriander and cayenne to skillet and cook 1 to 2 minutes, stirring constantly. Stir the spice mixture into slow cooker and continue to cook another 2½ hours on HIGH or 3 hours on LOW.

③ Carefully puree soup in batches. Just before serving, stir in remaining ½ teaspoon ginger, the cream, salt and pepper and serve over rice, if desired.

PER SERVING 218 calories; 6 g fat (3 g sat.); 11 g protein; 30 g carbohydrate; 14 g fiber; 590 mg sodium; 16 mg cholesterol

MEXICAN LASAGNA

MAKES 8 servings **PREP** 15 minutes **SLOW-COOK** 3½ hours on HIGH or 6 hours on LOW

- 1 head cauliflower, cored
- 3 plum tomatoes, chopped
- 1 can (15.5 ounces) black beans, rinsed and drained
- 1 cup frozen corn
- ⅓ cup chopped cilantro
- 2 teaspoons chili powder
- 2 teaspoons ground cumin
- 3½ cups shredded Monterey Jack cheese
- 1 jar (16 ounces) tomatillo salsa
- 6 fajita-size flour tortillas
  Sour cream (optional)

① Cut cauliflower into florets and slice them into ½-inch-thick slices (you should have about 6 cups). Place cauliflower, tomatoes, beans, corn and cilantro in a large bowl. Sprinkle with chili powder and cumin and stir to combine.

② Coat inside of oval slow cooker bowl with nonstick cooking spray. Spread a scant 3 cups cauliflower mixture over bottom of slow cooker, then sprinkle with 1 cup Monterey Jack cheese and a generous ½ cup salsa over top. Place 2 tortillas on top. Repeat layering two more times, setting aside last 2 tortillas. Cut these tortillas into 2-inch pieces and scatter over top.

③ Cover and cook on HIGH for 3 hours or LOW for 5½ hours or until cauliflower is tender. Top with remaining ½ cup cheese. Cover and cook another 30 minutes or until cheese has melted. Let sit for 10 minutes, then serve with sour cream, if desired.

PER SERVING 362 calories; 18 g fat (10 g sat.); 19 g protein; 30 g carbohydrate; 6 g fiber; 1,011 mg sodium; 44 mg cholesterol

Pineapple Upside-Down Cake

Serve when it's still a little warm—people will flip for this surprisingly easy dessert.

If you rush to pop the cake out too soon, the pineapple rings and cherries may stick to the pan. Allow the full 10 minutes for cooling. Before there were ovens, this retro treat—sometimes credited to Dole Pineapple, though the company neither confirms nor denies this—was cooked in a cast-iron skillet on the stovetop.

PINEAPPLE UPSIDE-DOWN CAKE

MAKES 12 servings **PREP** 20 minutes **BAKE** at 350° for 40 minutes

TOPPING
- ¼ cup (½ stick) unsalted butter
- ½ cup packed dark-brown sugar
- 1 can (20 ounces) pineapple rings in juice
- 10 to 12 maraschino cherries

CAKE
- 2 cups all-purpose flour
- 2 teaspoons baking powder
- ½ teaspoon salt
- ⅛ teaspoon ground nutmeg
- ½ cup (1 stick) unsalted butter, softened
- 1 cup granulated sugar
- 2 eggs
- ½ cup milk
- 1 teaspoon vanilla extract

① Heat oven to 350°. **Topping:** Melt butter in a 13 x 9-inch metal baking pan on stovetop over low heat. Remove from heat and stir in brown sugar (see step A). Drain pineapple rings, reserving ½ cup juice. Fit rings tightly into bottom of pan (see step B); you will need 10 to 12. Save any extra rings for snacking. Tuck a maraschino cherry in center of each ring.

② **Cake:** In medium-size bowl, whisk flour, baking powder, salt and nutmeg. In a large bowl, beat butter and sugar 2 minutes. Add eggs; beat until blended. On low speed, beat in half the flour mixture. Pour in reserved ½ cup pineapple juice and the milk; beat until blended. Beat in remaining flour mixture, then vanilla.

③ Spread batter into pan. Bake at 350° for 40 minutes or until toothpick inserted in center comes out clean. Cool cake in pan on rack 10 minutes. Place a baking sheet over cake; carefully invert (see step C). If any pineapple or cherries stick to pan, gently replace on cake top.

PER SERVING 316 calories; 13 g fat (8 g sat.); 4 g protein; 48 g carbohydrate; 1 g fiber; 186 mg sodium; 66 mg cholesterol

step by step

A

Once butter has melted, tilt pan to coat. Stir in brown sugar until it covers the bottom.

B

Fit pineapple snugly into pan; you will need to push rings up sides so 10 to 12 will fit.

C

Place a large baking sheet or platter over cake. Carefully turn cake over onto sheet.

SPRING IS THE SEASON TO GO GREEN. CELEBRATE IT WITH LIGHT AND FLAVORFUL DISHES FEATURING FRESH VEGGIES. SAMPLE GLUTEN-FREE DISHES AS WELL AS A BEVY OF BAKED GOODS.

SAUTÉED SHRIMP & RED CHARD, PAGE 85

APRIL

78

91

93

Baking—not frying—these homemade treats saves a whopping 12 grams of fat compared to store-bought.

VANILLA CAKE DOUGHNUTS

MAKES 6 doughnuts **PREP** 10 minutes
BAKE at 325° for 13 minutes

1¼ cups all-purpose flour
½ teaspoon baking soda
¼ teaspoon salt
½ cup low-fat buttermilk
⅓ cup packed dark-brown sugar
1 egg
4 teaspoons unsalted butter, melted
1 teaspoon vanilla extract

① Heat oven to 325°. Coat a 6-indentation doughnut pan with nonstick cooking spray.

② In large bowl, whisk flour, baking soda and salt. In small bowl, whisk buttermilk, sugar, egg, melted butter and vanilla extract until smooth. Add milk mixture to flour mixture; whisk until smooth.

③ Spoon batter into a large resealable plastic bag. Cut off a corner and squeeze into prepared indents, about two-thirds full. Bake at 325° for 13 minutes, until doughnuts spring back when pressed. Cool in pan on rack 3 minutes, then carefully turn out onto rack to cool.

CHOCOLATE CAKE DOUGHNUTS

MAKES 6 doughnuts **PREP** 10 minutes
BAKE at 325° for 13 minutes

1 cup all-purpose flour
¼ cup unsweetened cocoa powder
½ teaspoon baking soda
¼ teaspoon salt
½ cup low-fat buttermilk
½ cup packed dark-brown sugar
1 egg
4 teaspoons unsalted butter, melted
1 teaspoon vanilla extract

① Heat oven to 325°. Coat doughnut pan with nonstick cooking spray.

② In large bowl, whisk flour, cocoa, baking soda and salt. In small bowl, whisk buttermilk, sugar, egg, butter and vanilla until smooth. Add milk mixture to flour mixture; whisk until blended and smooth.

③ Spoon batter into a large resealable plastic bag. Cut off a corner and squeeze batter into prepared indents, about two-thirds full. Smooth tops. Bake at 325° for 13 minutes, until doughnuts spring back when lightly pressed. Cool in pan on rack 3 minutes, then carefully turn out directly onto rack to cool.

TOPPINGS

2¼ cups confectioners' sugar
3 tablespoons milk
Sprinkles, toasted coconut, mini chips, cinnamon-sugar
1 tablespoon unsweetened cocoa powder

① **For powdered doughnuts:** Place ¼ cup confectioners' sugar in a sifter and gently sift over cooled vanilla doughnuts. Flip doughnuts; cover with sugar.

② **For white-frosted doughnuts:** In small bowl, combine 1 cup of the confectioners' sugar and 1 tablespoon of the milk. Stir until smooth. Dip cooled doughnuts into bowl and allow excess frosting to drip back into bowl. Transfer to rack. Top with sprinkles, coconut or mini chips, if desired. Transfer any extra frosting to a plastic bag.

③ **For chocolate-frosted doughnuts:** Combine remaining 1 cup confectioners' sugar, the cocoa and remaining 2 tablespoons milk. Stir until smooth.

Dip cooled doughnuts into bowl and allow excess frosting to drip back into bowl. Transfer to rack. Top with sprinkles, coconut or mini chips, if desired. Transfer any extra frosting to a plastic bag.

④ **For drizzle:** Snip small corner off bags of frosting. Decoratively drizzle over cooled doughnuts.

⑤ **For cinnamon-sugar doughnuts:** Toss still-warm vanilla doughnuts in cinnamon-sugar to coat.

PER POWDERED OR CINNAMON-SUGAR 203 calories; 4 g fat (2 g sat.); 5 g protein; 37 g carbohydrate; 1 g fiber; 242 mg sodium; 43 mg cholesterol

PER FROSTED OR DRIZZLED VANILLA OR CHOCOLATE 206-248 calories; 4 g fat (2 g sat.); 5 g protein; 48 g carbohydrate; 1 g fiber; 243 mg sodium; 43 mg cholesterol

PER COCONUT 267 calories; 5 g fat (3 g sat.); 5 g protein; 50 g carbohydrate; 1 g fiber; 256 mg sodium; 44 mg cholesterol

Green Party

Seasonal meals that will have you vegging out in a whole new way.

**SCALLOPS WITH
ASPARAGUS SALAD,
PAGE 73**

CHERRY TOMATO
& PROSCIUTTO
FOCACCIA, PAGE 73

ONION, BACON
& SPINACH TART

ONION, BACON & SPINACH TART

MAKES 8 servings **PREP** 10 minutes
COOK 29 minutes **BAKE** at 375° for 15 minutes,
then at 325° for 20 minutes **BROIL** 2 minutes

- 1 refrigerated rolled piecrust (from a 15-ounce package)
- 4 slices bacon, cut crosswise into ¼-inch slices
- 6 cups baby spinach
- 1½ pounds yellow onions (about 4), halved and cut crosswise into ¼-inch slices (6 cups)
- ¾ teaspoon salt
- ¼ teaspoon dried thyme
- 3 eggs
- ¾ cup half-and-half
- ¼ teaspoon black pepper
- ¼ cup shredded Gruyère cheese

① Heat oven to 375°. Fit piecrust into 9-inch tart pan. Trim excess crust from top edge of tart pan; refrigerate while preparing filling.

② Heat a large nonstick skillet over medium heat. Add bacon to skillet and cook, stirring often, for 8 minutes. Add spinach to skillet and cook 1 minute, stirring until wilted. Using a slotted spoon, remove bacon mixture to a paper-towel-lined plate.

③ Return skillet to medium heat and add onions, ¼ teaspoon salt and the thyme. Cover and cook 25 minutes over medium heat, stirring occasionally, or until browned. Remove from heat and allow to cool, uncovered, 5 minutes.

④ Whisk together eggs, half-and-half, pepper and the remaining ½ teaspoon salt. Stir bacon mixture and onions into eggs; stir to combine. Pour egg mixture into crust. Bake at 375° for 15 minutes. Reduce heat to 325° and continue to bake 20 minutes.

⑤ Heat broiler. Sprinkle tart with Gruyère and broil for 1 to 2 minutes. Let stand 5 minutes before slicing and serving.

PER SERVING 295 calories; 17 g fat (7 g sat.); 8 g protein; 26 g carbohydrate; 3 g fiber; 483 mg sodium; 107 mg cholesterol

SPRING VEGETABLE RISOTTO

MAKES 4 servings **PREP** 15 minutes **COOK** 39 minutes

- ½ pound sugar snap peas, trimmed and cut into ½-inch pieces
- 3½ cups low-sodium chicken broth
- 1 tablespoon plus 1 teaspoon olive oil
- 4 leeks, cleaned and thinly sliced
- ½ teaspoon salt
- ¼ teaspoon black pepper
- 2 cloves garlic, minced
- 1 cup arborio rice
- ¾ cup white wine
- 3 large carrots, cut into ¼-inch pieces
- ¾ cup grated Parmesan cheese
- 1 tablespoon unsalted butter
- 1 teaspoon lemon juice

① Cook peas in boiling water about 4 minutes or until crisp-tender. Drain and rinse with cold water; set aside.

② Pour broth into a medium-size saucepan and bring to a simmer over medium heat; reduce heat to low and keep broth warm.

③ Heat 1 tablespoon of the olive oil in a large saucepan over medium heat. Add leeks, salt and pepper and cook 6 minutes, stirring frequently, or until softened. Stir in garlic and cook 1 minute.

④ Add remaining 1 teaspoon olive oil to saucepan. Stir in rice and cook 1 minute. Add wine to saucepan and stir until almost evaporated, about 3 minutes. Stir in warm broth, ½ cup at a time. Stir frequently until liquid is absorbed before adding the next ½ cup (about 22 minutes total). When you have about 10 minutes of cook time remaining, stir in carrots.

⑤ Add peas to saucepan and cook, stirring constantly, 2 minutes, or until heated through. Remove from heat and stir in Parmesan cheese, butter and lemon juice.

PER SERVING 385 calories; 12 g fat (5 g sat.); 14 g protein; 47 g carbohydrate; 6 g fiber; 1,111 mg sodium; 25 mg cholesterol

FARFALLE WITH PEAS & GOAT CHEESE

MAKES 6 servings   **PREP** 15 minutes   **COOK** 12 minutes

8   ounces farfalle pasta

1½ cups frozen peas, thawed

1   large red pepper, seeded and cut into ¼-inch strips

1   tablespoon cornstarch

2   tablespoons olive oil

3   cloves garlic, minced

2   teaspoons dried oregano

⅛   teaspoon red pepper flakes

½   cup white wine

1½ cups low-sodium chicken broth

½   teaspoon salt

1   bunch chives, cut into ½-inch pieces

¾   cup chopped walnuts, toasted

½   cup crumbled goat cheese

① Bring a medium-size pot of salted water to a boil. Cook pasta according to package directions, about 12 minutes, reserving ¼ cup of the pasta water. Add peas and red pepper to pasta pot for last 2 minutes of cook time. Drain pasta mixture and set aside.

② Meanwhile, stir together cornstarch and 1 tablespoon water; set aside. Heat olive oil in a large nonstick skillet over medium-high heat. Add garlic, oregano and red pepper flakes and cook 1 minute. Stir in wine and bring to a boil. Cook for about 2 minutes, stirring occasionally.

Stir in chicken broth and bring to a boil. Stir in cornstarch mixture and cook 2 minutes or until thickened. Stir in salt.

③ Add pasta mixture to skillet and stir together with sauce. Stir in chives, walnuts and ¼ cup of the goat cheese, adding pasta water by the tablespoonful if mixture appears dry. Sprinkle with remaining goat cheese. Serve immediately.

PER SERVING 547 calories; 25 g fat (4 g sat.); 17 g protein; 59 g carbohydrate; 7 g fiber; 574 mg sodium; 7 mg cholesterol

SCALLOPS WITH ASPARAGUS SALAD

MAKES 6 servings **PREP** 15 minutes
COOK 18 minutes

1	tablespoon cider vinegar
1	teaspoon Dijon mustard
1	shallot, minced
4	tablespoons extra virgin olive oil
1	pound new potatoes, cut into ¼-inch slices
1	pound asparagus
½	teaspoon salt
½	teaspoon black pepper
1½	pounds sea scallops (about 24 scallops)
1½	tablespoons unsalted butter
10	cups salad greens (about one 5-ounce container)

① In small bowl, whisk together cider vinegar, mustard and shallot. Gradually drizzle in 3 tablespoons olive oil, whisking continuously until dressing is emulsified; set aside until ready to use.

② Bring a medium-size pot of salted water to a boil over medium-high heat. Add potato slices to boiling water and cook 4 minutes; drain. Cut 1 inch off of bottoms of asparagus; discard. Cut stalks into 2-inch pieces.

③ Heat remaining 1 tablespoon oil in a large nonstick skillet over medium-high heat. Add potato slices to skillet and cover; cook 3 to 4 minutes, stirring occasionally.

Add asparagus pieces to skillet and stir to combine. Sprinkle potato mixture with ¼ teaspoon each salt and pepper. Cover and cook an additional 4 minutes, stirring occasionally. Remove asparagus and potatoes to a plate. Very carefully, wipe out hot skillet with tongs and paper towels.

④ Season scallops with remaining ¼ teaspoon each salt and pepper. Return skillet to medium-high heat and add half of butter, swirling to coat bottom. Add half of the scallops to the skillet and cook 1½ to 2 minutes on the first side, then flip and cook 1 minute on second side, adjusting heat as necessary so butter doesn't burn. Repeat process with remaining butter and scallops.

⑤ Toss salad greens with 2 tablespoons prepared dressing and divide among plates. Toss asparagus mixture with remaining dressing and divide among salad plates, then divide scallops among plates and serve immediately.

PER SERVING 306 calories; 13 g fat (3 g sat.); 24 g protein; 25 g carbohydrate; 5 g fiber; 431 mg sodium; 45 mg cholesterol

CHERRY TOMATO & PROSCIUTTO FOCACCIA

MAKES 8 servings **PREP** 15 minutes **BAKE** at 425° for 14 minutes, then at 325° for 15 minutes **ROAST** at 325° for 30 minutes

16	ounces frozen pizza dough, thawed
2	tablespoons grated Parmesan cheese
1½	pounds cherry tomatoes, halved
1	large shallot, minced
2	garlic cloves, minced
1	tablespoon balsamic vinegar
½	teaspoon salt
¼	teaspoon black pepper
2	cups baby arugula
8	ounces mozzarella cheese, shredded
1	package (3 ounces) thinly sliced prosciutto, cut or torn lengthwise into ½-inch strips
2	tablespoons fresh basil, sliced into ribbons

① Heat oven to 425°. Roll and stretch dough into a large rimmed baking sheet, at least 15 x 10 x 1 inches. Sprinkle with Parmesan cheese and bake at 425° for 14 minutes or until lightly browned. Remove from oven and set aside. Reduce oven temperature to 325°.

② While dough is baking, toss together tomatoes, shallot, garlic, vinegar, salt and pepper in a medium-size bowl. Spread tomatoes in an even layer in a rimmed baking sheet and roast at 325° for 30 minutes. Remove from oven and gently stir in arugula.

③ Sprinkle 1 cup of the mozzarella over dough and scatter tomato mixture over top using a slotted spoon. Distribute prosciutto slices over tomatoes. Sprinkle remaining mozzarella over top and bake at 325° for 15 minutes. Cool on wire rack 5 minutes, then sprinkle with basil.

PER SERVING 293 calories; 10 g fat (5 g sat.); 15 g protein; 35 g carbohydrate; 2 g fiber; 772 mg sodium; 28 mg cholesterol

Going Against the Grain

Need to go gluten-free—even temporarily? These recipes make it deliciously easy.

BAKED PENNE &
TURKEY MEATBALLS,
PAGE 79

CHICKEN
SCALOPPINE
AL MARSALA,
PAGE 79

THAI PORK WRAPS,
PAGE 79

TOMATILLO SHRIMP ENCHILADAS

MAKES 8 enchiladas **PREP** 30 minutes
COOK 6 minutes **MICROWAVE** 1 minute
BAKE at 375° for 15 minutes

- 2   tablespoons olive oil
- ½   medium red onion, peeled and thinly sliced
- ½   medium green bell pepper, seeded and thinly sliced
- 1¼   pounds medium shrimp, shelled, deveined and cut in half crossways
- 1   cup frozen corn, thawed
- 1   teaspoon chili powder
- ½   teaspoon ground cumin
- 8   corn tortillas
- 1   bottle (16 ounces) tomatillo salsa
- 3   tablespoons half-and-half
- 1   cup shredded reduced-fat Monterey Jack cheese

① Heat oil in a large nonstick skillet over medium-high heat. Add onion and pepper; cook 3 minutes, stirring occasionally. Add shrimp; cook an additional 3 minutes, until shrimp is opaque. Stir in corn, ¼ cup water, chili powder and cumin. Heat through.

② Heat oven to 375°. Coat a 13 x 9 x 2-inch baking dish with nonstick cooking spray.

③ Wrap 4 tortillas in damp paper towels. Microwave 30 seconds. Brush 1 side of each tortilla with salsa. Spoon ½ cup shrimp on each. Roll up and place in baking dish. Repeat with remaining tortillas and filling. Top with extra filling.

④ Mix remaining salsa with half-and-half. Spoon over enchiladas. Sprinkle with cheese. Bake at 375°, uncovered, for 15 minutes or until bubbly.

PER ENCHILADA 240 calories; 8 g fat (2 g sat.); 20 g protein; 20 g carbohydrate; 2 g fiber; 677 mg sodium; 115 mg cholesterol

SOUTHWESTERN PIZZA

MAKES two 9-inch pizzas (12 slices) **PREP** 10 minutes **BAKE** at 450° for 15 minutes

- 1   package (24 ounces; two in package) gluten-free pizza crusts (such as Whole Foods)
- 1   cup jarred tomato salsa
- 1¼   cups reduced-fat shredded mozzarella cheese
- 1⅓   cups black beans, drained and rinsed
- 1   small sweet red pepper, seeded and thinly sliced
- 2   scallions, trimmed and thinly sliced
- ¼   cup cilantro leaves for garnish (optional)

① Heat oven to 450°. Coat a large baking sheet with nonstick cooking spray.

② Place crusts on baking sheet. Spread each crust with ½ cup salsa, ½ cup of the cheese and ⅔ cup beans. Divide red pepper strips and scallions over pizzas. Top each with 2 tablespoons cheese.

③ Bake at 450° in lower third of oven for 13 to 15 minutes until cheese is melted. Remove from oven; garnish with cilantro, if desired. Serve warm.

PER SLICE 190 calories; 4 g fat (1 g sat.); 9 g protein; 31 g carbohydrate; 5 g fiber; 508 mg sodium; 13 mg cholesterol

GLAZED DRUMSTICKS WITH QUINOA

MAKES 6 servings **PREP** 20 minutes **BAKE** at 400° for 40 minutes **COOK** 15 minutes

1	tablespoon olive oil
½	cup apricot preserves
1	tablespoon grainy Dijon mustard
12	chicken drumsticks
¾	teaspoon salt
¼	teaspoon black pepper
2	cups reduced-sodium chicken broth
1	medium onion, chopped
2	large ribs celery, chopped
1	cup quinoa
⅓	cup dried apricots, chopped
¼	cup toasted pine nuts

① Heat oven to 400°.

② In a small bowl, stir together olive oil, preserves and mustard. Set aside 3 tablespoons for the quinoa.

③ Place the chicken in a roasting pan. Season with ¼ teaspoon of the salt and ⅛ teaspoon of the pepper. Bake at 400° for 20 minutes. Brush on remaining mustard mixture and bake for an additional 15 to 20 minutes or until internal temperature registers 170° on an instant-read thermometer. Remove from oven and let stand 5 minutes before serving.

④ While chicken is cooking, make quinoa dressing. Place chicken broth, onion, celery, quinoa, remaining ½ teaspoon salt and ⅛ teaspoon pepper in a medium-size saucepan. Bring to a boil; reduce heat to medium-low and simmer, covered, for 15 minutes. Stir in the apricots during the last few minutes of cook time. Take off heat and stir in reserved mustard mixture.

⑤ To serve, spoon the quinoa onto a serving platter and sprinkle with pine nuts. Place chicken on top of the quinoa.

PER SERVING 449 calories; 18 g fat (3 g sat.); 28 g protein; 45 g carbohydrate; 3 g fiber; 664 mg sodium; 94 mg cholesterol

BAKED PENNE & TURKEY MEATBALLS

MAKES 6 servings **PREP** 20 minutes **BAKE** at 400° for 55 minutes **COOK** 5 minutes

1   package (1.3 pounds) ground turkey
2   cups cornflakes, finely crushed
2   eggs, lightly beaten
¾   teaspoon Italian seasoning
½   teaspoon salt
¼   teaspoon black pepper
1   box (8 ounces) gluten-free rice penne (such as De Boles)
1   jar (26 to 28 ounces) gluten-free marinara sauce (such as Victoria)
1½   cups shredded reduced-fat mozzarella cheese

①   Heat oven to 400°. Line a baking sheet with nonstick foil.

②   In a large bowl, blend turkey, cornflakes, eggs, Italian seasoning, salt and pepper. Shape into 12 meatballs, ¼ cup each.

③   Transfer to prepared baking sheet; bake at 400° for 15 minutes. Turn and bake an additional 15 minutes. Meanwhile, cook pasta in boiling water for 1 minute less than package directions (about 5 minutes). Drain.

④   Coat a 13 x 9 x 2-inch baking dish with nonstick cooking spray; add pasta. Toss with the meatballs, marinara and 1 cup of the cheese. Scatter remaining ½ cup cheese over dish. Bake at 400°, uncovered, for 25 minutes or until bubbly. Let stand 10 minutes before serving.

PER SERVING 447 calories; 11 g fat (3 g sat.); 34 g protein; 54 g carbohydrate; 1 g fiber; 972 mg sodium; 153 mg cholesterol

CHICKEN SCALOPPINE AL MARSALA

MAKES 6 servings **PREP** 15 minutes **COOK** 27 minutes

¼   cup rice flour
6   thin-cut boneless, skinless chicken breasts, about 4 ounces each
3   tablespoons olive oil
1   package (8 ounces) sliced brown mushrooms
½   cup marsala wine
½   cup low-sodium beef broth
¼   teaspoon salt
⅛   teaspoon black pepper
1   package (10 ounces) brown rice couscous (such as Lundberg)
1   tablespoon unsalted butter
1   tablespoon chopped parsley

①   Place the rice flour on a large plate. Coat the chicken in the flour. Heat a large nonstick skillet over medium-high heat. Add 1 tablespoon of oil and sauté half the chicken for 1 to 2 minutes per side until lightly browned. Remove to a plate and keep warm. Repeat with a second tablespoon of the oil and the remaining chicken.

②   Add the remaining 1 tablespoon oil to the skillet and stir in the mushrooms. Cook for 2 to 3 minutes, until tender. Off heat, add in the marsala and cook for 1 minute, scraping any browned bits from the skillet. Add the broth, salt and pepper. Bring to a simmer and return the chicken and any accumulated juices to skillet. Gently simmer, covered, for 15 minutes.

③   Meanwhile, prepare couscous following package direction.

④   Stir butter and parsley into the sauce and serve with the cooked couscous.

PER SERVING 429 calories; 14 g fat (3 g sat.); 32 g protein; 43 g carbohydrate; 4 g fiber; 410 mg sodium; 78 mg cholesterol

THAI PORK WRAPS

MAKES 10 wraps **PREP** 10 minutes **COOK** 10 minutes

2   tablespoons vegetable oil
¾   pound boneless pork chops, cut with the grain, into ¼ x 2-inch strips
1   bag (16 ounces) coleslaw mix
2   cups shredded carrot
1   bunch scallions, trimmed and thinly sliced
4   cloves garlic, chopped
½   cup sweet red chili sauce (such as Thai Kitchen)
10   large Bibb lettuce leaves
½   cucumber, seeded, peeled and cut into matchsticks
    Fresh mint and lime wedges

①   In a large nonstick skillet, heat 1 tablespoon of the oil over medium-high heat. Add the pork and cook for 3 minutes until cooked through. Remove to plate and keep warm. Add remaining 1 tablespoon oil, the coleslaw mix, carrot, scallions and garlic. Cook 6 to 7 minutes, stirring occasionally, until tender. Stir in sweet chili sauce and reserved pork and heat through.

②   To serve, place about ½ cup filling in center of each lettuce leaf (See Note). Add some cucumber and mint. Spritz with lime, roll up and serve.

Note: Can also be served wrapped in rice flour tortillas.

PER WRAP 142 calories; 4 g fat (1 g sat.); 8 g protein; 16 g carbohydrate; 2 g fiber; 292 mg sodium; 21 mg cholesterol

Ciao Down

Simple, delicious pasta dishes that will bowl you over.

ANGEL HAIR WITH ARUGULA PESTO & SALMON

MAKES 8 servings **PREP** 10 minutes **COOK** 10 minutes

PESTO

2	cups baby arugula leaves
¾	cup basil leaves
½	cup toasted hazelnuts
2	cloves garlic, peeled
⅔	cup extra virgin olive oil
⅔	cup grated Parmesan
1¼	teaspoon salt

SALMON AND PASTA

1¼	pounds salmon fillet
1	cup dry white wine or vegetable broth
1	pound angel hair pasta

① **Pesto:** In food processor, combine arugula, basil, nuts and garlic. Process 1 minute. Gradually add oil and process until blended. Add cheese and salt; process until smooth. Set aside 1 cup for recipe. Refrigerate remainder for another use (up to 1 week).

② **Salmon and pasta:** Place salmon fillet in a large nonstick skillet. Add wine and bring to a boil over medium-high heat. Reduce heat to medium-low and simmer, covered, for 10 minutes or until fish flakes easily. Remove from poaching liquid; keep warm. Discard liquid.

③ Meanwhile, cook pasta following package directions, 3 minutes. Drain, reserving ½ cup of the water. Toss drained pasta with 1 cup pesto and ¼ cup of the pasta water, adding more water if needed. Remove skin from salmon; discard. Flake fish into pasta.

PER SERVING 530 calories; 25 g fat (4 g sat.); 27 g protein; 43 g carbohydrate; 2 g fiber; 500 mg sodium; 48 mg cholesterol

PASTA PRIMAVERA,
PAGE 85

SAUTÉED SHRIMP &
RED CHARD, PAGE 85

CHIPOTLE CHICKEN WAGON WHEELS

MAKES 6 servings **PREP** 15 minutes **COOK** 12 minutes

1   tablespoon vegetable oil
1½ **pounds boneless, skinless chicken breasts, cut into 1½-inch pieces**
½   **red onion, thinly sliced**
2   **cloves garlic, peeled and chopped**
1   **can (14½ ounces) diced tomatoes, drained**
¾   **cup fat-free half-and-half**
2   **chipotle peppers in adobo, seeded and chopped**
¾   **teaspoon salt**
2   **tablespoons chopped cilantro**
1   **pound wagon wheel pasta**

① Heat a large nonstick skillet over medium-high heat. Add oil and chicken. Cook 5 minutes, turning after 3 minutes.

Add onion and garlic; cook 3 minutes. Stir in tomatoes, half-and-half, chipotle and salt. Simmer, uncovered, 4 minutes, stirring occasionally. Add cilantro.

② Meanwhile, cook pasta following package directions, about 12 minutes. Drain, reserving ½ cup of the cooking water.

③ Toss pasta with sauce. Add reserved water as needed to thin out sauce.

PER SERVING 467 calories; 5 g fat (1 g sat.); 38 g protein; 65 g carbohydrate; 4 g fiber; 615 mg sodium; 67 mg cholesterol

SHELLS WITH WHITE BEANS & BEEF

MAKES 8 servings **PREP** 10 minutes
COOK 22 minutes

1   tablespoon olive oil
1   **pound beef fillet, cut into 1-inch cubes**
¾   **teaspoon salt**
½   **small onion, finely chopped**
2   **ribs celery with leaves, finely chopped**
3   **cloves garlic, finely chopped**
1   **can (28 ounces) crushed tomatoes**
2   **cans (15 ounces each) cannellini beans, drained and rinsed**
½   **teaspoon dried oregano**
½   **teaspoon dried basil**
¼   **teaspoon red pepper flakes**
1   **pound medium-size shells**
     Grated cheese (optional)

① Heat oil in a large nonstick lidded skillet over medium-high heat. Season beef with ¼ teaspoon of the salt. Add to skillet and cook for 2 minutes. Turn and cook for an additional 2 minutes. Remove beef from skillet to a plate with a slotted spoon. Keep warm.

② Add onion and celery to skillet and cook, stirring occasionally, for 5 minutes. Add garlic and cook for 1 minute. Stir in tomatoes, beans, oregano, basil, red pepper flakes and remaining ½ teaspoon salt. Bring to a boil. Reduce heat to medium-low and simmer, covered, for 12 minutes. Stir occasionally.

③ Meanwhile, cook pasta following package directions, about 8 minutes. Drain, reserving 1 cup of the cooking water. Place drained pasta back into pot. Add the bean mixture, cooked beef with accumulated juices and the reserved cooking water to the pasta.

④ Serve with grated cheese, if desired.

PER SERVING 483 calories; 13 g fat (5 g sat.); 25 g protein; 65 g carbohydrate; 8 g fiber; 545 mg sodium; 37 mg cholesterol

QUICKEST-EVER
SPICY MARINARA

PASTA PRIMAVERA

MAKES 6 servings **PREP** 20 minutes
COOK 14 minutes

½   pound asparagus, trimmed and cut into 1-inch pieces
½   pound green beans, trimmed and cut into 1-inch pieces
2   sweet orange peppers, cored, seeded and cut into ¼-inch strips
1   pound spaghetti
¾   cup half-and-half
¾   cup chicken broth
¾   teaspoon salt
¼   teaspoon black pepper
¼   teaspoon ground nutmeg
2   tablespoons olive oil
5   cloves garlic, sliced
2   cups grape tomatoes, halved
⅓   cup grated Parmesan
¼   cup flat-leaf parsley, chopped
    Shaved Parmesan, optional

① Bring a large pot of salted water to a boil. Add asparagus and green beans; cook 4 minutes. Add peppers and cook 1 more minute. Scoop out vegetables with a large slotted spoon and place in a colander. Rinse under cold water.

② Add pasta to boiling water and cook following package directions, about 9 minutes. Drain; return to pot.

③ While pasta is cooking, place half-and-half, chicken broth, salt, pepper and nutmeg in a small saucepan. Bring to a simmer over medium heat.

④ Heat a large nonstick skillet over medium-high heat. Add olive oil and garlic and cook 30 seconds. Add cooked veggies and tomatoes. Cook, stirring a few times, about 1 minute, 30 seconds. Spoon into pasta pot. Stir grated cheese into the half-and-half mixture. Add to pasta and gently stir in parsley until all ingredients are combined. Allow to stand for 5 minutes. Shave Parmesan on top, if desired.

PER SERVING 425 calories; 11 g fat (5 g sat.); 17 g protein; 67 g carbohydrate; 6 g fiber; 447 mg sodium; 18 mg cholesterol

SAUTÉED SHRIMP & RED CHARD

MAKES 6 servings **PREP** 10 minutes
COOK 10 minutes

4   tablespoons olive oil
6   cloves garlic, sliced
1¼ pounds medium shrimp, shelled and deveined
¾   teaspoon salt
¼   teaspoon black pepper
1   pound red chard, stems cut off and reserved (see Note); leaves cut into 1-inch slices
½   teaspoon dried oregano
1   package (17.5 ounces) whole-wheat spaghetti (such as De Cecco)
⅓   cup grated Parmesan

① Heat 2 tablespoons of the oil in a large nonstick skillet over medium-high heat. Add garlic and cook 30 seconds. Season shrimp with ¼ teaspoon of the salt and ⅛ teaspoon of the pepper. Add shrimp to skillet and cook 2 minutes per side. Remove to a plate and keep warm.

② Add chard leaves to skillet and season with the remaining ½ teaspoon of salt, ⅛ teaspoon pepper and the oregano. Reduce heat to medium-low. Cook 4 to 5 minutes until tender. Add shrimp back into skillet. Cover and set aside.

③ Meanwhile, cook pasta following package directions, about 10 minutes. Drain, reserving ½ cup cooking water. Toss pasta with shrimp mixture and remaining 2 tablespoons oil. Add enough of the pasta water to create a sauce. To serve, transfer to a large bowl and sprinkle with cheese.

Note: If desired, rinse and dry stems. Toss with a little olive oil, salt and pepper. Roast at 350° for 20 minutes or until tender. Cut into bite-size pieces and add to pasta.

PER SERVING 468 calories; 14 g fat (3 g sat.); 31 g protein; 61 g carbohydrate; 11 g fiber; 671 mg sodium; 122 mg cholesterol

QUICKEST-EVER SPICY MARINARA

MAKES 6 servings **PREP** 10 minutes
COOK 15 minutes

2   tablespoons olive oil
½   small onion, finely chopped
4   cloves garlic, finely chopped
2   tablespoons tomato paste
1   can (28 ounces) plum tomatoes in thick puree
1   teaspoon sugar
½   teaspoon salt
¼   to ½ teaspoon red pepper flakes
1   pound extra-large (or traditional-size) rigatoni
½   cup fresh basil
6   tablespoons part-skim ricotta cheese

① Heat a large nonstick skillet over medium heat. Add oil, onion and garlic and cook for 2 minutes, stirring occasionally so garlic doesn't burn. Add tomato paste and cook 1 minute. Add tomatoes and puree, sugar, salt and red pepper flakes. Break up tomatoes with a wooden spoon. Cook, uncovered, over medium heat for 12 minutes, stirring occasionally.

② While sauce is simmering, cook pasta following package directions, about 10 minutes. Drain, reserving ½ cup of the cooking water.

③ Tear basil into bite-size pieces and stir into sauce. Toss pasta with sauce, adding ¼ cup of reserved cooking water if needed to thin out sauce.

④ To serve, spoon pasta into individual serving bowls and top each with a tablespoon of ricotta.

PER SERVING 393 calories; 7 g fat (1 g sat.); 13 g protein; 67 g carbohydrate; 4 g fiber; 604 mg sodium; 8 mg cholesterol

Sweet Success

Spring bake sales abound—pick a winning recipe from these luscious options.

**CARROT CUPCAKES,
PAGE 91**

DOUBLE CHOCOLATE BROWNIES, PAGE 91

LEMON POPPYSEED COOKIES

LEMON POPPYSEED COOKIES

MAKES about 36 cookies **PREP** 20 minutes
CHILL 2 hours or overnight
BAKE at 350° for 13 minutes

2½ **cups all-purpose flour**
1 **teaspoon baking powder**
½ **teaspoon salt**
½ **cup (1 stick) unsalted butter, softened**
⅔ **cup sugar**
1 **egg**
2 **teaspoons lemon zest**
2 **tablespoons lemon juice**
2 **tablespoons poppyseeds**

① In a small bowl, whisk together flour, baking powder and salt; set aside.

② Beat butter and sugar on medium-high speed for 2 minutes or until smooth. Beat in egg, zest and juice until fluffy, 1 minute. Gradually beat in flour mixture on low, just until blended. Add poppy seeds; stir to combine. Divide dough in half. Flatten each into 6-inch square; wrap in plastic. Refrigerate 2 hours or overnight. Let stand at room temperature 15 minutes before rolling out dough.

③ Heat oven to 350°. Coat 2 baking sheets with nonstick cooking spray. Lightly flour dough. Roll half of dough on lightly floured surface to ¼-inch thickness. For variety, use 2 cutters, one about 2 inches and the other 2½ inches. Reroll scraps and repeat. Place cookies, 1 inch apart, on baking sheet. Repeat with other half of dough.

④ Bake at 350° for 10 to 13 minutes or until golden around edges. Remove to rack to cool completely.

PER COOKIE 73 calories; 3 g fat (2 g sat.); 1 g protein; 11 g carbohydrate; 0 g fiber; 46 mg sodium; 13 mg cholesterol

PB&J BARS

MAKES 18 servings **PREP** 15 minutes **BAKE** at 350° for 35 minutes

1¼ **cups all-purpose flour**
¼ **teaspoon baking powder**
⅛ **teaspoon salt**
6 **tablespoons (¾ stick) unsalted butter, softened**
½ **cup sugar**
1 **egg**
1 **cup creamy peanut butter**
½ **teaspoon vanilla extract**
1 **cup seedless strawberry jam**
⅔ **cup salted peanuts, chopped**

① Heat oven to 350°. Place nonstick aluminum foil in the bottom and overhanging sides of a 9 x 13 x 2-inch baking dish; set aside.

② In a medium bowl, stir together flour, baking powder and salt until well blended.

③ Beat butter and sugar on medium-high speed until fluffy, about 2 minutes. Add egg and beat until incorporated. Add peanut butter and beat until well blended, about 2 minutes.

④ On low speed, add in flour and beat just until blended. Stir in vanilla extract. Spread into prepared pan and bake at 350° for 30 minutes. Remove from oven and spread with jam and sprinkle with peanuts; bake an additional 5 minutes. Cool completely on wire rack, then lift from pan using aluminum foil; cut into 18 bars.

PER SERVING 247 calories; 14 g fat (4 g sat.); 6 g protein; 27 g carbohydrate; 1 g fiber; 92 mg sodium; 22 mg cholesterol

**CHOCOLATE CHIP
POUND CAKE**

CARROT CUPCAKES

MAKES 24 cupcakes **PREP** 20 minutes
BAKE at 350° for 27 minutes

CUPCAKES

- 1 cup (2 sticks) unsalted butter, melted and cooled
- 1¼ cups granulated sugar
- ¼ cup dark-brown sugar
- 4 eggs
- 2½ cups all-purpose flour
- ½ teaspoon salt
- ½ teaspoon cinnamon
- ¼ teaspoon ground nutmeg
- 1½ teaspoons baking powder
- ¾ teaspoon baking soda
- 1½ pounds carrots, peeled and grated on medium holes of box grater (about 3½ cups)
- ½ cup chopped raisins

CREAM CHEESE FROSTING

- ½ cup (1 stick) unsalted butter, softened
- 2 cups confectioners' sugar
- 8 ounces cream cheese, softened
- 2 teaspoons vanilla extract

① **Cupcakes:** Heat oven to 350°. Place cupcake liners in 24 indents of muffin pans; set aside.

② In large bowl, stir together butter, sugars and eggs until well blended. Stir in flour, salt, cinnamon, nutmeg, baking powder, baking soda, carrots and raisins.

③ Spoon ¼ cup batter into each cupcake liner. Bake at 350° for 25 to 27 minutes or until toothpick inserted in centers comes out clean. Cool cupcakes in pan on rack for 5 minutes, then remove and cool completely on rack.

④ **Frosting:** In a large bowl, beat butter and confectioners' sugar together on medium-high until blended. Add cream cheese and vanilla and beat on medium-high until no lumps remain. Divide frosting among cupcakes.

PER CUPCAKE 299 calories; 16 g fat (10 g sat.); 4 g protein; 37 g carbohydrate; 1 g fiber; 175 mg sodium; 76 mg cholesterol

DOUBLE CHOCOLATE BROWNIES

MAKES 16 brownies **PREP** 15 minutes
MICROWAVE 1 minute, 30 seconds
BAKE at 350° for 45 minutes

- 8 ounces 70% cacao bittersweet chocolate
- 1 cup (2 sticks) unsalted butter
- 1½ cups granulated sugar
- 1¼ cups all-purpose flour
- ½ teaspoon baking soda
- ¼ teaspoon salt
- 4 large eggs
- 2 teaspoons vanilla extract
- 2 teaspoons confectioners' sugar

① Heat oven to 350°. Line a 9-inch square baking pan with nonstick foil; set aside.

② Reserve 2 ounces of the chocolate. Chop remaining 6 ounces and place in a large microwave-safe bowl with butter. Microwave for 1 minute; stir. Microwave 30 seconds, then stir until smooth.

③ Stir sugar, flour, baking soda and salt into chocolate mixture until well blended. Add eggs and vanilla; stir until smooth. Chop remaining 2 ounces chocolate. Stir into batter. Pour into prepared pan, spreading level.

④ Bake at 350° for 45 minutes or until toothpick comes out clean when inserted in center. Cool on rack for 10 minutes. Lift brownie from pan using foil; place directly on rack to cool completely. Dust with confectioners' sugar.

PER BROWNIE 300 calories; 19 g fat (11 g sat.); 4 g protein; 34 g carbohydrate; 1 g fiber; 95 mg sodium; 83 mg cholesterol

CHOCOLATE CHIP POUND CAKE

MAKES 24 slices **PREP** 10 minutes
BAKE at 325° for 1 hour, 12 minutes

- 3½ cups all-purpose flour, plus more for dusting pans
- ½ teaspoon salt
- 4 eggs
- 4 egg yolks
- 1 tablespoon vanilla extract
- 1½ cups (3 sticks) unsalted butter, softened
- 2 cups sugar
- 1 bag (12 ounces) semisweet chocolate chips

① Heat oven to 325°. Coat two 9 x 5 x 3-inch loaf pans with nonstick cooking spray; dust with flour and shake out excess. Set aside.

② Stir together flour and salt; set aside. In small bowl, stir together eggs, egg yolks and vanilla; set aside.

③ Mix butter and sugar together on medium-high speed for 6 minutes or until very light and fluffy. Reduce speed to medium and gradually pour in egg mixture. Increase speed to medium-high and beat 3 minutes or until light and fluffy. On low speed, gradually add flour mixture and beat until just blended. Stir in chocolate chips.

④ Divide batter between prepared loaf pans and smooth tops. Bake at 325° for 1 hour, 12 minutes, or until toothpick inserted in center comes out clean. Cool in pans on wire rack for 30 minutes, then remove from pans and cool completely on rack.

PER SLICE 330 calories; 17 g fat (10 g sat.); 4 g protein; 42 g carbohydrate; 1 g fiber; 65 mg sodium; 99 mg cholesterol

Slow Cooker Suppers

Classic pork dishes with a healthy twist.

PORK POSOLE & CORN BREAD STEW

MAKES 8 servings **PREP** 15 minutes **COOK** 16 minutes **SLOW-COOK** 4½ hours on HIGH or 6½ hours on LOW

3   pounds boneless pork shoulder, well trimmed and cut into 1-inch chunks
½   teaspoon salt
½   teaspoon black pepper
1   tablespoon canola oil
4   large carrots, cut into ¼-inch pieces
2   onions, chopped
2   tablespoons flour
3   teaspoons chili powder
1   teaspoon dried oregano
4   garlic cloves, minced
1½ cups low-sodium chicken broth
1   box (8.5 ounces) corn muffin mix
2   eggs
    Zest of 1 lime plus 1 tablespoon lime juice

2   tablespoons plus 1 teaspoon chopped cilantro
1   can (15 ounces) white hominy, rinsed and drained

① Sprinkle pork with ¼ teaspoon each salt and pepper. Heat oil in a large skillet over medium-high heat. Cook pork for 5 minutes, stirring often, in batches, or until browned. Remove to slow cooker.

② Add carrots and onions to skillet and sprinkle with ¼ teaspoon each salt and pepper; cook for 5 minutes, stirring often. Stir in flour, chili powder, oregano and garlic; cook 1 minute then remove to slow cooker. Add broth to skillet and bring to a boil; pour into slow cooker. Cover; cook on HIGH for 4½ hours or LOW for 6½ hours.

③ When there is 1 hour of cook time remaining, stir together corn muffin mix, eggs, lime zest, 1 teaspoon cilantro and ¼ cup water. Remove cover; stir in hominy, lime juice and 2 tablespoons cilantro. Dollop corn muffin mixture on top. Place cotton dish towel over slow cooker bowl then top with cover; cook for remaining cook time or until top is firm.

PER SERVING 455 calories; 17 g fat (6 g sat.); 37 g protein; 38 g carbohydrate; 3 g fiber; 960 mg sodium; 159 mg cholesterol

ITALIAN PORK ROAST

MAKES 8 servings **PREP** 15 minutes
SLOW-COOK 3 hours on HIGH or 5½ hours on LOW **COOK** 1 minute

- 1 boneless pork loin roast (about 3 pounds), trimmed and tied
- 3 teaspoons Italian seasoning
- 1 can (14.5 ounces) diced tomatoes with basil, oregano and garlic, drained
- ⅓ cup plus 2 tablespoons low-sodium chicken broth
- ¾ teaspoon salt
- ½ teaspoon black pepper
- 1 large green pepper, seeded and chopped
- 2 tablespoons cornstarch
- 1½ teaspoons balsamic vinegar

① Rub pork with 1 teaspoon of the Italian seasoning and place in slow cooker bowl.

② Scatter tomatoes around pork. Pour ⅓ cup of the broth in bowl; top with 1½ teaspoons Italian seasoning, ½ teaspoon of the salt and ¼ teaspoon of the pepper. Cook 3 hours on HIGH or 5½ hours on LOW.

③ Add green pepper to slow cooker for last 45 minutes of cook time.

④ Blend remaining 2 tablespoons broth, the cornstarch and balsamic vinegar. Set aside. Remove pork to a serving platter; keep warm. Strain liquid from slow cooker into a small saucepan and place vegetables around pork on serving platter.

⑤ Bring liquid to a boil over medium-high heat. Whisk in cornstarch mixture, remaining ½ teaspoon Italian seasoning and ¼ teaspoon each salt and black pepper; cook 1 minute. Spoon sauce over pork.

PER SERVING 242 calories; 7 g fat (3 g sat.); 37 g protein; 5 g carbohydrate; 1 g fiber; 460 mg sodium; 107 mg cholesterol

ASIAN-STYLE RIBS

MAKES about 15 ribs **PREP** 15 minutes **SLOW-COOK** 6 hours on HIGH **COOK** 2 minutes

- ⅔ cup light-brown sugar
- ½ cup low-sodium soy sauce
- 2 tablespoons sesame oil
- 2 tablespoons rice vinegar
- 2 tablespoons minced fresh ginger
- 4 garlic cloves, crushed
- ½ teaspoon red pepper flakes
- 1 rack pork ribs (about 3 pounds), cut into sections of 3 to 4 ribs
- 2 tablespoons cornstarch
- 3 scallions, trimmed and thinly sliced
- 1 teaspoon sesame seeds

① In a small bowl, blend sugar, soy sauce, sesame oil, vinegar, ginger, garlic and red pepper.

② Place ribs in slow cooker bowl; add sauce. Cover; cook on HIGH for 6 hours or until meat is tender.

③ Transfer ribs to a platter. Strain sauce and discard excess fat. Combine cornstarch and ¼ cup water; blend with sauce in a saucepan. Bring to a boil over high heat and cook for 2 minutes, stirring, until thickened. Top ribs with ½ cup of sauce, scallions and sesame seeds; serve with remaining sauce.

PER RIB 324 calories; 23 g fat (8 g sat.); 15 g protein; 12 g carbohydrate; 0 g fiber; 395 mg sodium; 73 mg cholesterol

Jambalaya

This easy-to-make Cajun classic has roots in both Spanish and French cooking.

Evenly cooked vegetables are essential for delicious jambalaya. The onion, pepper and celery should all be cut uniformly so they cook at the same speed—otherwise, big pieces will be too crunchy and small ones, mushy. Chop the onion first following the steps below, then use those pieces as your guide.

JAMBALAYA

MAKES 6 servings **PREP** 15 minutes **COOK** 34 minutes

- 1   tablespoon vegetable oil
- 1   pound boneless, skinless chicken breasts, cut into 1-inch pieces
- 1   package (12 ounces, 4 links) spicy smoked chicken or pork sausage, such as habanero green chile or andouille, cut into coins
- 1   medium onion, diced (see steps A, B and C)
- 1   green bell pepper, seeded and diced
- 1   rib celery, trimmed and diced
- 1½   teaspoons Cajun seasoning
- 1   can (14 ounces) diced tomatoes with zesty mild green chiles, drained
- 1   cup long-grain white rice
- 1   can (15.5 ounces) light, low-sodium chicken broth

① Heat oil in large lidded skillet or sauté pan over medium-high heat. Add chicken and sausage and sauté, shaking pan and stirring frequently until chicken is no longer pink but not cooked completely, about 4 minutes.

② With a slotted spoon, remove chicken and sausage to a bowl. Reduce heat to medium and add onion, green pepper and celery to skillet. Cook vegetables until crisp-tender, about 5 minutes. Stir in Cajun seasoning, tomatoes and rice. Add broth.

③ Bring to a simmer, then cover pan and reduce heat to medium-low. Simmer 20 minutes, until almost all the liquid is absorbed. Stir chicken and sausage back into pan, along with any accumulated juices. Cook, uncovered, 5 minutes, until rice is tender.

PER SERVING 351 calories; 10 g fat (3 g sat.); 2 g protein; 34 g carbohydrate; 2 g fiber; 1,062 mg sodium; 91 mg cholesterol

step by step

A

Peel onion; cut in half from top to bottom. Lay one half on flat side and slice down into thin sections, leaving root intact.

B

Then, holding knife parallel to cutting board, cut onion crosswise into even slices (about two per onion half).

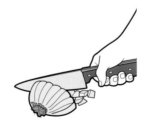

C

Finally, slice straight down through onion to form even pieces. Repeat with second half of onion.

ENJOY FRESH IDEAS FOR PREPARING HEALTHFUL FISH, BAKE UP SOME SUGAR-FREE DESSERTS AND ENTERTAIN WITH A SIMPLE AND DELICIOUS MENU OF FIVE-INGREDIENT DISHES.

MAY

105

113

119

Good Catch

Delicious and healthy ways to cook up salmon, flounder, snapper and more.

**TILAPIA WITH LEMONY
HERB SALAD, PAGE 103**

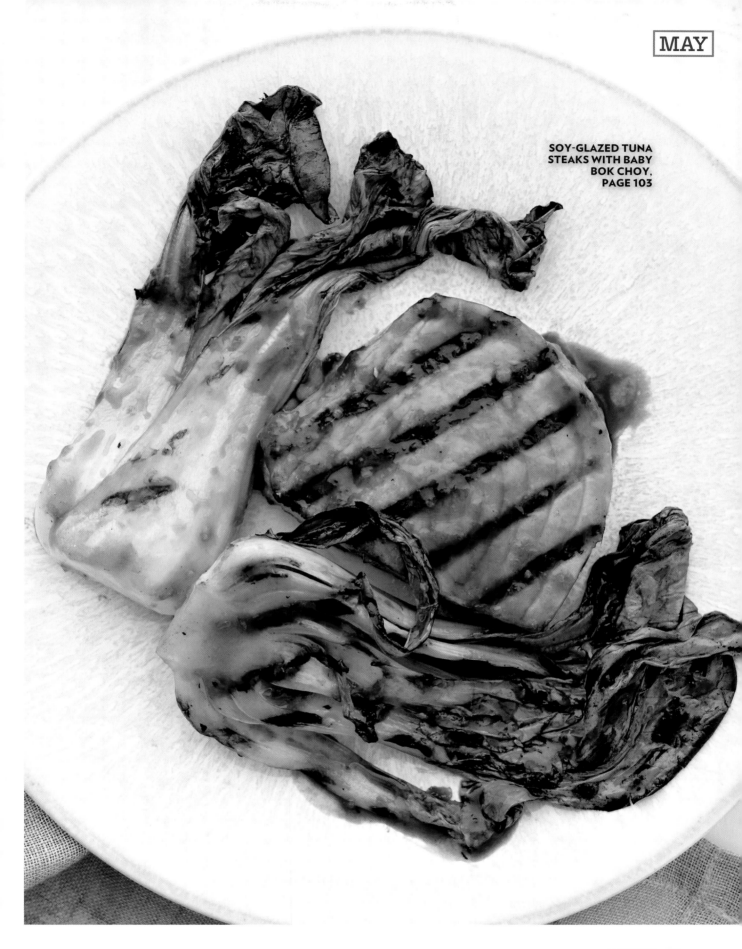

SOY-GLAZED TUNA STEAKS WITH BABY BOK CHOY, PAGE 103

RED SNAPPER WITH GAZPACHO SALSA

MAKES 4 servings **PREP** 15 minutes **COOK** 7 minutes

- 3   plum tomatoes, seeded and cut into ¼-inch pieces
- 1   yellow pepper, seeded and cut into ¼-inch pieces
- 1   small rib celery, cut into ¼-inch pieces
- ½   cucumber, seeded and cut into ¼-inch pieces
- ½   small red onion, minced
- ½   teaspoon salt
- ½   teaspoon black pepper
- 1½   tablespoons extra virgin olive oil
- 1   tablespoon white wine vinegar
- 2   red snapper fillets (about 9 ounces each) cut in half on the diagonal
- 2   tablespoons Wondra flour

① Stir together tomatoes, yellow pepper, celery, cucumber, onion, ¼ teaspoon each of the salt and black pepper, the olive oil and vinegar; set aside.

② Sprinkle fish with remaining ¼ teaspoon each salt and pepper. Place flour on plate. Dip flesh side of fish (not skin) in flour, shaking off excess. Heat a large nonstick skillet over medium-high heat. Coat pan generously with nonstick cooking spray. Add fish to pan, flesh side down, and cook 3 minutes. Flip and cook an additional 4 minutes or until fish flakes easily. Remove fish to serving platter and keep warm.

③ Meanwhile, heat a medium-size skillet over medium-high heat and add tomato mixture to pan. Cook 4 minutes, stirring often. Serve salsa with fish immediately.

PER SERVING 218 calories; 7 g fat (1 g sat.); 28 g protein; 10 g carbohydrate; 2 g fiber; 385 mg sodium; 47 mg cholesterol

COD & RATATOUILLE PACKETS

MAKES 4 servings **PREP** 15 minutes **BAKE** at 450° for 20 minutes

2 plum tomatoes, seeded and cut into ½-inch pieces

1 small zucchini (5 ounces), halved lengthwise and cut into ¼-inch-thick half-moons

1 small yellow squash (5 ounces), halved lengthwise and cut into ¼-inch-thick half-moons

½ of 1 large fennel bulb, trimmed, halved, cored and thinly sliced (about 2 cups)

½ small onion, thinly sliced

2 garlic cloves, minced

1 tablespoon chopped fresh thyme

¼ teaspoon salt

⅛ teaspoon black pepper

3 tablespoons low-sodium chicken broth

4 cod fillets, about 6 ounces each

4 teaspoons unsalted butter

① Heat oven to 450°.

② In a large bowl, stir together tomatoes, zucchini, squash, fennel, onion, garlic, ½ tablespoon of the thyme, ⅛ teaspoon of the salt, the pepper and broth; set aside.

③ Lay 4 large pieces of foil or parchment paper (each 16 inches long) on work surface. Place 1½ heaping cups vegetable mixture on lower half of each piece. Place fish on top of vegetables and sprinkle with remaining ½ tablespoon thyme and ⅛ teaspoon salt. Place 1 teaspoon butter on top of each fillet. Fold foil or parchment over fish and fold edges to create a sealed packet. Place packets on a rimmed baking sheet, overlapping if necessary.

④ Bake at 450° for 20 minutes or until fish is cooked through and veggies are tender. Cut open packets and slide contents onto plates; serve immediately.

PER SERVING 230 calories; 4 g fat (1 g sat.); 37 g protein; 9 g carbohydrate; 3 g fiber; 300 mg sodium; 55 mg cholesterol

BAKED FLOUNDER WITH CRABMEAT STUFFING

MAKES 4 servings **PREP** 15 minutes **COOK** 5 minutes **REFRIGERATE** 30 minutes **BAKE** at 400° for 20 minutes

½ small onion, minced
½ small red pepper, finely chopped
¾ teaspoon low-sodium Old Bay seasoning
¼ teaspoon salt
⅔ cup light cream
8 ounces imitation crabmeat, finely chopped
3 teaspoons chopped parsley
4 flounder fillets (about 4 ounces each)
¾ cup white wine or water
   Cooked brown rice (optional)

① Heat a medium-size nonstick skillet over medium heat. Coat pan with nonstick cooking spray, then add onion and red pepper and coat generously with spray; cover and cook 4 minutes or until softened, stirring occasionally.

② Remove cover and stir in ½ teaspoon of the Old Bay, ⅛ teaspoon of the salt and the light cream. Increase heat to medium-high and bring to a boil; cook for 1 minute or until reduced and thickened. Gently fold in crabmeat and 2 teaspoons of the parsley; refrigerate 30 minutes.

③ Heat oven to 400°. Coat a 13 x 9 x 2-inch baking dish with nonstick cooking spray. Place 1 of the flounder fillets skinned side up on work surface, then spoon ½ cup crab mixture onto end of fillet; roll up, creating a small bundle. Repeat using remaining fillets and crab. Transfer bundles to prepared baking dish, seam side down, and sprinkle with remaining ¼ teaspoon Old Bay, ⅛ teaspoon salt and 1 teaspoon parsley. Add wine or water to pan; transfer to oven.

④ Bake at 400° for 20 minutes or until fish is solid white and flakes easily with a fork. Remove to plates with a large spatula and serve with rice, if desired.

PER SERVING 281 calories; 9 g fat (5 g sat.); 27 g protein; 13 g carbohydrate; 1 g fiber; 803 mg sodium; 92 mg cholesterol

HERB-CRUSTED SALMON & ISRAELI COUSCOUS

MAKES 4 servings **PREP** 10 minutes
COOK 8 minutes **BROIL** 7 minutes

¾ teaspoon salt
1 cup Israeli couscous
2½ tablespoons panko bread crumbs
2 tablespoons chopped fresh dill
4 salmon fillets (about 4 ounces each)
¼ teaspoon black pepper
2 teaspoons Dijon mustard
3 cups baby spinach, roughly chopped
¼ cup low-sodium chicken broth

① Heat oven to broil. Place nonstick foil on a rimmed baking sheet and set aside.

② Bring 1¼ cups water to a boil in a medium-size pot. Add ½ teaspoon of the salt and the couscous. Cover and cook 8 minutes, stirring occasionally; set aside.

③ Meanwhile, stir together bread crumbs and 1 tablespoon dill; set aside. Sprinkle salmon with remaining ¼ teaspoon salt and the pepper and place on prepared baking sheet. Place directly under broiler and cook for 5 minutes.

④ Remove salmon from oven and lower rack so it's 6 inches from heating element. Brush salmon with mustard and sprinkle with bread crumb mixture, pressing to adhere. Generously spritz each fillet with nonstick cooking spray and return to oven; broil 2 minutes.

⑤ Stir remaining 1 tablespoon dill, spinach and chicken broth into couscous; let sit 5 minutes. Serve with salmon.

PER SERVING 307 calories; 7 g fat (1 g sat.); 27 g protein; 31 g carbohydrate; 2 g fiber; 318 mg sodium; 63 mg cholesterol

TILAPIA WITH LEMONY HERB SALAD

MAKES 4 servings **PREP** 15 minutes
COOK 8 minutes

1 garlic clove, minced
1 teaspoon lemon zest plus 1 tablespoon lemon juice
¼ teaspoon Dijon mustard
1 tablespoon chopped fresh parsley
1 tablespoon olive oil
4 tilapia fillets, trimmed to 6 ounces each
1 teaspoon lemon-herb seasoning (such as McCormick)
6 cups arugula
2 cups parsley leaves
Lemon wedges (optional)

① In a small bowl, stir together garlic, lemon zest and juice, Dijon and chopped parsley. Slowly whisk in olive oil; set aside.

② Sprinkle tilapia with lemon-herb seasoning. Heat large nonstick skillet over medium-high heat. Spritz both sides of tilapia with nonstick cooking spray and place in skillet. Cook 3 to 4 minutes per side or until fish flakes easily with a fork. Remove fish from skillet to a serving platter.

③ In a large bowl, toss together arugula and parsley leaves; drizzle with prepared dressing and serve with tilapia and lemon wedges, if desired.

PER SERVING 215 calories; 7 g fat (2 g sat.); 36 g protein; 4 g carbohydrate; 2 g fiber; 190 mg sodium; 85 mg cholesterol

SOY-GLAZED TUNA STEAKS WITH BABY BOK CHOY

MAKES 4 servings **PREP** 10 minutes
GRILL 10 minutes

3 tablespoons low-sodium soy sauce
5 teaspoons mirin
2 tablespoons grated fresh ginger
2 tablespoons sugar
2 garlic cloves, minced
1 teaspoon cornstarch
6 baby bok choy (about 1½ pounds), halved lengthwise, washed and large leaves removed
4 tuna steaks, about 4 ounces each (¾ to 1 inch thick)

① Combine ¼ cup water, 2 tablespoons of the soy sauce, the mirin, ginger, sugar and garlic in a small saucepan. Bring to a boil over medium-high heat. Stir together remaining tablespoon soy sauce and cornstarch, then stir into saucepan. Cook for 3 minutes over medium heat or until thickened. Divide sauce into 2 separate bowls, 5 tablespoons in one bowl and 3 tablespoons in the other.

② Prepare grill with medium-hot coals or heat gas grill to medium-high. Brush cut side of bok choy with about half of the 5 tablespoons of sauce and place cut side down on grill. Cook for 4 to 5 minutes per side, brushing often with sauce.

③ Meanwhile, place tuna on grill and brush with about half of the 3 tablespoons of sauce from second bowl. Cook about 4 minutes per side, constantly brushing with sauce. Remove bok choy and tuna from grill and serve immediately.

PER SERVING 238 calories; 6 g fat (1 g sat.); 30 g protein; 14 g carbohydrate; 2 g fiber; 609 mg sodium; 43 mg cholesterol

STUFFED FLANK STEAK

STUFFED FLANK STEAK

MAKES 6 servings **PREP** 15 minutes
COOK 5 minutes **ROAST** at 425° for 35 minutes

1   flank steak, about 1½ pounds
1   package (10 ounces) frozen chopped spinach, thawed and squeezed dry
4   ounces sun-dried tomato- or herb-garlic-flavored feta cheese, crumbled
2   tablespoons seasoned bread crumbs
2   tablespoons olive oil
1   egg, lightly beaten
¾   teaspoon salt
½   teaspoon black pepper

① Heat oven to 425°. Place a rack in a shallow baking pan. Coat with cooking spray.

② Lay steak on work surface. Starting at a long side, slice steak in half without cutting through all the way. Open like a book and flatten to an even thickness.

③ In a bowl, combine spinach, feta, bread crumbs, 1 tablespoon of the oil and the beaten egg.

④ Season steak with ½ teaspoon of the salt and ¼ teaspoon of the pepper. Press spinach mixture onto steak, leaving a 1-inch border. Beginning on a short end, roll up to enclose filling. Tie steak with cotton twine at 2-inch intervals.

⑤ Rub steak with remaining 1 tablespoon oil and season with remaining ¼ teaspoon each salt and pepper.

⑥ Heat a large nonstick skillet over medium-high heat. Brown meat on all sides, about 5 minutes total. Transfer steak to prepared rack.

⑦ Roast at 425° for 35 minutes or until internal temperature registers 135° on an instant-read thermometer. Remove meat from oven; let rest, covered, 10 minutes before slicing.

PER SERVING 271 calories; 14 g fat (5 g sat.); 32 g protein; 5 g carbohydrate; 2 g fiber; 708 mg sodium; 79 mg cholesterol

ORZO PILAF

MAKES 6 servings **PREP** 10 minutes
COOK 17 minutes

2   tablespoons olive oil
½   cup chopped onion
4   cups reduced-sodium chicken broth
2   cups orzo
½   teaspoon salt
¼   teaspoon black pepper
2   tablespoons capers
2   tablespoons chopped parsley

① Heat oil in a medium-size saucepan over medium heat. Add onion and cook 5 minutes, stirring occasionally.

② Add broth, orzo, salt and pepper and stir to combine. Bring to a boil over medium-high heat. Cover and reduce heat to low. Cook for 12 minutes or until most of liquid is absorbed and orzo is tender. Stir halfway through cooking time.

③ Mix in capers and parsley and serve.

PER SERVING 269 calories; 6 g fat (1 g sat.); 11 g protein; 44 g carbohydrate; 2 g fiber; 376 mg sodium; 3 mg cholesterol

ROASTED ASPARAGUS

MAKES 6 servings **PREP** 10 minutes
COOK at 450° for 10 minutes

2   bunches asparagus, about 2 pounds total
3   tablespoons olive oil
4   cloves garlic, finely chopped
½   teaspoon salt
½   teaspoon black pepper
2   tablespoons lemon juice
    Lemon wedges for serving

① Heat oven to 450°. Coat 2 baking sheets with nonstick cooking spray. Trim and discard tough ends of asparagus. Place spears in a large bowl and toss with olive oil, garlic, salt and pepper.

② Place half of the asparagus on each baking sheet. Roast at 450° for 10 minutes, turning halfway through.

③ To serve, place on a platter and sprinkle with lemon juice and lemon wedges.

PER SERVING 97 calories; 7 g fat (1 g sat.); 3 g protein; 8 g carbohydrate; 3 g fiber; 194 mg sodium; 0 mg cholesterol

CHIPOTLE CHEESE PUFFS

MAKES about 50 pieces **PREP** 20 minutes **REFRIGERATE** 15 minutes **BAKE** at 400° for 15 minutes

1 **cup shredded sharp cheddar cheese**
½ **cup shredded Parmesan cheese**
¾ **teaspoon chipotle chili powder**
1 **sheet frozen puff pastry, thawed (from a 17.5 ounce package)**
1 **egg, lightly beaten with 1 tablespoon water**

① Heat oven to 400°. Coat a large baking sheet with nonstick cooking spray.

② In a small bowl, mix together cheeses and chili powder. Set aside.

③ Place pastry sheet on a lightly floured work surface. Roll out to a 12 x 10-inch rectangle. Lightly brush with egg wash. Starting at a short end, sprinkle ¾ cup of the cheese mixture over one-half of the pastry. Fold other half over cheese like a book. Gently press down over cheese. Place on a small baking sheet and refrigerate for 15 minutes.

④ Place pastry on a cutting board and trim sides evenly. Cut into approximately fifty 1-inch squares. Lightly brush tops with egg wash and sprinkle on remaining cheese. Gently press cheese down so it adheres to pastry. Bake at 400° for 13 to 15 minutes, until golden. Serve immediately.

PER PIECE 35 calories; 2 g fat (1 g sat.); 1 g protein; 2 g carbohydrate; 0 g fiber; 56 mg sodium; 8 mg cholesterol

TIRAMISU BUNDT CAKE

MAKES 16 servings **PREP** 10 minutes **BAKE** at 350° for 40 minutes

1 box (18.25 ounces) white cake mix
1 pint coffee ice cream, such as Häagen-Dazs, melted
3 eggs
1 container (12 ounces) whipped vanilla frosting
1 teaspoon instant coffee granules dissolved in 1 tablespoon water
   Cinnamon sugar for dusting, optional

① Heat oven to 350°. Coat a 10-cup bundt pan with nonstick cooking spray.

② In a large bowl, beat cake mix, melted ice cream and eggs on low speed for 1 minute. Beat 2 minutes on medium speed. Scrape into prepared pan.

③ Bake at 350° for 35 to 40 minutes or until wooden pick inserted in center of cake comes out clean. Cool in pan on wire rack for 20 minutes. Invert onto wire rack to cool completely.

④ In a large bowl, beat together frosting and instant coffee mixture.

⑤ Place cake on stand and spread with frosting. Refrigerate until ready to serve. Dust with cinnamon sugar, if desired.

PER SERVING 314 calories; 14 g fat (5 g sat.); 4 g protein; 43 g carbohydrate; 0 g fiber; 271 mg sodium; 70 mg cholesterol

Sugar-Free Desserts

It's a piece of cake to bake with maple syrup, honey or even fruit juice concentrate. Sweet!

BLUEBERRY TARTS,
PAGE 113

RICH CHOCOLATE CAKE,
PAGE 113

**BANANA HONEY
NUT LOAF**

BANANA HONEY NUT LOAF

MAKES 12 slices **PREP** 20 minutes
BAKE at 350° for 55 minutes

TOPPING

¾ cup all-purpose flour
¼ cup (½ stick) unsalted butter
¼ cup finely chopped walnuts
1 tablespoon honey
   Pinch of salt

BANANA LOAF

2 cups all-purpose flour
2 teaspoons baking powder
½ teaspoon salt
⅛ teaspoon baking soda
⅛ teaspoon ground nutmeg
2 large eggs
⅔ cup honey
⅔ cup vegetable oil
2 large over-ripe bananas, mashed
1 teaspoon vanilla extract
½ cup walnuts, chopped

① Heat oven to 350°. Coat a 9 x 5 x 3-inch loaf pan with nonstick cooking spray.

② **Topping:** In a medium-size bowl, blend together flour and butter with your fingertips. Stir in nuts, honey and salt, then work mixture together with your hands to make crumbs (mixture will be very moist). Set aside.

③ **Banana Loaf:** In a large bowl, whisk together flour, baking powder, salt, baking soda and nutmeg. Make a well in the center of the dry ingredients. In medium-size bowl, whisk eggs, honey, oil, mashed banana and vanilla. Pour into well in flour mixture and stir until just combined. Stir in nuts and transfer batter to prepared pan. Sprinkle with topping.

④ Bake loaf at 350° for 55 minutes. Cool in pan on wire rack for 20 minutes, then remove from pan directly to rack and cool completely.

PER SLICE 360 calories; 19 g fat (4 g sat.); 5 g protein; 44 g carbohydrate; 2 g fiber; 202 mg sodium; 45 mg cholesterol

VANILLA SNACK CAKE

MAKES 24 servings **PREP** 10 minutes **BAKE** at 325° for 45 minutes

CAKE

3½ cups all-purpose flour
3¼ teaspoons baking powder
¾ teaspoon salt
1 cup (2 sticks) unsalted butter, softened
1½ cups agave syrup
4 large eggs
2 teaspoons vanilla extract
½ cup milk

FROSTING

2 packages (8 ounces each) cream cheese, softened
½ cup (1 stick) unsalted butter, softened
6 tablespoons agave syrup

① **Cake:** Heat oven to 325°. Coat a 13 x 9 x 2-inch baking pan with nonstick cooking spray. In medium bowl, whisk flour, baking powder and salt.

② With mixer on medium speed, beat butter and agave syrup in bowl until light and fluffy. Add eggs, one at a time, beating after each. Beat in vanilla.

③ On low, beat flour mixture alternately with milk into butter mixture, beating after each addition. Pour into prepared pan.

④ Bake at 325° for 45 minutes, or until toothpick inserted in center comes out clean. Cool cake completely.

⑤ While cake cools, prepare **Frosting.** Beat cream cheese and butter in a large bowl until smooth. Beat in agave syrup until good spreading consistency. Spread onto cooled cake. Store in refrigerator.

PER SERVING 313 calories; 19 g fat (12 g sat.); 5 g protein; 32 g carbohydrate; 1 g fiber; 203 mg sodium; 86 mg cholesterol

COCONUT OATMEAL RAISIN COOKIES

MAKES about 2 dozen cookies **PREP** 15 minutes **BAKE** at 350° for 15 minutes

- 1   cup old-fashioned oats
- ¾   cup all-purpose flour
- ½   cup shredded natural unsweetened coconut (see Note)
- ½   cup golden raisins
- ¾   teaspoon pumpkin pie spice
- ½   teaspoon baking soda
- 1   stick (½ cup) unsalted butter, softened
- ¾   cup Splenda (not Splenda for baking, which has sugar)
- 1   large egg
- 1   teaspoon vanilla extract

① Heat oven to 350°. Coat 2 large baking sheets with nonstick cooking spray.

② In a medium-size bowl, combine oats, flour, coconut, raisins, pumpkin pie spice and baking soda.

③ In a large bowl, beat together butter and Splenda until combined. Beat in egg. Stir in oat mixture and vanilla.

④ Drop cookie dough by slightly heaping tablespoonfuls onto prepared baking sheets. With wet hands, press down cookies to form flattened 3-inch circles.

Let stand on countertop for 5 minutes. Transfer cookie sheets to oven and bake at 350° for 13 to 15 minutes, until cookies are lightly browned around edges. Transfer to wire rack to cool completely.

Note: Look for unsweetened coconut in the bulk bins or health food section of your market.

PER COOKIE 91 calories; 5 g fat (4 g sat.); 2 g protein; 9 g carbohydrate; 1 g fiber; 31 mg sodium; 19 mg cholesterol

BLUEBERRY TARTS

MAKES 4 tarts (8 servings) **PREP** 20 minutes
CHILL 2 hours or overnight **BAKE** at 375° for
35 minutes

PASTRY

1½ cups all-purpose flour
¼ teaspoon salt
½ cup (1 stick) cold unsalted butter,
     cut in pieces
1 tablespoon maple syrup

BLUEBERRY FILLING

2 6-ounce packages fresh blueberries
    (about 2 cups)
½ cup maple syrup
¼ cup cornstarch
1 teaspoon lemon zest

① **Pastry:** In medium bowl, whisk
together flour and salt. Add butter and mix
into flour with a pastry blender or your
fingers until crumbly. In a small bowl, stir
together maple syrup and ¼ cup plus
1 teaspoon cold water. Add water mixture
to flour mixture and toss together with a
fork until dough begins to come together.
Gather dough into a ball; divide in 4 equal
pieces. Flatten each into a disc, wrap in
plastic and refrigerate 2 hours.

② **Blueberry Filling:** Heat oven to 375°.
Place blueberries in a large bowl. In small
bowl, stir together maple syrup, cornstarch
and lemon zest. Gently combine with
blueberries. Set aside.

③ Roll out 1 pastry disc to an 8-inch
circle. Transfer to a nonstick baking sheet.
Fold over ½ inch of dough all around
pastry, forming a decorative edge. Repeat
with remaining pastry. Divide blueberry
mixture evenly among pastry rounds,
about ½ cup in each (spread berry mixture
in single layer).

④ Bake tarts at 375° for 35 minutes, until
pastry is browned and filling is set.

PER SERVING (½ TART) 281 calories; 12 g fat
(7 g sat.); 3 g protein; 42 g carbohydrate;
2 g fiber; 77 mg sodium; 30 mg cholesterol

RICH CHOCOLATE CAKE

MAKES 12 servings **PREP** 20 minutes
COOK 6 minutes **BAKE** at 325° for 50 minutes

1 can (12 ounces) frozen apple juice
    concentrate, thawed
¾ cup sweet pitted prunes
1 stick (½ cup) unsalted butter
2 cups all-purpose flour
¾ cup unsweetened cocoa powder,
    plus more for dusting
2 teaspoons baking powder
1 teaspoon baking soda
½ teaspoon salt
3 eggs
½ cup 2% milk
2 teaspoons vanilla extract
1 container (6 ounces) fresh
    raspberries
    Sugar-free vanilla ice cream

① Heat oven to 325°. Coat a 9-inch
springform pan with nonstick cooking
spray.

② In a medium-size saucepan, heat
1¼ cups of the apple juice concentrate with
the prunes and butter over medium heat.
Cook until butter is melted and mixture
just begins to simmer, about 6 minutes.
Remove from heat and let stand 5 minutes.

③ Meanwhile, whisk together flour, ¾ cup
cocoa, baking powder, baking soda and
salt in a large bowl. Carefully transfer
apple juice mixture to a blender and mix
until prunes are pureed.

④ Beat eggs in a large bowl until blended.
With mixer on medium speed, slowly add
apple juice mixture. Beat until evenly
blended. On low speed, beat in half the
flour mixture, then milk, then remaining
flour mixture. Stir in vanilla; spread into
prepared pan. Bake at 325° for 50 minutes
or until toothpick inserted in center of cake
comes out with moist crumbs. Cool in pan
on wire rack 10 minutes; then remove pan
and cool completely.

⑤ Meanwhile, combine raspberries,
remaining apple juice concentrate and
2 tablespoons water in a mini chopper.
Pulse until pureed. Strain through a sieve;
discard solids. Once cake has cooled, dust
top with a little cocoa powder. Slice and
serve with raspberry puree and sugar-free
ice cream.

PER SERVING 271 calories; 10 g fat (6 g sat.); 6 g
protein; 42 g carbohydrate; 4 g fiber; 302 mg
sodium; 73 mg cholesterol

Slow Cooker Suppers

A week's worth of easy springtime dishes.

**CHICKEN &
CORN CHILI**

CHICKEN & CORN CHILI

MAKES 6 servings **PREP** 10 minutes
SLOW-COOK 4 hours on HIGH or 6 hours on
LOW plus 5 minutes

1   large onion, chopped
1   pound boneless, skinless chicken
    breasts
2   cups low-sodium chicken broth
1   green pepper, seeded and chopped
1   jalapeño chile, seeded and chopped
1¾ teaspoons ground cumin
½   teaspoon ground cayenne
¾   teaspoon salt
1   can (14.5 ounces) diced tomatoes
    with jalapeños, drained
1½ cups frozen corn, thawed
2   cans (15 ounces each) cannellini
    beans, drained and rinsed
2   tablespoons stone-ground cornmeal
    Shredded Monterey Jack cheese

① Combine onion, chicken, broth, green
pepper, jalapeño, 1½ teaspoons cumin,
¼ teaspoon cayenne and ¼ teaspoon salt
in slow cooker bowl. Cover and cook for
4 hours on HIGH or 6 hours on LOW.

② Remove the chicken to a cutting board
and allow to cool slightly. Shred the
chicken and return it to the slow cooker
with remaining ¼ teaspoon each of the
cumin and cayenne, the tomatoes, corn
and beans. Gently mash some of the
beans against the side of the bowl to
thicken the chili.

③ Stir in the cornmeal and the remaining
½ teaspoon salt. Let sit 5 minutes to soften
the cornmeal. Sprinkle with Monterey Jack
cheese and serve.

PER SERVING 287 calories; 3 g fat (1 g sat.); 27 g
protein; 38 g carbohydrate; 9 g fiber; 736 mg
sodium; 45 mg cholesterol

SPICED SHREDDED BEEF BRISKET

MAKES 8 servings **PREP** 10 minutes **SLOW-COOK** 5 hours on HIGH or 10 hours on LOW plus
15 minutes on HIGH

1   cup beef broth
1   jar (8 ounces) hoisin sauce
¼   cup white vinegar
2   teaspoons Chinese five-spice powder
2   teaspoons garlic powder
2   ribs celery, cut into 2-inch-long
    matchsticks
2   large carrots, cut into 2-inch-long
    matchsticks
1   thin-cut beef brisket (2 pounds),
    well trimmed of excess fat
½   teaspoon salt
¼   teaspoon black pepper
1   head bok choy, trimmed and thinly
    sliced
8   soft sandwich buns

① Whisk beef broth, hoisin sauce, ½ cup
water, vinegar, five-spice powder and
garlic powder in a small bowl. Place celery

and carrot strips in slow cooker bowl.
Add the brisket (slicing in half to fit, if
necessary); season on all sides with salt
and pepper. Pour in beef broth mixture.
Cover; cook for 5 hours on HIGH or
10 hours on LOW.

② Remove meat to a cutting board. Cool
slightly. Skim any fat off top of sauce in
cooker and discard. Add bok choy to slow
cooker and cook for 15 minutes on HIGH.

③ Meanwhile, shred beef with two forks,
cutting long pieces in half, if desired. Add
back to slow cooker and stir to coat with
sauce. Serve immediately with soft
sandwich buns.

PER SERVING 479 calories; 15 g fat (4 g sat.); 42 g
protein; 43 g carbohydrate; 2 g fiber; 727 mg
sodium; 108 mg cholesterol

TURKEY LASAGNA

MAKES 8 servings **PREP** 10 minutes **COOK** 10 minutes
SLOW-COOK 4 hours on HIGH or 5 hours on LOW

1   medium onion, chopped
2   cloves garlic, minced
1¼ pounds ground turkey
1   teaspoon dried oregano
½   teaspoon salt
¼   teaspoon black pepper
1   container (15 ounces) low-fat ricotta
1   cup Italian-blend shredded cheese
12   lasagna noodles (12 ounces) broken in half
1   package (10 ounces) frozen chopped broccoli, thawed and squeezed dry
1   jar (26 ounces) chunky tomato sauce

① In a large nonstick skillet, cook onion and garlic over medium-high heat, stirring often, for 4 minutes or until softened. Add turkey to skillet and cook, breaking up large chunks, for about 6 minutes or until no longer pink; drain fat. Stir oregano, salt and pepper into turkey.

② In a small bowl, combine ricotta and ½ cup of the Italian shredded cheese.

③ In slow cooker bowl, layer half the uncooked noodles, overlapping as necessary. Spread half of both the meat mixture and broccoli over noodles, then top with about half of the tomato sauce and ¼ cup water. Gently spread ricotta mixture on top, and continue layering with remaining noodles, meat, broccoli, sauce and an additional ¼ cup water.

④ Cover and cook for 4 hours on HIGH or 5 hours on LOW. Sprinkle remaining ½ cup of Italian cheese on top for last 15 minutes of cooking time or until melted.

PER SERVING 333 calories; 14 g fat (6 g sat.); 27 g protein; 24 g carbohydrate; 3 g fiber; 826 mg sodium; 85 mg cholesterol

SHRIMP STIR-FRY

MAKES 6 servings **PREP** 10 minutes
SLOW-COOK 1¾ hours on HIGH or 3½ hours on LOW

1   pound carrots, peeled and cut diagonally into ½-inch slices
1   medium sweet red pepper, seeded and cut into ½-inch slices
¾   cup low-sodium chicken broth
¼   cup low-sodium teriyaki sauce
2   tablespoons cornstarch
1   tablespoon oyster sauce
2   teaspoons sugar
1   pound shrimp, peeled and deveined
8   ounces snow peas, trimmed
1   can (8 ounces) bamboo shoots, drained
     Sliced scallions (optional)
3   cups cooked brown rice

① Place carrots and red pepper slices in slow cooker bowl. In a small bowl, blend broth, teriyaki sauce, cornstarch, oyster sauce and sugar. Pour into slow cooker and cook on HIGH for 1¾ hours or LOW for 3½ hours.

② Stir shrimp, snow peas and bamboo shoots into slow cooker for the final 20 minutes of cook time. Sprinkle with scallions, if desired, and serve with brown rice.

PER SERVING 277 calories; 3 g fat (1 g sat.); 21 g protein; 42 g carbohydrate; 6 g fiber; 349 mg sodium; 115 mg cholesterol

SUMMER FRUIT COMPOTE

MAKES 6 cups **PREP** 15 minutes **SLOW-COOK** 3½ hours on HIGH or 5½ hours on LOW plus 15 minutes

3 cups fresh pineapple chunks

2 medium pears, peeled, cored and cut into ½-inch chunks (about 2 cups)

2 cups frozen sliced peaches

1 cup frozen pitted cherries

¾ cup dried apricots, quartered

⅔ cup frozen orange juice concentrate, thawed

1 tablespoon packed dark-brown sugar

1 teaspoon vanilla extract

2 tablespoons cornstarch

½ cup sliced almonds, toasted
   Vanilla ice cream (optional)

① Stir together pineapple chunks, pears, peaches, cherries, apricots, orange juice, brown sugar and vanilla extract in slow cooker bowl. Cover and cook for 3½ hours on HIGH or 5½ hours on LOW.

② Uncover and remove 2 tablespoons liquid. In a small bowl, stir together liquid and cornstarch. Stir cornstarch mixture back into slow cooker; cook 15 minutes more or until thickened. Sprinkle with almonds. Serve warm, with ice cream, if desired.

PER SERVING 139 calories; 2 g fat (0 g sat.); 2 g protein; 29 g carbohydrate; 3 g fiber; 3 mg sodium; 0 mg cholesterol

Good Eggs

They're cheap, protein-rich and extremely versatile. Breakfast for dinner, anyone?

Those indentations in your fridge aren't the best place to store eggs—the temperature there varies too much because of the opening and closing of the door. Leave them in their original container and keep on a shelf. This way you also have a record of the "best by" date. To test freshness, place eggs in a bowl of water. If they float, toss.

POACHED EGGS

MAKES 4 eggs **PREP** 5 minutes
COOK 4 minutes

1   teaspoon white vinegar (helps keep egg white together)
4   large eggs

① Half-fill a 10-inch nonstick skillet with water; add the vinegar. Bring to a simmer over medium to medium-high heat.

② Crack one of the eggs into a measuring cup or small bowl and carefully drop into simmering water. Repeat with all eggs. Cook 4 minutes, until whites are firm but yolks are still soft. Remove with a slotted spoon.

HARD-COOKED

MAKES 6 eggs **PREP** 2 minutes
COOK 10 minutes **STAND** 12 minutes

6   large week-old eggs
1   tablespoon vegetable oil

① Place eggs in a medium-size saucepan. Add oil and enough water to cover eggs by 1 inch. Heat over medium-high heat until just boiling, about 10 minutes.

② Cover saucepan; remove from heat. Let stand 12 minutes. Drain and then cover with ice water. Cool completely, then roll eggs over paper towels and remove shells.

OMELET

MAKES 1 serving **PREP** 5 minutes
COOK 8 minutes

    Broccoli, spinach, onion and/or mushrooms
2   large eggs
    Pinch of salt and pepper
2   tablespoons grated cheddar cheese

① Coat an 8-inch nonstick skillet with nonstick cooking spray. Add desired vegetables and cook 5 minutes, until softened. Remove from pan.

② Add more nonstick spray to skillet. Scramble eggs, adding salt and pepper. Pour eggs into pan; cook 30 seconds until eggs begin to set. Use a spatula to push egg toward center of pan; tilt pan to let uncooked egg fill empty areas. Repeat until all areas are set, about 90 seconds. Cook 1 minute, then top one half with cooked vegetables and shredded cheese. Fold omelet onto itself and transfer to plate.

step by step

POACHED Use a small bowl or measuring cup to drop each egg into a 10-inch skillet filled with simmering water. Cook 4 minutes.

HARD-COOKED Place eggs in a pan; add water to cover and 1 tablespoon oil. Bring to a boil, remove from heat and cover.

OMELET Pour beaten eggs into heated skillet; cook 30 seconds. Push cooked egg to center, tilt pan and allow uncooked egg to fill empty spots.

STAY COOL WITH 25 FRESH AND HEARTY MAIN-DISH SALADS, FIRE UP THE GRILL FOR A SUMMER PARTY—AND SAVOR THE SEASON'S SWEETEST BERRIES IN A SELECTION OF DELECTABLE DESSERTS.

CHEESECAKE BROWNIE BARS, PAGE 145

JUNE

125

136

147

25 Simple Salad Suppers

Hearty, healthy veggie-packed meals that you can toss together in no time.

PANZANELLA,
PAGE 125

**BEEF KEBABS
& TANGY SLAW,
PAGE 133**

MIXED BABY GREENS

1. STEAK SALAD

MAKES 6 servings **PREP** 10 minutes
GRILL 12 minutes **LET REST** 5 minutes

① Heat grill or broiler. Spread 1½ lb. flank steak on a cutting board. In a small bowl, combine 1 tsp. Italian seasoning, ½ tsp. *each* garlic powder and salt, ¼ tsp. pepper and a pinch of cayenne. Coat steak with 2 tsp. olive oil and then rub spice mixture into steak. Grill or broil for 6 minutes per side, turning once, for a total of 12 minutes. Transfer to a clean board and let rest 5 minutes.

② Meanwhile, in a large bowl, combine 1½ packages (5 oz. each) baby arugula, ½ lb. bing cherries, pitted, and ½ cup crumbled blue cheese. Toss gently with ½ cup bottled low-fat blue cheese dressing (such as Bolthouse). Slice steak against the grain (starting on a small side) into thin slices. Toss with salad mixture.

PER SERVING 288 calories; 15 g fat (6 g sat.); 29 g protein; 9 g carbohydrate; 1 g fiber; 503 mg sodium; 46 mg cholesterol

2. PANZANELLA

MAKES 6 servings **PREP** 10 minutes
BAKE at 400° for 10 minutes **STAND** 5 minutes

① Heat oven to 400°. Cut a 12-oz. baguette into 1-inch pieces. Spread onto a baking sheet and spritz with nonstick cooking spray. Bake at 400° for 10 minutes, until lightly toasted. Remove from oven and let cool.

② In small bowl, whisk together ¼ cup white wine vinegar, 2 tsp. Dijon or spicy brown mustard, ½ tsp. sugar and ⅛ tsp. each salt and pepper. While whisking, add ¼ cup olive oil in a thin stream.

③ In large bowl, toss together bread cubes, 6 cups packed mixed baby greens, 4 oz. cubed tomato-basil cheddar and 8 oz. mixed heirloom tomatoes, sliced. Drizzle with dressing and toss to combine. Let sit 5 minutes to soften; serve.

PER SERVING 287 calories; 15 g fat (5 g sat.); 10 g protein; 30 g carbohydrate; 2 g fiber; 475 mg sodium; 20 mg cholesterol

3. MIXED GREENS WITH SEAFOOD SALAD

MAKES 4 servings **PREP** 15 minutes
CHILL 20 minutes

① In a medium-size bowl, combine ½ lb. cooked, peeled shrimp, chopped; ½ lb. imitation crabmeat, chopped; ½ cup minced red onion; 2 ribs celery, trimmed and finely chopped; 6 tbsp. light mayo; 1 tsp. fresh lemon juice; and ⅛ tsp. pepper. Stir until blended; chill at least 20 minutes.

② Place 8 cups (10-oz. pkg.) mixed baby greens in a large bowl or on a platter. Toss with ⅓ cup bottled creamy balsamic vinaigrette. Top with seafood salad and serve.

PER SERVING 252 calories; 12 g fat (2 g sat.); 14 g protein; 21 g carbohydrate; 3 g fiber; 1,004 mg sodium; 102 mg cholesterol

4. LEMON-BASIL ARUGULA

MAKES 6 servings **PREP** 15 minutes

① In a large bowl, combine two 5-oz. packages baby arugula; ¼ lb. small mozzarella balls, quartered; ⅓ cup pitted kalamata olives, halved; ½ of a small red onion, thinly sliced; and 1 can (15.5 oz.) butter beans, drained and rinsed.

② In mini chopper, combine ½ cup fresh basil leaves, ¼ cup fresh lemon juice, 2 tbsp. honey, 1 tbsp. Dijon mustard and ⅛ tsp. each salt and pepper. Pulse until basil is chopped and mixture is well combined. With blender running, add 3 tbsp. extra virgin olive oil in a thin stream. Toss dressing with salad; top with ¼ cup French's fried onions.

PER SERVING 280 calories; 17 g fat (5 g sat.); 10 g protein; 24 g carbohydrate; 4 g fiber; 688 mg sodium; 13 mg cholesterol

5. BABY GREENS WITH CHICKEN & GOAT CHEESE

MAKES 4 servings **PREP** 10 minutes
COOK 4 minutes

① Heat a small pot of water to boiling. Add ½ lb. trimmed and halved green beans and cook 4 minutes. Drain and rinse with cold water.

② In large bowl, combine 6 cups packed baby salad greens, 2 cups sliced or shredded rotisserie chicken (skin removed), the green beans, ¾ cup corn kernels, ½ cup goat cheese crumbles and ¼ cup sunflower seeds. Drizzle with ¼ cup bottled peppercorn ranch.

PER SERVING 320 calories; 18 g fat (4 g sat.); 23 g protein; 18 g carbohydrate; 5 g fiber; 500 mg sodium; 50 mg cholesterol

6. FRISÉE WITH BACON & POACHED EGG

MAKES 6 servings **PREP** 10 minutes
COOK 11 minutes

① In small bowl, whisk together 1 tbsp. white wine vinegar, ¾ tsp. Dijon mustard, ½ tsp. light mayo and ⅛ tsp. each salt and pepper. Slowly whisk in 3 tbsp. extra virgin olive oil.

② Cut 5 slices turkey bacon crosswise into ½-inch pieces and cook them in a large nonstick skillet over medium-high heat for 7 minutes or until crispy; drain on a paper-towel-lined plate.

③ Combine 8 cups chopped frisée (2 large heads), 5 oz. thinly sliced radishes (about 12) and the bacon in a large serving bowl. Drizzle with dressing and toss to coat. Divide salad among plates.

④ Bring a large skillet three-quarters full of water to a simmer; crack 6 eggs into separate measuring cups and pour separately into water; cook for 4 minutes; remove with a slotted spoon and place on top of individual servings.

PER SERVING 250 calories; 18 g fat (4 g sat.); 14 g protein; 13 g carbohydrate; 10 g fiber; 544 mg sodium; 235 mg cholesterol

7. FRISÉE WITH PEARS, CHEDDAR & PECANS

MAKES 6 servings **PREP** 15 minutes

① Cut 2 ripe pears in half and core them. Peel one pear half, cut into chunks and place in blender with 2 tbsp. red wine vinegar, ½ tsp. Dijon mustard and ¼ tsp. each salt and pepper. Puree until smooth. With machine running, slowly pour in 4 tbsp. olive oil; set aside.

② Cut remaining (unpeeled) pear halves into ¼-inch slices and place in a large bowl with 8 cups chopped frisée (2 small heads); 1 head radicchio (½ lb.), cored and thinly sliced; 1 cup shredded reduced-fat cheddar cheese; and ⅓ cup toasted chopped pecans. Drizzle with dressing and toss gently; serve immediately.

PER SERVING 275 calories; 19 g fat (4 g sat.); 10 g protein; 23 g carbohydrate; 12 g fiber; 378 mg sodium; 13 mg cholesterol

8. ESCAROLE, ORANGE & AVOCADO SALAD WITH SCALLOPS

MAKES 6 servings **PREP** 10 minutes
COOK 4 minutes

① In large bowl, combine 8 cups chopped escarole (1 large head); 2 cans (11 oz. each) mandarin oranges, drained and liquid reserved; ½ head of fennel, thinly sliced; and 1 diced avocado.

② Whisk together 3 tbsp. reserved mandarin liquid, 1 minced shallot, 1½ tbsp. lemon juice, ½ tsp. sugar and ¼ tsp. each salt and pepper. Slowly whisk in 3 tbsp. extra virgin olive oil.

③ Heat 1 tbsp. olive oil in a large nonstick skillet over medium-high heat. Add 1½ lb. large scallops to pan and cook 1½ to 2 minutes per side. Top salad with scallops and drizzle with citrus dressing; toss to coat and serve immediately.

PER SERVING 313 calories; 15 g fat (2 g sat.); 22 g protein; 24 g carbohydrate; 7 g fiber; 324 mg sodium; 37 mg cholesterol

9. FRISÉE, FIGS & PROSCIUTTO WITH WALNUT VINAIGRETTE

MAKES 4 servings **PREP** 15 minutes

① In a small bowl, whisk together 1½ tbsp. white wine vinegar, 2 tsp. raspberry jam, 2 tsp. minced shallot, ½ tsp. Dijon mustard, ⅛ tsp. each salt and pepper. Slowly whisk in 2 tbsp. walnut oil and 1 tbsp. olive oil.

② Combine in a large serving bowl 8 cups chopped frisée (about 2 large heads); ⅔ cup dried figs, cut into ¼-inch pieces; ⅓ cup toasted, chopped walnuts; and 2 oz. prosciutto, torn into long ribbons. Toss with prepared dressing.

PER SERVING 358 calories; 19 g fat (2 g sat.); 13 g protein; 42 g carbohydrate; 18 g fiber; 634 mg sodium; 11 mg cholesterol

10. ITALIAN ESCAROLE SALAD

MAKES 6 servings **PREP** 10 minutes

① In a small bowl, whisk together 2 tbsp. balsamic vinegar, 1 tbsp. white wine vinegar and ⅛ tsp. each salt and pepper; slowly whisk in 3 tbsp. olive oil.

② In large serving bowl, combine 8 cups chopped escarole (1 large head); 1 can (13.75 oz.) drained artichoke hearts; 3 oz. thinly sliced salami cut into ¼-inch ribbons; 1 jar (12.4 oz.) roasted red peppers; cut into ½-inch pieces; and 6 oz. fresh mozzarella; cut into ½-inch pieces. Drizzle with prepared dressing and serve.

PER SERVING 285 calories; 19 g fat (7 g sat.); 13 g protein; 16 g carbohydrate; 6 g fiber; 138 mg sodium; 34 mg cholesterol

ROMAINE & ICEBERG

11. MEXICAN CHICKEN SALAD

MAKES 8 servings **PREP** 15 minutes
REFRIGERATE 1 hour **GRILL** 8 minutes

① In small bowl, whisk together 6 tbsp. olive oil, ¼ cup lime juice, ¼ cup chopped cilantro, 2 minced garlic cloves, 1 minced shallot, ¾ tsp. sugar and ½ tsp. ground cumin. Place 4 tbsp. in a large resealable bag; set remaining dressing aside. Add 1 lb. thinly sliced chicken cutlets to bag; seal and squeeze to coat chicken. Refrigerate at least 1 hour.

② In very large serving bowl, combine 3 hearts of romaine, chopped (10 cups); 3 plum tomatoes, seeded and chopped; 1 can (15.5 oz.) black beans, drained and rinsed; 1 cup shredded pepper Jack cheese; and 1 cup frozen corn, thawed.

③ Heat grill to medium-high and grill chicken 3 to 4 minutes per side or until done; discard marinade. Chop chicken into 1-inch pieces and add to serving bowl. Drizzle with reserved dressing and toss well to combine.

PER SERVING 290 calories; 17 g fat (4 g sat.); 21 g protein; 15 g carbohydrate; 5 g fiber; 309 mg sodium; 45 mg cholesterol

12. GREEK CHOPPED SALAD

MAKES 4 servings **PREP** 15 minutes

① In a small bowl, whisk together 3 tbsp. lemon juice, 2 tbsp. chopped red onion, 3 tsp. chopped oregano, 1 minced garlic clove and ⅛ tsp. each salt, pepper and sugar. Slowly whisk in 4 tbsp. olive oil.

② In a large serving bowl, combine 2 hearts of romaine, chopped into ½-inch pieces (8 cups); 1 medium-size cucumber, peeled, seeded and cut into ½-inch pieces; 2 cups cherry tomatoes, quartered; 1 can (14 oz.) chickpeas, drained and rinsed;

½ cup chopped parsley; ⅓ cup chopped pitted kalamata olives; and 5 oz. feta cheese, crumbled. Drizzle with dressing and toss well to coat; serve immediately.

PER SERVING 330 calories; 21 g fat (5 g sat.); 13 g protein; 26 g carbohydrate; 8 g fiber; 840 mg sodium; 10 mg cholesterol

13. BUFFALO CHICKEN SALAD

MAKES 4 servings **PREP** 15 minutes
COOK 8 minutes

① Coat large nonstick skillet with nonstick cooking spray. Cook 1 lb. chicken breast tenders in skillet over medium heat about 8 minutes, flipping halfway through, or until cooked through; remove from heat and stir together with 3 tbsp. hot sauce (such as Frank's).

② In small bowl, stir together ½ cup crumbled blue cheese, 3 tbsp. reduced-fat sour cream, 3 tbsp. 2% milk and 3 tbsp. light mayo.

③ Combine 1 chopped romaine heart and ½ head chopped iceberg lettuce in a large serving bowl and add 2 stalks celery, cut into ¼ x 2-inch matchsticks, and 1 cup shredded carrots. Drizzle dressing over salad. Toss well to combine. Top with chicken.

PER SERVING 284 calories; 12 g fat (5 g sat.); 33 g protein; 11 g carbohydrate; 3 g fiber; 497 mg sodium; 89 mg cholesterol

14. ROMAINE WITH TURKEY & DRIED CRANBERRIES

MAKES 4 servings **PREP** 15 minutes

① In small bowl, blend ¼ cup whole-berry cranberry sauce, 2 tbsp. light mayo, 1½ tbsp. red wine vinegar and 2 tsp. Dijon mustard.

② In serving bowl, combine 2 hearts of romaine, chopped (8 cups); one ½-inch-thick slice smoked turkey (about 8 oz.), diced; ½ cup chopped toasted pecans; and ½ cup dried cranberries. Drizzle with dressing and serve.

PER SERVING 293 calories; 16 g fat (2 g sat.); 13 g protein; 28 g carbohydrate; 5 g fiber; 683 mg sodium; 28 mg cholesterol

15. CRISPY PEANUT TOFU SALAD

MAKES 4 servings **PREP** 15 minutes
COOK 12 minutes

① In small bowl, blend 3 tbsp. chunky peanut butter, 2 minced garlic cloves, 2 tbsp. hot water, 1 tbsp. light-brown sugar, 1 tbsp. rice vinegar, 2 tsp. low-sodium soy sauce and ⅛ tsp. red pepper flakes.

② Place 8 cups chopped iceberg lettuce (1 large head) in a large bowl and add 1 sweet red pepper, thinly sliced, and 1 bunch scallions, thinly sliced.

③ Drain 1 package (14 oz.) firm tofu and cut into 1-inch squares. Pat dry with paper towels. Place ½ cup cornstarch in a pie plate and coat tofu with cornstarch.

④ Heat 1 tbsp. vegetable oil in a large nonstick skillet over medium-high heat and cook tofu for 10 to 12 minutes, turning often, or until golden brown. Add tofu to bowl; drizzle with dressing.

PER SERVING 302 calories; 14 g fat (1 g sat.); 14 g protein; 31 g carbohydrate; 4 g fiber; 380 mg sodium; 0 mg cholesterol

FRESH SPINACH

16. SPINACH NIÇOISE

MAKES 6 servings **PREP** 10 minutes
COOK 6 minutes

① Whisk together ¼ cup olive oil, 3 tbsp. red wine vinegar, 1 minced shallot, ½ tsp. Dijon mustard and ¼ tsp. each salt and pepper.

② Bring a medium-size pot of salted water to a boil. Add 10 oz. new potatoes, cut into ¼-inch-thick slices, to boiling water for 6 minutes; drain and run under cool water.

③ Place 12 oz. baby spinach in a large serving bowl with potatoes, 3 plum tomatoes, cut into ½-inch wedges; 6 oz. green beans, steamed and cut in half; ½ cup chopped black olives; and 3 cans (5 oz.) albacore tuna in water, drained. Drizzle with dressing; toss well to coat. Place salad mixture on serving platter and crumble 1 additional can of albacore tuna in water, drained, over top. Add 3 hard-cooked eggs, peeled and cut into wedges, and serve immediately.

PER SERVING 295 calories; 15 g fat (3 g sat.); 23 g protein; 17 g carbohydrate; 5 g fiber; 371 mg sodium; 136 mg cholesterol

17. SPINACH WITH GRILLED PORTOBELLOS & ONION

MAKES 4 servings **PREP** 15 minutes
GRILL 10 minutes

① Whisk together 3 tbsp. extra virgin olive oil, 1 tbsp. balsamic vinegar, 2 minced garlic cloves, ½ tsp. light mayo and ⅛ tsp. each salt and pepper.

② Place 12 oz. baby spinach and 1 can (15.5 oz.) rinsed and drained cannellini beans in a large serving bowl; set aside.

③ Heat grill to medium-high. Slice 1 large yellow onion across equator into ½-inch-thick slices and secure with toothpicks. Grill 5 minutes per side. Meanwhile, clean 4 portobello mushroom caps and place each in the center of a 12-inch square of aluminum foil; brush caps with dressing and fold foil over caps. Place foil packets on grill; cook 10 minutes.

④ Remove onions and mushrooms from grill (pouring any liquid inside packets into dressing) and chop; add to serving bowl. Drizzle with dressing and toss well to combine. Sprinkle with ⅓ cup crumbled blue cheese; serve.

PER SERVING 303 calories; 15 g fat (4 g sat.); 11 g protein; 34 g carbohydrate; 10 g fiber; 605 mg sodium; 9 mg cholesterol

18. CURRIED CHICKEN & BABY SPINACH

MAKES 4 servings **PREP** 10 minutes
COOK 1 minute

① Heat 1 tsp. vegetable oil in a medium-size nonstick skillet over medium-high heat. Add 1 tbsp. grated ginger, 2 minced garlic cloves and 1½ tsp. curry powder to skillet and stir; cook 1 minute. Remove to a small bowl and stir in ¾ cup 2% Greek yogurt, ¼ cup skim milk, 1 tsp. lemon juice and ½ tsp. salt; stir.

② Place 12 oz. baby spinach in a large serving bowl and stir in 4 cups cooked, shredded chicken, ⅓ cup toasted and chopped cashews and ½ cup chopped dried apricots. Toss with dressing and serve immediately.

PER SERVING 320 calories; 9 g fat (2 g sat.); 35 g protein; 27 g carbohydrate; 5 g fiber; 595 mg sodium; 68 mg cholesterol

19. SPINACH WITH ASPARAGUS & GOAT CHEESE

MAKES 4 servings **PREP** 15 minutes
COOK 12 minutes

① Trim 1 inch off of bottom of 1 lb. asparagus; cut spears into 2-inch pieces.

② Whisk together 3 tbsp. sherry vinegar, 2 tbsp. olive oil, 1 large minced shallot and ½ tsp. dried thyme.

③ Place 12 oz. baby spinach in a large serving bowl; crumble 3 oz. goat cheese on top; set aside.

④ Cook 4 slices bacon in a large nonstick skillet over medium-high heat for 8 minutes, flipping halfway through. Cool and crumble into serving bowl. Carefully wipe out skillet and return to medium heat. Add asparagus to skillet with ⅓ cup water and cover; cook 4 minutes or until bright green and tender. Add to serving bowl. Drizzle salad with dressing and toss to combine.

PER SERVING 286 calories; 21 g fat (7 g sat.); 11 g protein; 15 g carbohydrate; 7 g fiber; 404 mg sodium; 25 mg cholesterol

20. CARIBBEAN SHRIMP, MANGO & SPINACH SALAD

MAKES 4 servings **PREP** 10 minutes

① Whisk together 2 tbsp. lime juice, 3 tbsp. vegetable oil, 1 tbsp. dark-brown sugar, 1 small jalapeño, seeded and minced, ½ tsp. cumin and ¼ tsp. each salt and pepper.

② Place 9 oz. baby spinach in a large serving bowl. Stir in 1 large mango, peeled and cut into ½-inch pieces, 1 lb. medium-size cooked and peeled shrimp and 4 thinly sliced scallions. Drizzle with dressing and serve.

PER SERVING 294 calories; 13 g fat (1 g sat.); 25 g protein; 22 g carbohydrate; 5 g fiber; 420 mg sodium; 172 mg cholesterol

RED, GREEN AND NAPA CABBAGE

21. VIETNAMESE PORK SALAD

MAKES 6 servings **PREP** 15 minutes
MARINATE 20 minutes **SOAK** 8 minutes
GRILL 6 minutes

① Slice 2 boneless, center-cut pork chops in half horizontally to form 4 thin-cut chops. Pound to even thinness. In small bowl, mix together ⅓ cup rice vinegar, ¼ cup mirin, 3 tbsp. fish sauce, 1½ tbsp. olive oil, 1½ tbsp. sugar and ½ tsp. Thai chili garlic sauce (such as Sriracha). Combine ¼ cup dressing with pork in a resealable bag; marinate 20 minutes.

② Soak 3 ounces rice vermicelli noodles (from 8-oz. pkg) following package directions, 8 minutes. Drain and rinse.

③ Heat grill pan. Grill pork for 3 minutes, then flip and grill an additional 2 to 3 minutes. Remove to a cutting board and cut into thin strips. In large bowl, combine ½ head napa cabbage, cored and sliced; ½ cup cilantro leaves; ½ cup mint leaves; and 2 scallions, trimmed and sliced, with the noodles. Toss with remaining dressing and top with pork.

PER SERVING 226 calories; 5 g fat (1 g sat.); 20 g protein; 20 g carbohydrate; 2 g fiber; 845 mg sodium; 42 mg cholesterol

22. CHINESE SHRIMP SALAD

MAKES 4 servings **PREP** 10 minutes **BAKE** at 400° for 13 minutes **BROIL** 3 minutes

① Heat oven to 400°. Spread 2 packages (8 oz. each) frozen popcorn shrimp on a large baking sheet; spread ½ cup sliced almonds on medium-size sheet. Bake shrimp at 400° for 13 minutes; bake almonds at 400° for 3 minutes. Increase heat to broil. Broil shrimp 3 minutes or until browned and crispy.

② Meanwhile, in a large bowl, toss together ½ head napa cabbage (¾ lb.), cored and shredded; ½ head green cabbage (¾ lb.), cored and shredded; the toasted almonds; and ⅓ cup bottled miso-sesame dressing (such as Masa's) or any low-calorie Asian dressing. Stir in hot shrimp, top with ½ cup crispy chow mein noodles and serve immediately.

PER SERVING 412 calories; 14 g fat (2 g sat.); 25 g protein; 48 g carbohydrate; 7 g fiber; 758 mg sodium; 91 mg cholesterol

23. APPLE & KIELBASA SALAD

MAKES 4 servings **PREP** 10 minutes
COOK 8 minutes

① In small bowl, mix together 2 tbsp. cider vinegar, 1 tbsp. grainy mustard, 1 tsp. sugar, ¼ tsp. pepper and ⅛ tsp. salt. Whisk in 3 tbsp. olive oil until blended. Set aside.

② Coat a large nonstick skillet with nonstick cooking spray. Heat over medium-high heat and then add ¾ lb. turkey kielbasa, sliced. Cook 4 minutes, turning, until browned. Remove to a plate. Add 1 package (10 oz.) shredded red cabbage, 3 Granny Smith apples, cored and grated, 2 tbsp. cider vinegar and ½ tsp. caraway seeds. Cook 4 minutes. Remove from heat; stir in kielbasa and dressing.

PER SERVING 303 calories; 17 g fat (4 g sat.); 14 g protein; 26 g carbohydrate; 5 g fiber; 928 mg sodium; 56 mg cholesterol

24. HAM & RAISIN CONFETTI

MAKES 6 servings **PREP** 20 minutes
CHILL ½ hour

① In a large bowl, combine ½ head green cabbage (1 lb.), cored and shredded; 1 cup shredded carrots; ⅔ cup golden raisins; and ½ lb. thinly sliced deli ham; cut into thin strips.

② In small bowl, whisk together ¾ cup creamy poppyseed dressing (such as Brianne's), ½ cup reduced-fat sour cream and ⅛ tsp. each salt and pepper. Pour over cabbage mixture; toss to combine. Refrigerate at least ½ hour.

PER SERVING 314 calories; 17 g fat (3 g sat.); 9 g protein; 30 g carbohydrate; 3 g fiber; 665 mg sodium; 27 mg cholesterol

25. BEEF KEBABS & TANGY SLAW

MAKES 4 servings **PREP** 10 minutes
MARINATE 25 minutes
GRILL OR BROIL 5 minutes

① Soak 8 bamboo skewers in warm water. In small bowl, blend ½ cup white vinegar, ¼ cup honey, 1 tbsp. Dijon mustard and ¼ tsp. each salt and pepper. Add ¼ cup olive oil in a thin stream.

② In glass dish, combine ⅓ cup of the dressing with 1 lb. sirloin steak, cut into 1-inch pieces (about 24). Refrigerate 25 minutes.

③ In large bowl, combine 1 small red cabbage (1¼ lb.) cored and shredded; 1 small sweet red pepper, cored and cut into thin strips; and ½ of a red onion, peeled and thinly sliced. Toss with remaining dressing.

④ Heat grill or broiler. Thread meat onto skewers alternating with 1-inch pieces of sweet red pepper. Grill or broil for 3 minutes, then turn over and grill or broil an additional 2 minutes or until desired doneness. Serve slaw topped with 2 skewers each.

PER SERVING 383 calories; 18 g fat (3 g sat.); 25 g protein; 34 g carbohydrate; 5 g fiber; 325 mg sodium; 35 mg cholesterol

Grilling USA

Get fired up for the best of BBQ, from California to the Carolinas.

**GRILLED GEORGIA
PEACHES, PAGE 139**

PACIFIC RIM CEDAR PLANK
SALMON, PAGE 139

CAROLINA SHREDDED CHICKEN

MAKES 6 servings **PREP** 25 minutes **COOK** 10 minutes **GRILL** 18 minutes

CHICKEN

6	bone-in chicken thighs, skin removed (about 2 pounds)
½	teaspoon seasoned salt
¼	teaspoon paprika

SAUCE

1	tablespoon vegetable oil
1	small onion, diced
⅔	cup vinegar
½	cup ketchup
¼	cup packed light-brown sugar
1	tablespoon spicy brown mustard
6	sandwich buns

① Heat gas grill to medium-high or charcoal grill to medium-hot coals.

② **Chicken:** Sprinkle chicken on all sides with seasoned salt and paprika. When grill is ready, place chicken on grill grate. Cook, turning once, for 18 minutes, or until thigh registers 180° on an instant-read thermometer.

③ Meanwhile, prepare **Sauce:** Heat oil in a medium-size saucepan over medium heat. Add onion and cook 5 minutes. Stir in vinegar, ketchup, brown sugar and mustard. Bring to a boil, then reduce heat and simmer 5 minutes.

④ Remove chicken from grill and allow to cool slightly. With two forks or your hands, shred meat from bones. Add shredded chicken to sauce and heat through. Divide chicken evenly among sandwich buns, a heaping ⅓ cup on each. Serve with Coleslaw.

PER SERVING 390 calories; 10 g fat (2 g sat.); 34 g protein; 37 g carbohydrate; 1 g fiber; 670 mg sodium; 125 mg cholesterol

COLESLAW In a large bowl, stir together 1 bag (16 ounces) shredded coleslaw blend, 1 cup Miracle Whip, 2 tablespoons vinegar, 1 teaspoon sugar and ⅛ teaspoon each salt and pepper until blended.

MIDWESTERN PORK CHOPS & BEER BRATS

MAKES 4 servings **PREP** 20 minutes **MARINATE** 2 hours **COOK** 5 minutes **GRILL** 12 minutes

2   cans or bottles beer
2   small onions, sliced
2   tablespoons cider vinegar
2   cloves garlic, smashed
2   teaspoons fresh thyme
½   teaspoon sugar
¼   teaspoon pepper
2   tablespoons vegetable oil
4   bone-in pork loin chops (10 to 12 ounces each)
4   reduced-calorie bratwurst (uncooked if available)

① In bowl, blend 1 cup beer, 1 sliced onion, the vinegar, garlic, thyme, sugar and pepper. Whisk in oil. Transfer to a resealable plastic bag and add the pork chops. Marinate, refrigerated, 2 hours.

② Heat gas grill to medium-high or charcoal grill to medium-hot coals. Pour remaining beer into a medium-size saucepan and add remaining sliced onion. Add bratwurst. Simmer gently, 5 minutes (if brats are precooked, simply heat through).

③ Add pork chops to grill; cover and cook 5 minutes. Uncover grill and turn chops over. Add brats to the grill and continue to cook chops and brats for 5 to 7 minutes more, until pork registers 155° on an instant-read thermometer and brats are nicely browned. Serve chops and brats with Macaroni Salad.

PER SERVING 547 calories; 30 g fat (4 g sat.); 38 g protein; 28 g carbohydrate; 2 g fiber; 1,070 mg sodium; 120 mg cholesterol

MACARONI SALAD Cook 8 ounces (½ package) macaroni in boiling water following package directions, 7 minutes. Drain and rinse. In a small bowl, whisk ½ cup light mayonnaise; 1 carrot, grated; 1 rib celery, chopped; 1½ tablespoons white vinegar; 1 tablespoon pickle relish; 1 teaspoon sugar; and ⅛ teaspoon pepper. Stir into drained macaroni and refrigerate until serving.

TEXAS RIBEYE STEAKS & POTATO SALAD

MAKES 4 servings **PREP** 10 minutes **COOK** 10 minutes **GRILL** 10 minutes

1 **tablespoon taco seasoning (from a 1- to 1.5-ounce packet)**
1 **teaspoon chili powder**
2 **bone-in ribeye steaks (1 pound each)**

① Heat gas grill to medium; heat charcoal grill so that most of the coals are stacked to one side. Mix together 1 tablespoon of the taco seasoning (save remaining for potato salad) and the chili powder. Rub mixture into steaks.

② Place steaks on grill (for charcoal grill, place steaks in the center of the grill where the heat is moderate). Cover and cook for 5 minutes. Turn over and grill an additional 5 minutes or until steaks register 145° to 150° on an instant-read thermometer. Remove to a platter and cover with foil. Let rest at least 5 minutes before slicing and serving with the potato salad.

PER SERVING 661 calories; 33 g fat (14 g sat.); 50 g protein; 40 g carbohydrate; 5 g fiber; 807 mg sodium; 136 mg cholesterol

POTATO SALAD Boil 2 pounds peeled and cut-up all-purpose potatoes 10 minutes or until tender. Drain and rinse; cool completely. Stir in 1 sweet red pepper, cored and diced; and 3 scallions, trimmed and sliced. In small bowl, whisk ¾ cup reduced-fat sour cream, ¼ cup light mayo and 4 teaspoons packaged taco seasoning. Gently stir into potato mixture and top with ¼ cup shredded cheddar, if desired. Refrigerate until serving.

EAST COAST FLOUNDER PACKETS & GRILLED CORN

MAKES 6 servings **PREP** 10 minutes
SOAK 30 minutes **GRILL** 40 minutes

- 6   ears corn on the cob, silks removed, husks left on
- 6   flounder fillets, about 2 pounds total
- ¾   teaspoon Old Bay seasoning
- 1½   teaspoons olive oil
- 6   slices lemon
     Butter, for serving (optional)

① Place corn in a sink full of cold water; weigh down with a heavy bowl; soak 30 minutes.

② Meanwhile, heat gas grill to medium-high heat, or charcoal grill to medium-hot coals (mounding slightly on one side).

③ Transfer soaked corn to heated grill. Grill corn, turning frequently, 20 minutes. If using gas grill, move corn to warming tray. If using charcoal, transfer corn to a large platter and cover with a clean cloth to keep warm.

④ Tear off six 10-inch-square pieces of foil. Place one flounder fillet in center of one foil square. Season with ⅛ teaspoon of the Old Bay seasoning. Tuck ends under fillet, top with ¼ teaspoon of the olive oil and one lemon slice. Seal foil tightly to form packet; repeat with remaining fish, Old Bay, oil and lemon.

⑤ Reduce heat to medium on a gas grill. Place fish packets on grill; on charcoal grill, group packets on side with less charcoal. Grill packets 18 to 20 minutes or until fish is white throughout. Serve with corn and butter alongside.

PER SERVING 241 calories; 5 g fat (1 g sat.); 33 g protein; 20 g carbohydrate; 3 g fiber; 206 mg sodium; 73 mg cholesterol

PACIFIC RIM CEDAR PLANK SALMON

MAKES 4 servings **PREP** 10 minutes
SOAK 10 minutes **COOK** 6 minutes
GRILL 25 minutes

- 1   cedar plank (see Note)
- ¼   cup packed light-brown sugar
- 2   tablespoons soy sauce
- 3   cloves garlic; 1 minced, the other 2 sliced
- ½   teaspoon sesame oil
- 1¼   pounds salmon fillet (one piece)
- 1   tablespoon olive oil
- 1   pound baby bok choy, trimmed and chopped
- ⅛   teaspoon salt
- ⅛   teaspoon pepper

① Soak plank in cool water for 10 minutes, weighing down with a heavy object to keep submerged.

② Heat gas grill to medium or charcoal grill to medium coals.

③ In small bowl, stir together brown sugar, soy sauce, the clove of minced garlic and the sesame oil. Set aside 2 tablespoons sauce for serving.

④ Once plank is done soaking, place salmon fillet on plank, skin side down, and brush with half of remaining sauce. Transfer plank to grill and cover. Grill 10 minutes; if plank chars too much, mist with water.

⑤ Uncover grill; baste salmon with remaining sauce. Cover grill and continue to cook 15 minutes or until fish registers 130° on an instant-read thermometer and flakes easily with a fork.

⑥ Meanwhile, heat oil in a large nonstick skillet over medium heat. Add the 2 sliced garlic cloves and cook 1 to 2 minutes. Add bok choy, salt and pepper and cook an

additional 2 to 4 minutes, until tender and cooked through.

⑦ To serve, slide a spatula between fillet and skin and transfer to a platter. Drizzle with the 2 tablespoons reserved sauce; serve with bok choy on the side.

Note: Visit madeinoregon.com to buy a 3-pack of cedar planks for $13.

PER SERVING 339 calories; 14 g fat (2 g sat.); 34 g protein; 17 g carbohydrate; 2 g fiber; 324 mg sodium; 90 mg cholesterol

GRILLED GEORGIA PEACHES

MAKES 6 servings **PREP** 5 minutes
GRILL 5 minutes

- 3   peaches, halved and pitted
- 3   tablespoons unsalted butter, melted
- 3   tablespoons packed dark-brown sugar
- ⅛   teaspoon ground cinnamon
     Vanilla ice cream (optional)

① Heat gas grill to medium-high heat, charcoal grill to medium-hot coals. Brush cut sides of peaches with a little butter. In small bowl, blend remaining butter, the sugar and cinnamon.

② Grill peaches, cut side down, 3 minutes. Flip over and carefully brush with butter mixture (remove from the grill to do this). Return peaches to grill, cut side up. Grill 2 minutes, until butter is bubbly. Serve warm, with ice cream, if desired.

PER SERVING 98 calories; 6 g fat (4 g sat.); 1 g protein; 12 g carbohydrate; 1 g fiber; 4 mg sodium; 15 mg cholesterol

The Berry Best

Fresh-picked ideas for summer's sweetest fruit.

STRAWBERRY SORBET, PAGE 145

**CHUNKY GINGERED
STRAWBERRY SAUCE,
PAGE 145**

Plump, juicy and sweet, strawberries are one of June's greatest gifts. Enjoy them in a gorgeous trifle based on purchased poundcake—or in a melty, banana-stuffed s'more.

STRAWBERRY SHORTCAKE TRIFLE

MAKES 8 servings **PREP** 10 minutes
REFRIGERATE 6 hours or overnight

1   quart strawberries (about 4 cups), hulled and sliced
¼   cup sugar
1   container (8 ounces) light frozen whipped topping (such as Cool Whip Lite), thawed
⅓   cup prepared strawberry topping (such as Smucker's)
1   store-bought 13-ounce marbled pound cake (such as Entenmann's), cut into 1-inch cubes
    Strawberries for garnish, optional

① In a large bowl, mix together strawberries and sugar. Cover and refrigerate for 2 hours.

② In a medium-size bowl, stir together the whipped topping and strawberry topping. Place half of the cake cubes in a large glass bowl. Spoon half of the berries and accumulated juices evenly over the cake. Spread half of the topping mixture over the berries. Repeat layering. Cover and refrigerate for 4 hours or overnight.

③ Garnish with additional strawberries, if desired.

PER SERVING 314 calories; 12 g fat (5 g sat.); 3 g protein; 52 g carbohydrate; 2 g fiber; 185 mg sodium; 27 mg cholesterol

STRAWBERRY BANANA S'MORES

MAKES 12 servings **PREP** 10 minutes **MICROWAVE** 15 seconds per batch

12   graham cracker boards
6   ounces milk chocolate
12   large marshmallows, cut in half crosswise
6   large strawberries, hulled and thinly sliced
1   large banana, thinly sliced on the diagonal
12   teaspoons strawberry preserves

① Break each graham cracker in half along perforation to form 2 squares.

② Place 12 of the squares on a flat work surface. Layer a ½-ounce piece of chocolate and 2 marshmallow halves on each cracker. In batches of 4, place them on a microwave-safe plate and microwave for 15 seconds, until marshmallows puff up.

③ Place a few strawberry slices and a banana slice on top of each square. Spread 1 teaspoon of preserves on one side of each remaining graham cracker and place, preserve side down, over fruit. Press down gently; serve immediately.

PER SERVING 198 calories; 6 g fat (3 g sat.); 2 g protein; 34 g carbohydrate; 2 g fiber; 70 mg sodium; 3 mg cholesterol

CHEESECAKE BROWNIE BARS

MAKES 32 servings **PREP** 25 minutes
MICROWAVE about 2 minutes **BAKE** at 350°
for 1 hour, 5 minutes **STAND** 2 hours
CHILL 2 hours

CHEESECAKE

¼ cup cornstarch
½ cup sugar
3 packages (8 ounces each) ⅓-less-fat cream cheese, softened
3 large eggs
¾ cup sour cream
⅔ cup milk
1 teaspoon vanilla extract

BROWNIE

1 cup (2 sticks) unsalted butter
5 squares (1 ounce each) unsweetened chocolate
1¾ cups sugar
4 large eggs
1¾ cups all-purpose flour
1½ teaspoons baking powder
½ teaspoon salt
2 teaspoons vanilla extract
1 bag (12 ounces) bittersweet chocolate chips

TOPPING

3 tablespoons strawberry jelly
1 package (12 ounces) strawberries, hulled and chopped
¼ cup hot fudge sauce, heated
1 container (8 ounces) frozen whipped topping, thawed
Chopped hazelnuts, for garnish (optional)

① Heat oven to 350°. Line a 13 x 9 x 2-inch baking pan with foil. Coat foil with nonstick cooking spray. Set aside.

② **Cheesecake:** In large bowl, whisk cornstarch and sugar until blended. Add cream cheese, and beat until smooth. Beat in eggs, sour cream and milk. Stir in vanilla; set aside.

③ **Brownie:** In large microwave-safe bowl, combine butter and chocolate. Microwave for 1 minute, 30 seconds. Stir. If necessary, continue heating in 30-second increments, stirring after each, until chocolate is melted.

④ Whisk in sugar, then eggs. Whisk in flour, baking powder and salt until smooth. Stir in vanilla and chocolate chips. Spread evenly into prepared pan. Pour cream cheese mixture over brownie mixture. Spread gently until smooth.

⑤ Bake at 350° for 1 hour and 5 minutes or until center is set. Cool on wire rack to room temperature, about 2 hours. Transfer to refrigerator and continue to cool 2 hours.

⑥ **Topping:** Heat jelly in microwave-safe bowl for 15 seconds. Stir in berries. Heat fudge sauce in a glass cup in microwave for 25 seconds, until drizzling consistency.

⑦ Cut cheesecake brownie into 32 squares. Dollop each square with about 1 tablespoon whipped topping, then some of the strawberries and fudge topping. Sprinkle with nuts, if desired.

PER SERVING 326 calories; 21 g fat (12 g sat.); 6 g protein; 33 g carbohydrate; 2 g fiber; 178 mg sodium; 80 mg cholesterol

STRAWBERRY SORBET

MAKES 6 cups **PREP** 10 minutes
COOK 1 minute **FREEZE** 6½ hours

¾ cup sugar
2 quarts strawberries, hulled (about 8 cups)
½ cup lemon-lime soda
Chocolate-lined wafers (such as Pirouline) or mint for garnish (optional)

① In a medium-size heavy bottom saucepan, stir together ¾ cup water and sugar. Bring to a boil over medium-high heat. Boil for 1 minute. Turn off heat and stir until sugar is dissolved. Allow to cool.

② In a food processor, puree the strawberries and soda. Add in the sugar syrup and process until combined. Pour into a 13 x 9 x 2-inch metal baking pan and freeze for 4 to 4½ hours, until frozen solid.

③ Scrape into a food processor and process briefly until smooth but not melted. Spoon back into metal pan and freeze for an additional 1 to 2 hours before serving.

④ Form into balls with an ice cream scoop; serve in dessert dishes with chocolate wafers or mint leaves, if desired.

PER SERVING 130 calories; 1 g fat (0 g sat.); 1 g protein; 35 g carbohydrate; 4 g fiber; 4 mg sodium; 0 mg cholesterol

CHUNKY GINGERED STRAWBERRY SAUCE

MAKES 2 cups (8 servings) **PREP** 10 minutes
COOK 5 minutes

1 quart strawberries (about 4 cups), hulled and chopped
½ cup sugar
1 tablespoon candied ginger, chopped
½ teaspoon vanilla extract

① Set aside ½ cup of the chopped strawberries. In a medium-size heavy-bottom saucepan, stir together the remaining strawberries (about 3½ cups), the sugar and ginger. Bring to a simmer. Continue to cook for 5 minutes, stirring occasionally. Remove from heat and mash berries, until crushed, with the back of a wooden spoon.

② Stir in the vanilla extract and reserved strawberries. Allow to cool completely.

③ Serve as a topping for ice cream or waffles (see Note).

Note: To serve with waffles, toast frozen waffles following package directions. Top with ¼ cup of sauce and a dollop of sweetened whipped cream.

PER SERVING 65 calories; 0 g fat (0 g sat.); 0 g protein; 18 g carbohydrate; 1 g fiber; 2 mg sodium; 0 mg cholesterol

Slow Cooker Suppers

A week's worth of healthy chicken meals.

CHICKEN STEW WITH CORN & KIELBASA

CHICKEN STEW WITH CORN & KIELBASA

MAKES 6 servings **PREP** 15 minutes
SLOW COOK 3¼ hours on HIGH or 4½ hours on LOW

- 1½ cups plus 2 tablespoons low-sodium chicken broth
- 3 cloves garlic, minced
- 1 teaspoon dried thyme
- ¼ teaspoon cayenne pepper
- 4 bone-in skinless chicken breasts (about 3 pounds)
- 1 large onion, chopped
- 7 ounces turkey kielbasa sausage, halved lengthwise and thinly sliced
- 1 cup frozen corn
- 1 green pepper, seeded and chopped
- 2 tablespoons cornstarch
- ½ teaspoon salt
- ¼ teaspoon black pepper
- 4 cups mashed sweet potatoes (optional)

① Stir together 1½ cups of the broth, garlic, thyme and cayenne; set aside.

② Place chicken, onion and kielbasa in slow cooker bowl. Pour broth mixture over top. Cover and cook on HIGH for 2½ hours or LOW for 3½ hours.

③ Remove cover and stir in corn and green pepper. Cover; cook 30 minutes.

④ Remove chicken from slow cooker. Shred meat into bite-size pieces, discarding bones.

⑤ Stir together remaining 2 tablespoons broth and cornstarch. Whisk cornstarch mixture, salt and pepper into slow cooker; cook on HIGH for 15 minutes or on LOW for 30, or until thick. Stir shredded chicken into sauce. Serve with sweet potatoes, if desired.

PER SERVING 266 calories; 5 g fat (1 g sat.); 42 g protein; 12 g carbohydrate; 2 g fiber; 764 mg sodium; 111 mg cholesterol

CHEESY CHICKEN HASH

MAKES 8 servings **PREP** 20 minutes **SLOW COOK** 3 hours on HIGH or 5 hours on LOW

- 1 can (12 ounces) evaporated milk
- 3 tablespoons steak sauce–style marinade (such as A.1.)
- 2 tablespoons yellow mustard
- ¼ teaspoon salt
- ¼ teaspoon black pepper
- 1 bag (28 ounces) frozen Potatoes O'Brien (such as Ore-Ida)
- 1 pound ground chicken
- 1 large onion, finely chopped
- ½ cup shredded Swiss cheese
- ¼ cup chopped fresh parsley

① Coat slow cooker bowl with nonstick cooking spray. Whisk together evaporated milk, marinade, mustard, salt and pepper; set aside.

② Add potatoes, chicken and onion to slow cooker bowl and stir to combine. Pour marinade mixture over top. Cover and cook on HIGH for 2½ hours or LOW for 4½ hours, stirring once halfway through.

③ Remove cover and stir. Sprinkle with cheese and parsley and replace cover for 30 minutes or until cheese has melted; serve immediately.

PER SERVING 269 calories; 11 g fat (5 g sat.); 16 g protein; 27 g carbohydrate; 2 g fiber; 331 mg sodium; 88 mg cholesterol

ORANGE CHICKEN WITH ANGEL HAIR PASTA

CHICKEN TAGINE

MAKES 4 servings **PREP** 10 minutes
SLOW COOK 2½ hours on HIGH or 5 hours on LOW

1¾ pounds boneless, skinless chicken thighs, trimmed and cut into 1-inch pieces
2 large onions, thinly sliced
½ cup dried apricots, coarsely chopped
⅓ cup raisins
1¼ cups low-sodium chicken broth
2 tablespoons tomato paste
2 tablespoons lemon juice
2 tablespoons flour
1½ teaspoons ground cumin
1½ teaspoons ground ginger
1 teaspoon ground cinnamon
½ teaspoon black pepper
2 cups cooked couscous

① Place chicken, onions, apricots and raisins in slow cooker bowl.

② In a small bowl, whisk together chicken broth, tomato paste, lemon juice, flour, cumin, ginger, cinnamon and black pepper. Pour over chicken in slow cooker. Cover and cook on HIGH for 2½ hours or LOW for 5 hours.

③ Serve over cooked couscous.

PER SERVING 482 calories; 11 g fat (3 g sat.); 45 g protein; 54 g carbohydrate; 5 g fiber; 345 mg sodium; 195 mg cholesterol

ORANGE CHICKEN WITH ANGEL HAIR PASTA

MAKES 6 servings **PREP** 15 minutes **SLOW COOK** 3 hours on HIGH or 5 hours on LOW

⅔ cup sweet-and-sour sauce
⅓ cup orange juice
2 tablespoons quick-cooking tapioca
1 package (3 pounds) chicken pieces, skin removed, wings set aside
¼ teaspoon salt
½ pound angel hair

① In a small bowl, stir together sweet-and-sour sauce, orange juice and tapioca. Place chicken in slow cooker bowl and pour orange juice mixture over top. Cover and cook on HIGH for 3 hours or LOW for 5 hours.

② Using a slotted spoon, remove chicken to a serving platter and keep warm. Stir salt into orange sauce. Pour sauce into a gravy boat; set aside and keep warm.

③ Prepare angel hair pasta according to package directions. Drain, return to pot and stir in ½ cup orange sauce. Serve chicken with pasta and remaining sauce.

PER SERVING 360 calories; 7 g fat (2 g sat.); 49 g protein; 22 g carbohydrate; 0 g fiber; 439 mg sodium; 159 mg cholesterol

CHICKEN WITH FIGS & BLUE CHEESE

MAKES 6 servings **PREP** 20 minutes **COOK** 13 minutes **SLOW COOK** 2 hours on HIGH or 5 hours on LOW

1½ cups low-sodium chicken broth
¼ cup balsamic vinegar
1 tablespoon grated orange zest
¾ teaspoon salt
½ teaspoon black pepper
1 package (8 ounces) dried mission figs, stems removed
2 tablespoons vegetable oil
2 pounds boneless, skinless chicken thighs
1 large onion, thinly sliced
2 tablespoons flour
1 tube (16 ounces) prepared polenta
⅔ cup crumbled blue cheese

① In a small bowl, stir together broth, vinegar, orange zest and ¼ teaspoon each salt and pepper; set aside. Coarsely chop figs.

② Heat oil in a large nonstick skillet over medium-high heat. Add chicken to skillet and cook 5 minutes per side or until browned. Remove chicken to slow cooker and add onion to skillet. Sprinkle with ¼ teaspoon each salt and pepper and cook, stirring often, for 2 minutes. Stir in flour and cook 1 minute. Pour in broth mixture and bring to a boil. Pour skillet contents into slow cooker and add figs.

③ Cover and cook on HIGH for 2 hours or LOW for 5 hours.

④ Meanwhile, prepare polenta following package directions. Sprinkle remaining ¼ teaspoon salt into chicken mixture. Serve polenta with chicken and fig mixture; divide blue cheese among servings.

PER SERVING 459 calories; 17 g fat (5 g sat.); 37 g protein; 42 g carbohydrate; 5 g fiber; 997 mg sodium; 160 mg cholesterol

TRY THESE EASY, CROWD-PLEASING RECIPES FOR CRISPY FRIED CHICKEN—OR FIRE UP THE GRILL FOR FIVE TASTY GRILLED SUPPERS SIMPLE ENOUGH TO MAKE ANY DAY OF THE WEEK.

SKINLESS FRIED CHICKEN AND OLD-FASHIONED COLESLAW, PAGE 155

JULY

159

167

170

Southern Comfort

Five great takes on fried chicken, the ultimate summer food.

CRISPY BUTTERMILK FRIED CHICKEN

MAKES 8 pieces **PREP** 15 minutes **COOK** 16 minutes per batch

- 3 cups all-purpose flour
- 3 teaspoons salt
- 2 teaspoons black pepper
- 1½ teaspoons sugar
- 1½ teaspoons paprika
- 1½ cups buttermilk
- 2 eggs
- 1½ teaspoons baking powder
- ¾ teaspoon baking soda
- 1 broiler-fryer chicken (about 3½ pounds), cut into 8 pieces
- 4 cups peanut oil

① In a 13 x 9 x 2-inch baking pan, whisk together flour, salt, pepper, sugar and paprika. In a medium-size bowl, whisk together buttermilk, eggs, baking powder and baking soda until smooth.

② Dip each piece of chicken into buttermilk mixture, shaking off excess. Roll in flour mixture and then dip into buttermilk and flour mixture a second time. Place on a baking sheet fitted with a wire rack. Refrigerate while heating oil.

③ Heat oven to 175°. Place oil in a large lidded heavy-bottom Dutch oven. Heat oil to 360° over medium-high heat. Place half of the chicken pieces, skin sides down, in the oil. Cover and reduce heat to medium.

Fry chicken for 7 to 8 minutes or until golden brown. Check after 4 minutes to be sure chicken is browning evenly. Rearrange if necessary. Flip chicken over and fry an additional 7 to 8 minutes or until golden and internal temperature registers 170° on an instant-read thermometer. Transfer chicken to a baking sheet fitted with a wire rack and place in oven to keep warm.

④ Return oil to 360° and fry remaining chicken pieces. Serve warm.

PER PIECE 633 calories; 39 g fat (9 g sat.); 29 g protein; 39 g carbohydrate; 2 g fiber; 1,211 mg sodium; 139 mg cholesterol

CREAMY DILLED POTATO SALAD, PAGE 157

SOUTHWEST-STYLE
FRIED WINGS

SOUTHWEST-STYLE FRIED WINGS

MAKES 12 wings **PREP** 15 minutes
COOK 10 minutes

WINGS

1½ cups all-purpose flour
2 teaspoons chili powder
1 teaspoon ground cumin
1 teaspoon salt
¼ teaspoon cayenne pepper
1 cup buttermilk
12 chicken wings (about 2½ pounds)
2 cups peanut oil

DIP

1 cup prepared Ranch dressing
2 tablespoons buttermilk
2 scallions, chopped

① **Wings**: In shallow dish, whisk together flour, chili powder, cumin, salt and cayenne. Pour buttermilk into a medium-size bowl.

② Dip each wing into the buttermilk, shaking off excess. Roll in the flour mixture and place on a baking sheet fitted with wire rack. Refrigerate while heating oil.

③ Place oil in large lidded heavy-bottom skillet. Heat oil to 365° over medium-high heat. Add chicken and fry, covered, for about 5 minutes, until browned and crispy. Turn and fry an additional 5 minutes. If chicken is browning unevenly, move around in skillet with tongs. Transfer chicken to paper towels.

④ **Dip:** In a small bowl, mix together the Ranch dressing, buttermilk and scallions. Serve with the wings.

PER WING (Includes 1½ tablespoons dip.) 272 calories; 20 g fat (4 g sat.); 11 g protein; 10 g carbohydrate; 0 g fiber; 366 mg sodium; 35 mg cholesterol

SKINLESS FRIED CHICKEN

MAKES 8 pieces **PREP** 15 minutes
COOK 22 minutes

1½ cups all-purpose flour
2 teaspoons reduced-sodium Old Bay seasoning
1 teaspoon salt
1 teaspoon black pepper
1 cup buttermilk
1 broiler-fryer chicken (about 3½ pounds), cut into 8 pieces and skin removed
2 cups peanut oil

① In a shallow dish, whisk together flour, Old Bay seasoning, salt and pepper. Place buttermilk in a medium-size bowl.

② Dip each piece of chicken into the buttermilk, shaking off excess. Roll in flour mixture and place on baking sheet fitted with wire rack. Refrigerate while heating oil.

③ Place oil in large lidded heavy-bottom skillet. Heat oil to 365° over medium-high heat. Add chicken, flesh sides down. Fry, covered, about 20 to 22 minutes or until browned and crispy, turning chicken several times. Internal temperature should register 170° on an instant-read thermometer. Transfer chicken to paper towels.

PER PIECE 388 calories; 19 g fat (4 g sat.); 39 g protein; 13 g carbohydrate; 0 g fiber; 412 mg sodium; 120 mg cholesterol

OLD-FASHIONED COLESLAW

MAKES 12 servings **PREP** 10 minutes
REFRIGERATE 4 hours or overnight

2 packages (12 ounces each) shredded broccoli slaw
4 cups shredded red cabbage
1 cup shredded carrots
1 cup light mayonnaise
½ cup reduced-fat sour cream
¾ cup buttermilk
2 tablespoons yellow mustard
¾ teaspoon salt
½ teaspoon black pepper

① In a large bowl, stir together the broccoli slaw, red cabbage and carrots. In a medium-size bowl, whisk together the mayonnaise, sour cream, buttermilk, mustard, salt and pepper.

② Fold the mayonnaise mixture into the vegetables and stir until well combined. Cover and refrigerate 4 hours or overnight.

PER SERVING 114 calories; 8 g fat (2 g sat.); 3 g protein; 8 g carbohydrate; 2 g fiber; 380 mg sodium; 13 mg cholesterol

CHINESE FIVE SPICE OVEN-FRIED CHICKEN

MAKES 8 pieces **PREP** 15 minutes **BAKE** at 450° for 45 minutes

1½ cups panko bread crumbs
1 teaspoon Chinese five spice
1 teaspoon salt
¼ cup honey
1 tablespoon lemon juice
1 broiler-fryer chicken (about 3½ pounds), cut into 8 pieces, skin removed

① Heat oven to 450°. Fit a large rimmed baking sheet with a wire rack. Coat rack with nonstick cooking spray.

② In a shallow dish, whisk together panko, Chinese five spice and salt. In a medium-size bowl, whisk together honey, 1 tablespoon warm water and lemon juice.

③ Dip each piece of chicken into the honey mixture, shaking off excess. Roll in the panko mixture, pressing to adhere, and place on the prepared rack.

④ Bake chicken pieces at 450° for 15 minutes. Spritz chicken with nonstick cooking spray and bake an additional 30 minutes or until internal temperature registers 170° on an instant-read thermometer.

⑤ Remove chicken from oven and serve immediately.

PER PIECE 266 calories; 5 g fat (1 g sat.); 38 g protein; 16 g carbohydrate; 0 g fiber; 383 mg sodium; 119 mg cholesterol

CREAMY DILLED POTATO SALAD

MAKES 12 servings **PREP** 20 minutes
COOK 20 minutes **REFRIGERATE** 4 hours
or overnight

- 2½ pounds small red- and white-skinned potatoes (about 1-inch diameter), unpeeled
- 1 medium-size onion, chopped
- 6 hard-cooked eggs, peeled and chopped
- 1 cup chopped dill pickles
- 1 cup light mayonnaise
- 3 tablespoons brine from pickles
- 1 teaspoon garlic salt
- ¼ teaspoon black pepper
- 2 tablespoons chopped fresh dill

① Place potatoes in a large pot of lightly salted water. Boil for 15 to 20 minutes or until tender. Drain well.

② Cut the potatoes in half (cut larger potatoes in quarters so all pieces are about the same size). Place the potatoes, onion, eggs and pickles in a large bowl. Stir gently to combine.

③ In a small bowl, whisk together mayonnaise, brine, garlic salt, pepper and dill. Spoon mayo mixture into potato mixture and stir gently.

④ Cover and refrigerate 4 hours or overnight.

PER SERVING 176 calories; 9 g fat (2 g sat.); 5 g protein; 19 g carbohydrate; 2 g fiber; 424 mg sodium; 113 mg cholesterol

ITALIAN FRIED CHICKEN

MAKES 8 pieces **PREP** 15 minutes
COOK 22 minutes

- ½ cup all-purpose flour
- ½ cup seasoned bread crumbs
- ½ cup grated Parmesan cheese
- 1 teaspoon garlic salt
- 2 eggs
- 2 tablespoons milk
- ½ teaspoon salt
- 1 broiler-fryer chicken (about 3½ pounds), cut into 8 pieces
- 2 cups peanut oil

① In a shallow dish, whisk together flour, bread crumbs, Parmesan and garlic salt. In a medium-size bowl, whisk together eggs, milk and salt.

② Dip each piece of chicken into the egg mixture, shaking off excess. Roll in flour mixture and place on a baking sheet fitted with wire rack. Refrigerate while heating oil.

③ Place oil in a large lidded heavy-bottom skillet. Heat oil to 365° over medium-high heat. Add chicken, skin-side down. Fry, covered, about 22 minutes, turning every 4 minutes, or until internal temperature registers 170° on an instant-read thermometer. Transfer chicken to paper towels.

PER PIECE 410 calories; 32 g fat (8 g sat.); 24 g protein; 6 g carbohydrate; 0 g fiber; 326 mg sodium; 113 mg cholesterol

CHUNKY CORNBREAD

MAKES 12 servings **PREP** 10 minutes
BAKE at 375° for 30 minutes

- ¾ cup all-purpose flour
- ½ cup cornmeal
- 2 tablespoons sugar
- 1 teaspoon baking powder
- ¾ teaspoon salt
- ½ cup milk
- 4 tablespoons butter, melted
- 1 egg
- 1 can (11 ounces) Mexicorn (corn kernels with mild red and green peppers), drained

① Heat oven to 375°. Spray an 8-inch square baking pan with nonstick cooking spray.

② In a large bowl, whisk together flour, cornmeal, sugar, baking powder and salt. In a medium bowl, whisk together milk, butter and egg.

③ Pour the milk mixture into the flour mixture and stir until evenly moistened. Fold in the Mexicorn. Spoon batter into prepared baking pan and spread evenly.

④ Bake at 375° for 30 minutes or until top of cornbread is golden. Allow to cool in pan on wire rack 10 minutes.

⑤ To serve, gently remove from pan; cut into 12 squares.

PER SERVING 126 calories; 5 g fat (3 g sat.); 3 g protein; 19 g carbohydrate; 1 g fiber; 333 mg sodium; 29 mg cholesterol

Slim Pickings

Easy, delicious meals—and all 350 calories or less. Need we say more?

BAKED POTATOES
FLORENTINE,
PAGE 163

CHICKEN STIR-FRY WITH MUSHROOMS & BOK CHOY

MAKES 6 servings **PREP** 15 minutes **COOK** 11 minutes

¾ cup low-sodium, 99% fat-free chicken broth

3 tablespoons teriyaki sauce

3 tablespoons rice vinegar

2 tablespoons cornstarch

1½ teaspoons sugar

⅛ teaspoon red pepper flakes

2 teaspoons canola oil

2 teaspoons sesame oil

1 pound boneless, skinless chicken breast for stir-fry (thin strips)

1 package (3.5 ounces) shiitake mushroom caps, cleaned and sliced (1½ to 2 cups)

1 package (9.5 ounces) soba noodles

1 pound bok choy, trimmed and sliced into bite-size pieces

1 sweet red pepper, seeded and cut into thin strips

① In a measuring cup, whisk broth, teriyaki, vinegar, cornstarch, sugar and red pepper flakes. Set aside.

② Bring a large pot of water to boiling. Heat the canola and sesame oils in a large nonstick skillet over medium-high heat. Add chicken and cook 4 minutes, stirring occasionally. Remove to a plate. Add mushrooms and cook 2 minutes.

③ Meanwhile, add soba noodles to boiling water and cook 3 to 4 minutes. Drain.

④ Add bok choy and red pepper strips to skillet. Cook 2 minutes. Return chicken to pan along with broth mixture. Cook 2 to 3 minutes until thickened. Gently stir in soba noodles and serve.

PER SERVING 325 calories; 5 g fat (1 g sat.); 26 g protein; 45 g carbohydrate; 2 g fiber; 805 mg sodium; 44 mg cholesterol

SLOW COOKER CORN & CRAB CHOWDER

MAKES 10½ cups (4 servings) **PREP** 15 minutes **SLOW-COOK** 5 hours on HIGH or 7 hours on LOW

2 cans (14.5 ounces each) low-sodium, 99% fat-free chicken broth (3½ cups)
½ pound all-purpose potatoes, peeled and diced
1 cup baby carrots, cut into ¼-inch pieces
1 medium-size onion, chopped
2 ribs celery, trimmed and diced
½ teaspoon fresh thyme leaves, chopped
¼ teaspoon Old Bay seasoning
5 ears corn on the cob, husks removed
1 sweet red pepper, seeded and diced
1 can (12 ounces) evaporated skim milk

2 tablespoons cornstarch
¼ teaspoon salt
1 container (8 ounces) pasteurized crab claw meat (such as Phillips)

① Combine chicken broth, potatoes, carrots, onion, celery, thyme and Old Bay in a large oval slow cooker. Place corn on the cob on top of vegetables. Cover and cook on HIGH for 4 hours or LOW for 6 hours.

② In a bowl, stir together red pepper, evaporated milk, cornstarch and salt.

③ Uncover slow cooker and remove corn to a cutting board. Stir red pepper mixture into slow cooker, replace cover and cook on either HIGH or LOW for 1 hour.

④ Meanwhile, when cool enough to handle, cut kernels from cobs. Stir corn kernels and crabmeat into soup and heat through. Serve warm.

PER SERVING 340 calories; 5 g fat (0 g sat.); 27 g protein; 54 g carbohydrate; 5 g fiber; 921 mg sodium; 61 mg cholesterol

PORK TACOS WITH PINEAPPLE SALSA

MAKES 10 tacos (5 servings) **PREP** 15 minutes **MARINATE** 15 minutes **GRILL OR BROIL** 6 minutes **MICROWAVE** 1 minute

DRESSING

¼ cup lime juice
1 teaspoon sugar
⅛ teaspoon salt
⅛ teaspoon pepper
3 tablespoons extra virgin olive oil
2 tablespoons chopped cilantro

SALSA

2 cups pineapple chunks, diced
2 plum tomatoes, seeded and chopped
2 cloves garlic, minced
1 jalapeño pepper, seeded and finely diced

PORK TACOS

1 pork tenderloin, about 1¼ pounds, sliced ½ inch thick
¼ teaspoon salt
1 package white corn tortillas (10 per package)

① Heat grill or broiler. **Dressing:** In a small bowl, whisk together lime juice, sugar, salt and pepper. Slowly whisk in olive oil until blended. Stir in cilantro.

② **Salsa:** In medium bowl, combine pineapple, tomatoes, garlic and jalapeño. Stir in 2 tablespoons of the dressing.

③ **Pork Tacos:** Combine remaining dressing (about ⅓ cup) with the pork in a resealable plastic bag. Marinate in refrigerator about 15 minutes. Grill or broil pork about 6 minutes, turning, or until desired doneness. Slice into thin strips, and sprinkle with salt. Wrap tortillas in damp paper towels and microwave 1 minute. To serve, fill warm tortillas with pork strips and salsa and fold up.

PER SERVING 343 calories; 13 g fat (2 g sat.); 25 g protein; 30 g carbohydrate; 3 g fiber; 256 mg sodium; 69 mg cholesterol

PENNE WITH SAUSAGE & PEAS

MAKES 6 servings **PREP** 10 minutes
COOK 12 minutes

- 4 cups whole-wheat penne pasta, uncooked (12 ounces)
- 2 tablespoons olive oil
- 1 package (12 ounces) fully cooked roasted garlic chicken sausage, sliced on the diagonal
- 2 cloves garlic, chopped
- 1 pound tomatoes, seeded and chopped
- ¼ teaspoon salt
- ½ cup low-sodium, 99% fat-free chicken broth
- 1 cup frozen peas, thawed
- 2 tablespoons freshly grated Parmesan cheese

① Heat a large pot of lightly salted water to boiling. Add pasta and cook as per package directions, 12 minutes. Drain.

② Meanwhile, heat 1 tablespoon of the oil in a large nonstick skillet over medium-high heat. Add the sausage and cook 3 minutes, turning a few times, until browned. Scoop out sausage with a slotted spoon onto a plate.

③ Reduce heat to medium and add remaining 1 tablespoon oil and the garlic. Cook 30 seconds. Stir in tomatoes and salt and cook 2 minutes. Stir in chicken broth, peas and browned sausage. Heat through.

④ Place cooked pasta in a large bowl. Add sausage mixture and 1 tablespoon of Parmesan. Toss to combine. Top with remaining tablespoon Parmesan and serve warm.

PER SERVING 350 calories; 10 g fat (2 g sat.); 20 g protein; 50 g carbohydrate; 7 g fiber; 561 mg sodium; 62 mg cholesterol

BAKED POTATOES FLORENTINE

MAKES 4 servings **PREP** 5 minutes
MICROWAVE 16 minutes **COOK** 8 minutes
BAKE at 400° for 10 minutes **BROIL** 2 minutes

4	Idaho baking potatoes, about 8 ounces each, scrubbed
1	tablespoon olive oil
1	large onion, chopped
1	bag (9 ounces) baby spinach, coarsely chopped
½	teaspoon salt
⅛	teaspoon pepper
1	large egg, separated
1	package (4 ounces) crumbled feta cheese

① Heat oven to 400°. Pierce potatoes with a fork. Place on paper towels in microwave. Microwave on HIGH for 16 minutes, turning over halfway through.

② Meanwhile, heat oil in a large nonstick skillet over medium heat. Add onion and cook 5 minutes. Stir in half the spinach and cook down slightly. Add remaining spinach and cook until wilted, about 3 minutes. Season with ¼ teaspoon of the salt and the pepper. Remove skillet from heat; transfer mixture to a large bowl and cool slightly.

③ Line a small baking sheet with aluminum foil; place potatoes on foil. Carefully cut open potatoes; sprinkle with remaining ¼ teaspoon salt.

④ Beat the egg white to stiff peaks. Once the spinach mixture has cooled slightly, stir in egg yolk and all but 2 tablespoons of the feta cheese. Fold the egg white into the spinach mixture. Divide spinach mixture evenly among potatoes (about ½ cup in each). Sprinkle all with remaining cheese.

⑤ Bake at 400° for 10 minutes. Increase heat to broil. Run potatoes under broiler for 2 minutes.

PER POTATO 345 calories; 11 g fat (5 g sat.); 12 g protein; 53 g carbohydrate; 7 g fiber; 739 mg sodium; 78 mg cholesterol

GRILLED SHRIMP & COLD RICE SALAD

MAKES 4 servings **PREP** 10 minutes **COOK** 15 minutes **STAND** 10 minutes **GRILL** or **BROIL** 4 minutes

1	cup wild, brown and red rice mix (such as Rice Select)
½	cup sweetened, dried cranberries
¾	teaspoon salt
8	ounces broccoli florets, cut in half if large
¼	cup cider vinegar
1	tablespoon Dijon mustard
1	tablespoon honey
2	tablespoons olive oil
1	pound peeled and deveined medium-size shrimp

① In a medium-size saucepan, combine 1½ cups water, rice, cranberries and ½ teaspoon of the salt. Bring to a boil over high heat, stir once, then cover and reduce heat to medium-low. Cook 10 minutes, then add broccoli florets to pan. Recover and cook an additional 5 minutes. Remove from heat; let stand 10 minutes.

② Meanwhile, combine remaining ¼ teaspoon salt, the vinegar, mustard and honey in a measuring cup or bowl. Whisk in olive oil until blended. Place shrimp in a bowl. Add 2 tablespoons of the dressing and toss to coat. Toss remaining dressing with rice mixture in a large bowl. Refrigerate while heating grill and cooking shrimp.

③ Heat grill pan, grill or broiler. Grill or broil shrimp 4 minutes, turning once, or until cooked through.

④ To serve, spoon about 1 cup rice salad onto plate. Top with shrimp.

PER SERVING 339 calories; 8 g fat (1 g sat.); 22 g protein; 44 g carbohydrate; 3 g fiber; 742 mg sodium; 168 mg cholesterol

Grill Talk

Five simple suppers yield nearly a week of stress-free summer meals.

TURKEY PIZZA BURGERS, PAGE 169

**SWEET & SPICY
GRILLED VEGETABLES
WITH CHICKEN SAUSAGE,
PAGE 169**

GRILLED SHRIMP PITAS

COCOA-CHILE-RUBBED STEAK & SWEET POTATOES

MAKES 6 servings **PREP** 20 minutes **GRILL** sweet potatoes for 45 minutes; steak for 6 minutes

5 teaspoons McCormick cocoa-chile blend
1½ teaspoons ground cumin
1½ teaspoons garlic salt
3 large sweet potatoes, about 10 ounces each, scrubbed
2 tablespoons vegetable oil
1 large red onion, chopped
1½ pounds flatiron or skirt steak
Lime wedges and chopped cilantro (optional)

① Heat gas grill to medium-high or prepare charcoal grill with medium-hot coals. Lightly coat grill rack with oil or cooking spray.

② In a small bowl, stir together the cocoa-chile blend, cumin and garlic salt. Set aside.

③ Cut potatoes in half lengthwise and then crosswise into 1-inch slices. Brush cut sides with 1 tablespoon of the oil and sprinkle each with ¼ teaspoon of the cocoa-chile mixture. Place 2 halves in foil and sprinkle about 3 tablespoons of the onion over each. Wrap tightly and place on the grill. Close lid and grill for 35 to 45 minutes or until tender.

④ Brush steak with remaining oil. Rub remaining chile mixture over both sides of steak. Grill for 2 to 3 minutes per side for medium-rare.

⑤ Slice the steak and serve with sweet potatoes, and lime wedges and chopped cilantro, if desired.

PER SERVING 328 calories; 15 g fat (9 g sat.); 24 g protein; 23 g carbohydrate; 3 g fiber; 357 mg sodium; 55 mg cholesterol

GRILLED SHRIMP PITAS

MAKES 6 servings **PREP** 20 minutes
MARINATE 15 minutes **GRILL** 6 minutes

SAUCE

1 container (7 ounces) reduced-fat plain Greek yogurt (such as Fage)
4 ounces herb-seasoned feta cheese, crumbled
½ seedless cucumber, peeled, halved and thinly sliced
1 tablespoon lemon juice

SHRIMP

3 tablespoons olive oil
2 tablespoons lemon juice
2 tablespoons chopped fresh mint
2 tablespoons chopped fresh oregano
2 cloves garlic, finely chopped
½ teaspoon salt
¼ teaspoon black pepper
1½ pounds large shrimp, shelled and deveined
3 cups iceberg salad mix
6 whole-wheat pitas, about 6-inch diameter
Sliced red onion and plum tomatoes (optional)

① **Sauce:** In a medium-size bowl, stir together yogurt, crumbled feta, cucumber and lemon juice. Cover and refrigerate until ready to use.

② **Shrimp:** Combine olive oil, lemon juice, mint, oregano, garlic, salt and pepper in a large resealable plastic bag. Add shrimp, seal bag and shake to coat shrimp with marinade. Refrigerate for 15 minutes.

③ Heat gas grill to medium-high or prepare a charcoal grill with medium-hot coals. Lightly coat grill rack with oil or nonstick cooking spray. Place shrimp in a grilling basket and grill for 3 minutes. Baste once with the remaining marinade. Turn shrimp and grill for an additional 2 to 3 minutes or until shrimp is cooked.

④ To serve, equally divide the salad, sauce and shrimp over each pita. Add onion and tomato, if desired.

PER SERVING 406 calories; 15 g fat (5 g sat.); 31 g protein; 40 g carbohydrate; 5 g fiber; 972 mg sodium; 183 mg cholesterol

CITRUSY TEQUILA
CHICKEN THIGHS

CITRUSY TEQUILA CHICKEN THIGHS

MAKES 6 servings **PREP** 10 minutes
MARINATE 4 hours or overnight
COOK 1 minute **GRILL** 30 minutes

CHICKEN

½ cup orange juice
¼ cup lime juice
¼ cup tequila
2 tablespoons canola oil
1 teaspoon salt
½ teaspoon McCormick Smokehouse pepper
6 large skinless bone-in chicken thighs

RICE SALAD

3 tablespoons olive oil
3 tablespoons leftover marinade
¼ teaspoon salt
3 cups cooked rice
½ each red and yellow sweet peppers
2 scallions, trimmed and thinly sliced
1 tablespoon chopped cilantro

① **Chicken**: Place orange juice, lime juice, tequila, canola oil, salt and pepper in a large resealable plastic bag. Add chicken and seal. Marinate in refrigerator for 4 hours or overnight.

② Heat gas grill to medium-high or prep charcoal grill with medium-hot coals and set up one side for indirect grilling. Lightly coat grill rack with oil or nonstick cooking spray.

③ Remove chicken from plastic bag and pour marinade into a small saucepan. Boil for 1 minute and reserve. Place chicken on direct heat and grill for 5 minutes per side. Remove to indirect heat and grill for 20 minutes or until internal temperature reaches 160° on an instant-read thermometer. Baste every 5 minutes with the reserved marinade.

④ **Rice Salad:** In a large bowl, whisk olive oil, 3 tablespoons of the marinade and salt. Stir in rice, peppers, scallions and cilantro. Serve at room temperature with chicken.

PER SERVING 405 calories; 18 g fat (3 g sat.); 25 g protein; 31 g carbohydrate; 1 g fiber; 568 mg sodium; 110 mg cholesterol

TURKEY PIZZA BURGERS

MAKES 6 servings **PREP** 10 minutes
GRILL 8 minutes

1⅓ pounds lean ground turkey
9 tablespoons prepared marinara sauce
1 teaspoon dried Italian seasoning
½ teaspoon garlic salt
½ teaspoon onion salt
6 tablespoons shredded reduced-fat mozzarella cheese
12 fresh basil leaves
6 hamburger rolls or hard rolls

① Heat gas grill to medium-high or prepare charcoal grill with medium-hot coals and set up one side for indirect grilling. Lightly coat grill rack with oil or nonstick cooking spray.

② In a large bowl, mix together turkey, 3 tablespoons of the marinara sauce, Italian seasoning, garlic salt and onion salt. Form into 6 equal patties. Grill for 4 minutes per side or until internal temperature registers 160° on an instant-read thermometer.

③ Turn off grill. Top each burger with 1 tablespoon marinara sauce, 1 tablespoon of cheese and 2 basil leaves. Close grill and wait 5 minutes until cheese melts. If using charcoal, place burgers over indirect heat. Serve on buns.

PER SERVING 303 calories; 12 g fat (4 g sat.); 25 g protein; 24 g carbohydrate; 2 g fiber; 706 mg sodium; 82 mg cholesterol

SWEET & SPICY GRILLED VEGETABLES WITH CHICKEN SAUSAGE

MAKES 6 servings **PREP** 20 minutes
GRILL 20 minutes total

SAUCE

¾ cup peach preserves
¼ cup light soy sauce
2 tablespoons ginger root, finely chopped
2 cloves garlic, finely chopped
1 teaspoon Asian hot chili sauce, such as Sriracha

VEGETABLES AND SAUSAGE

1 medium-size eggplant, halved lengthwise and cut into ½-inch-thick slices
2 large zucchini, cut diagonally into ⅓-inch-thick slices
2 summer squash, cut diagonally into ⅓-inch-thick slices
3 assorted sweet peppers, seeds removed, each cut into 4 pieces
4 tablespoons vegetable oil
1 package (12 ounces) cooked chicken and apple sausages
½ pound whole-wheat spaghetti, cooked following package directions

① **Sauce:** In a small bowl, whisk together the preserves, soy sauce, ginger, garlic and chili sauce. Stir in the 2 tablespoons water. Set aside.

② Heat gas grill to medium-high or prepare a charcoal grill with medium-hot coals. Lightly coat grill rack with oil or nonstick cooking spray.

③ **Vegetables and Sausage:** In a large bowl, toss the vegetables with the vegetable oil. Grill in batches for about 5 minutes per side, brushing the sauce over the vegetables every few minutes. Brush the sausage with the sauce and grill for about 3 minutes per side, until nicely browned. Remove to cutting board and slice into chunks on the bias.

④ Toss the pasta with the remaining sauce and serve alongside vegetables and sausage.

PER SERVING 483 calories; 19 g fat (4 g sat.); 17 g protein; 68 g carbohydrate; 10 g fiber; 859 mg sodium; 50 mg cholesterol

Slow Cooker Suppers

Six simple summer meals—light yet satisfying.

BBQ PORK SANDWICHES

MAKES 8 servings **PREP** 5 minutes **SLOW-COOK** 3 hours on HIGH or 5 hours on LOW

1 **boneless pork loin roast (about 2½ pounds), trimmed and cut in half lengthwise**
1¼ **cups prepared low-sodium barbecue sauce**
4 **cups packaged coleslaw mix**
½ **cup reduced-fat coleslaw dressing**
8 **hamburger buns**

① Place roast and 1 cup water in slow cooker. Cover and cook on HIGH for 3 hours or LOW for 5 hours.

② Remove pork from slow cooker and discard water. When cool enough to handle, shred pork into bite-size pieces; discard any excess fat. Stir pork together with barbecue sauce.

③ Stir together coleslaw mix and dressing. Place ½ cup pork mixture on buns and top with ½ cup coleslaw. Serve immediately.

PER SERVING 456 calories; 16 g fat (5 g sat.); 31 g protein; 47 g carbohydrate; 2 g fiber; 1,050 mg sodium; 74 mg cholesterol

TURKEY BREAST WITH YOGURT-CILANTRO SAUCE

MAKES 6 servings **PREP** 10 minutes
SLOW-COOK 3 hours on HIGH or 5 hours on LOW
COOK 1 minute

- 1   boneless turkey breast for London Broil (about 2½ pounds; such as Shady Brook Farms)
- 1   onion, chopped
- 3   sprigs cilantro
- ¾   cup low-sodium chicken broth
- ½   teaspoon salt
- ½   teaspoon black pepper
- 2   tablespoons cornstarch
- ⅓   cup low-fat plain yogurt
- ¼   cup chopped cilantro
- 6   cups mixed salad (optional)

① Coat slow cooker bowl with nonstick cooking spray. Place turkey into bowl and top with onion. Add cilantro sprigs then pour in broth. Sprinkle turkey with ¼ teaspoon each salt and pepper. Cover; cook on HIGH for 3 hours or LOW for 5 hours.

② Remove turkey to a cutting board and keep warm. Strain liquid into a saucepan. In a small bowl, stir together cornstarch and 3 tablespoons liquid from saucepan. Bring to a boil over medium-high heat. Whisk cornstarch mixture into saucepan and cook 1 minute or until thickened.

③ Remove sauce to a serving bowl and stir in remaining ¼ teaspoon each salt and pepper, yogurt and chopped cilantro. Cut turkey into slices and serve with sauce and a side salad, if desired.

PER SERVING 235 calories; 3 g fat (0 g sat.); 48 g protein; 7 g carbohydrate; 1 g fiber; 388 mg sodium; 76 mg cholesterol

CREAMY SUMMER VEGETABLE STEW

MAKES 4 servings **PREP** 10 minutes **SLOW-COOK** 4 hours on LOW

- 8   ounces frozen pearl onions
- 2   cups baby carrots, halved
- 1½   cups frozen corn
- ½   cup vegetable broth
- 2   tablespoons red wine vinegar
- 2   teaspoons herbes de Provence
- ½   pound zucchini, cut into ¼-inch half-moons
- 1   can (15.5 ounces) chickpeas, drained and rinsed
- ½   cup light cream
- 1½   tablespoons cornstarch
- ¼   teaspoon salt
- ¼   teaspoon black pepper
- 2   plum tomatoes, seeded and chopped
- 2   tablespoons grated Asiago cheese
- 2   cups cooked white rice (optional)

① Place onions, carrots, corn, broth, vinegar and 1½ teaspoons herbes de Provence in slow cooker. Cover and cook on LOW for 3 hours.

② Stir in zucchini and chickpeas; cook for 45 minutes. In a small bowl, stir together cream, cornstarch, salt, pepper and remaining ½ teaspoon herbes de Provence; set aside.

③ Stir in cream mixture and tomatoes and cook an additional 15 minutes or until thickened. Sprinkle with Asiago and serve with rice, if desired.

PER SERVING 311 calories; 9 g fat (4 g sat.); 11 g protein; 48 g carbohydrate; 9 g fiber; 681 mg sodium; 23 mg cholesterol

SWEET & SOUR STUFFED CABBAGE ROLLS

MAKES 6 servings (18 rolls) **PREP** 20 minutes **COOK** 15 minutes **SLOW-COOK** 5 hours on LOW

1	small head green cabbage, cored
1	tablespoon vegetable oil
1	medium-size onion, finely chopped
2	garlic cloves, minced
1	teaspoon cinnamon
¼	teaspoon nutmeg
2	cans (8 ounces each) tomato sauce
2	tablespoons light-brown sugar
2	tablespoons red wine vinegar
2	slices reduced-calorie wheat bread
⅓	cup skim milk
1	pound lean ground beef
¼	teaspoon salt
¼	teaspoon black pepper
6	cups cooked egg noodles

① Bring large pot of salted water to a boil. Boil cabbage for 12 to 15 minutes, removing 9 leaves as they become pliable. Drain well, then remove tough stem from leaves; cut leaves in half. Remove remaining cabbage from water and shred. Place shredded cabbage in bottom of slow cooker.

② Meanwhile, heat oil in a large nonstick skillet over medium heat; cook onion 5 minutes. Add garlic, cinnamon and nutmeg; cook 1 minute. Remove half of onion mixture; set aside. Stir tomato sauce, sugar and vinegar into skillet and remove from heat.

③ Pulse bread and milk in food processor until a paste is formed. Add reserved onion mixture, beef, salt and pepper to food processor and pulse until well combined.

④ With stem ends of cabbage leaves facing you, place 2 heaping tablespoons of meat mixture in center of leaf and roll up. Place rolls, seam sides down, in slow cooker. Pour sauce over top. Cover; cook on LOW for 5 hours. Serve with noodles.

PER SERVING 368 calories; 9 g fat (2 g sat.); 25 g protein; 47 g carbohydrate; 5 g fiber; 603 mg sodium; 91 mg cholesterol

SEAFOOD PESTO PASTA

MAKES 6 servings **PREP** 10 minutes
SLOW-COOK 2 hours on HIGH or 4 hours
on LOW **COOK** 7 minutes

3	**cups frozen chopped broccoli**
1	**pound frozen bay scallops**
¾	**pound frozen raw, peeled medium-size shrimp**
⅔	**cup low-sodium chicken broth**
½	**cup white wine**
3	**sprigs parsley**
1	**thick slice onion**
1	**thick slice lemon**
½	**pound angel hair pasta**
7	**tablespoons reduced-fat basil pesto (such as Buitoni)**

① Coat slow cooker bowl with nonstick cooking spray. Arrange broccoli on bottom of bowl, then top with frozen scallops and shrimp. Pour broth and wine over top, then add parsley, onion and lemon. Cover and cook on HIGH for 2 hours or LOW for 4 hours. Drain and discard parsley, onion and lemon.

② Meanwhile, cook pasta according to package, 7 minutes; reserve ½ cup water. Drain pasta; place in large serving bowl.

③ Add seafood and pesto to pasta; toss well to combine, adding pasta water by the tablespoonful, if needed.

PER SERVING 352 calories; 8 g fat (2 g sat.); 33 g protein; 36 g carbohydrate; 4 g fiber; 384 mg sodium; 116 mg cholesterol

WILD RICE WITH CHICKEN & SUGAR SNAP PEAS

MAKES 6 servings **PREP** 10 minutes **SLOW-COOK** 5 hours on LOW

1½	**cups wild rice mix**
2¾	**cups vegetable broth**
1	**pound chicken breast tenders, cut into 1-inch pieces**
1	**shallot, finely chopped**
1	**carrot, finely chopped**
1	**celery rib, finely chopped**
8	**ounces sugar snap peas, trimmed and halved**
2	**tablespoons raspberry vinegar**
½	**cup chopped toasted walnuts**
¼	**cup chopped parsley**
½	**teaspoon salt**
¼	**teaspoon black pepper**
1	**head Boston lettuce**

① Rinse rice under cold water. Place rice in slow cooker bowl and add the broth, chicken, shallot, carrot and celery. Cover and cook on LOW for about 5 hours or until rice kernels are open but not mushy.

② Remove cover and stir in snap peas, vinegar, walnuts, parsley, salt and pepper.

③ Remove 12 small bowl-shape leaves from head of lettuce; rinse and pat dry. Spoon about ½ cup rice mixture into each lettuce cup and serve.

PER SERVING 338 calories; 9 g fat (1 g sat.); 24 g protein; 42 g carbohydrate; 5 g fiber; 696 mg sodium; 44 mg cholesterol

STAY COOL WITH VEGGIE-PACKED MAIN DISHES THAT TAKE 20 MINUTES TO MAKE, SWEET AND SAVORY RECIPES THAT CELEBRATE SUMMER BERRIES— AND CHILLED AND FROZEN DESSERTS.

CURRIED CHICKEN SALAD WITH BLACKBERRIES, PAGE 187

AUGUST

177

178

194

These are spectacular when summer is at its steamiest and fresh fruit is in abundance. For the best results, assemble the parfaits just before serving to ensure that the toasted coconut and the cookies stay nice and crisp.

TROPICAL PARFAITS

MAKES 6 servings **PREP** 20 minutes **COOK** 5 minutes

FRUIT

1	ripe mango, peeled, pitted and diced
1	cup pineapple chunks, diced
1	cup raspberries
1	cup blueberries
2	kiwifruit, peeled and diced
2	tablespoons honey

YOGURT LAYER

1½	cups 2% plain Greek yogurt (such as Fage)
2	tablespoons honey
6	tablespoons sweetened shredded coconut
6	rolled cookies

① **Fruit:** In a large bowl, combine mango, pineapple, raspberries, blueberries, kiwi and honey. Stir gently to combine and set aside.

② **Yogurt Layer:** In a medium-size bowl, whisk together the yogurt and 2 tablespoons honey. Chill until layering.

③ Place coconut in a small nonstick skillet. Heat over medium heat until toasted, stirring occasionally, 3 to 5 minutes. Remove from heat and cool.

④ Spoon 2 tablespoons fruit into bottom of an 8-ounce glass. Top with 1 tablespoon yogurt and a little coconut. Repeat layering one more time, finishing with coconut. Garnish with a cookie. Fill 5 more glasses with remaining fruit, yogurt, coconut and cookies and serve.

PER SERVING 249 calories; 7 g fat (5 g sat.); 7 g protein; 45 g carbohydrate; 4 g fiber; 66 mg sodium; 8 mg cholesterol

Green Light

A fresh twist on fast food— delicious, veggie-packed dishes ready in 20 minutes max.

CURRY CHICKEN & GREEN BEANS

MAKES 6 servings **PREP** 15 minutes **COOK** 18 minutes

1¼ pounds green beans, trimmed
1 tablespoon vegetable oil
2 cloves garlic, finely chopped
2 tablespoons green curry paste (such as Thai Kitchen)
1 can (13½ ounces) light coconut milk
1 cup low-sodium chicken broth
1 tablespoon fish sauce
2 teaspoons sugar
2 teaspoons cornstarch
½ teaspoon salt
1½ pounds boneless, skinless chicken thighs, cut into 1-inch pieces
1 large onion, halved and thinly sliced

2 sweet orange peppers, seeded and thinly sliced
½ cup Thai basil leaves
4½ cups cooked jasmine rice

① Bring a large pot of lightly salted water to a boil. Add green beans; cover and cook for 4 minutes or until crisp-tender. Drain and set aside.

② Heat oil in a large, deep nonstick skillet over medium-high heat. Add garlic and cook 30 seconds. Add curry paste and cook an additional 30 seconds. Whisk in coconut milk, chicken broth, fish sauce, sugar, cornstarch and salt. Bring to a boil; reduce heat and simmer 4 minutes. Add chicken and onion; cook, stirring, for 7 minutes.

③ Stir in peppers and reserved green beans. Cook 2 minutes to heat through. Tear in the basil. Serve with cooked jasmine rice.

PER SERVING 473 calories; 13 g fat (5 g sat.); 34 g protein; 54 g carbohydrate; 7 g fiber; 693 mg sodium; 56 mg cholesterol

MIDDLE EASTERN STUFFED
ZUCCHINI, PAGE 183

KUNG PAO STEAK
& VEGETABLES,
PAGE 183

GRILLED TURKEY WITH CORN, TOMATO & SWEET PEPPER SALSA

MAKES 4 servings **PREP** 15 minutes
REFRIGERATE 1 hour **GRILL** 4 minutes

1½ pounds ripe tomatoes, seeded and chopped
1½ cups fresh corn kernels
1 large sweet red pepper, seeded and chopped
¾ cup fresh cilantro leaves, coarsely chopped
1 jalapeño pepper, seeded and finely chopped
2 tablespoons extra virgin olive oil
2 tablespoons lime juice
¾ teaspoon salt
1¼ pounds turkey cutlets
¼ teaspoon black pepper
   Lime wedges

① In a large bowl, stir together tomatoes, corn, red pepper, cilantro, jalapeño, olive oil, lime juice and ½ teaspoon of the salt. Cover and refrigerate for 1 hour.

② Heat grill to medium-high. Season the turkey with the remaining ¼ teaspoon salt and the pepper.

③ Grill turkey about 2 minutes per side or until cooked through. Serve warm or at room temperature with the salsa and extra lime wedges.

PER SERVING 462 calories; 12 g fat (4 g sat.); 34 g protein; 53 g carbohydrate; 7 g fiber; 461 mg sodium; 67 mg cholesterol

SWORDFISH À LA SICILIANA

MAKES 4 servings **PREP** 15 minutes **COOK** 19 minutes **GRILL** 10 minutes

2 tablespoons olive oil
1½ pounds eggplant, ends trimmed and cut into 1-inch pieces
4 cloves garlic, finely chopped
2 pounds plum tomatoes, seeded and chopped
½ teaspoon salt
½ teaspoon red pepper flakes
1 cup fresh basil leaves
2 swordfish steaks (about 12 ounces each), 1 inch thick
¼ teaspoon salt
¼ teaspoon black pepper
   Cooked angel hair pasta (optional)

① Heat oil in a large nonstick skillet over medium heat. Add eggplant and cook, covered, for 8 minutes, stirring occasionally.

Add garlic and cook 1 minute. Stir in tomatoes, salt and red pepper flakes. Simmer 10 minutes, covered, stirring occasionally. Tear in basil leaves.

② Meanwhile, heat grill or broiler to medium-high. Cut each swordfish steak in half and season both sides with salt and pepper. Grill or broil for 4 to 5 minutes per side, until fish is cooked through.

③ Spoon sauce over fish and serve with pasta, if desired.

PER SERVING 345 calories; 14 g fat (3 g sat.); 36 g protein; 21 g carbohydrate; 9 g fiber; 594 mg sodium; 62 mg cholesterol

CAPRESE PASTA

MAKES 6 servings **PREP** 10 minutes
COOK 9 minutes

1   pound cavatappi pasta
1½ pounds heirloom tomatoes, cored,
     seeded and chopped
¼   cup extra virgin olive oil
¼   cup pitted black olives, chopped
2   tablespoons capers
2   tablespoons balsamic vinegar
½   pound fresh mozzarella cheese,
     cut into ½-inch pieces
1   cup fresh basil, torn

① Cook pasta following package
directions, about 9 minutes; drain.

② In a large bowl, stir together the
tomatoes, olive oil, olives, capers and
balsamic vinegar. Add pasta to the bowl
and stir to combine. Fold in mozzarella
and basil.

③ Serve warm or at room temperature.

PER SERVING 494 calories; 19 g fat (7 g sat.);
18 g protein; 62 g carbohydrate; 4 g fiber;
252 mg sodium; 27 mg cholesterol

MIDDLE EASTERN STUFFED ZUCCHINI

MAKES 4 servings **PREP** 15 minutes
MICROWAVE 8 minutes **COOK** 10 minutes
BAKE at 400° for 10 minutes

- 4 medium zucchini (about 6 ounces each)
- 1 tablespoon olive oil
- 1 green pepper, seeded and chopped
- ½ medium-size onion, chopped
- 2 cloves garlic, chopped
- 1 pound ground chicken
- ¼ cup golden raisins
- ½ teaspoon salt
- ¼ teaspoon black pepper
- ¼ teaspoon ground cinnamon
- ½ cup shredded cheddar cheese
- 2 tablespoons pine nuts

① Cut zucchini in half lengthwise. Using a small spoon, carefully scoop out flesh, leaving a ¼-inch-thick shell around edges. Discard flesh.

② Place half of the zucchini, cut sides down, in an 11 x 7 x 2-inch glass baking dish. Add ½ cup water and cover with plastic wrap, venting one corner. Microwave 4 minutes. Place cooked zucchini in a large baking dish. Repeat with remaining zucchini.

③ Meanwhile, heat oven to 400°. In a large nonstick skillet, heat oil over medium heat. Add green pepper, onion and garlic; cook 5 minutes, stirring occasionally. Crumble in chicken. Stir in raisins, salt, pepper and cinnamon. Cook 5 minutes, stirring occasionally. Turn off heat and stir in cheese.

④ Fill each zucchini half with about ⅓ cup stuffing, then sprinkle the pine nuts over tops. Bake at 400° for 10 minutes. Serve immediately.

PER SERVING 379 calories; 23 g fat (8 g sat.); 26 g protein; 22 g carbohydrate; 4 g fiber; 473 mg sodium; 152 mg cholesterol

KUNG PAO STEAK & VEGETABLES

MAKES 6 servings **PREP** 15 minutes
COOK 13 minutes

- ¼ cup low-sodium soy sauce
- 3 tablespoons rice vinegar
- 1 teaspoon sugar
- 1 teaspoon chili paste
- 1 tablespoon vegetable oil
- 1¼ pounds skirt steak, thinly sliced against the grain
- ½ of an onion, peeled and chopped
- 3 cloves garlic, finely chopped
- 4 cups broccoli florets (about 1 small head; see Note)
- 1 sweet red pepper, seeded and chopped
- 6 ounces Baby Bella mushroom caps (stems removed), quartered
- 2 ribs celery, sliced
- ¼ cup peanuts
- 4½ cups cooked white rice

① Whisk together soy sauce, vinegar, sugar and chili paste; set aside.

② Heat oil in a large nonstick skillet over medium-high heat. Add beef; cook for 2 minutes. Remove to a plate; keep warm.

③ Add onion and garlic to skillet and cook 1 minute. Add broccoli, red pepper, mushrooms and celery; cover and cook, stirring occasionally, for 8 minutes or until broccoli is tender.

④ Stir in beef, any accumulated juices and soy sauce mixture. Heat through, about 2 minutes. Sprinkle peanuts over the top.

⑤ Serve immediately with cooked white rice.

PER SERVING 420 calories; 14 g fat (4 g sat.); 28 g protein; 46 g carbohydrate; 4 g fiber; 518 mg sodium; 54 mg cholesterol

Note: If desired, peel broccoli stems and slice into coins. Add to skillet with florets.

With their bright, beautiful colors, these veggie-packed dishes are gorgeous to look at and so good for you too. An array of global flavor profiles—Middle Eastern, Chinese, Italian, Thai and Southwestern—makes them interesting to eat as well.

The More the Berrier

Fruit desserts—and savory dishes too—done just ripe.

VERY RASPBERRY PIE,
PAGE 189

**SUGAR SNAP PEA
& BERRY SALAD,
PAGE 189**

PORK CHOPS WITH RASPBERRY SAUCE

PORK CHOPS WITH RASPBERRY SAUCE

MAKES 4 servings **PREP** 15 minutes
COOK 20 minutes **BAKE** at 350° for 10 minutes

1	cup fresh raspberries
⅓	cup sugar
¼	cup raspberry vinegar
⅛	teaspoon ground ginger
⅛	teaspoon ground nutmeg
⅛	teaspoon ground cloves
1	tablespoon butter
4	rib pork chops, 1 inch thick, about 7 ounces each
½	teaspoon salt
½	teaspoon black pepper
½	teaspoon rubbed sage

① In a medium saucepan, combine raspberries, sugar, vinegar, ginger, nutmeg and cloves. Stir in ½ cup water and bring to a boil, crushing raspberries with a wooden spoon. Simmer, uncovered, 10 minutes, stirring occasionally. Take off heat; stir in butter. Keep warm.

② Heat oven to 350°. Place a grill pan over medium-high heat. Season the pork chops with salt, pepper and sage. Lightly grease grill pan and grill pork chops 5 minutes per side. Place chops in baking dish and bake for 10 minutes or until internal temperature registers 150° on an instant-read thermometer. Allow to stand for 5 minutes. Serve pork chops with warm sauce on the side.

PER SERVING 307 calories; 13 g fat (6 g sat.); 31 g protein; 16 g carbohydrate; 2 g fiber; 374 mg sodium; 94 mg cholesterol

Nutrition-wise, blueberries, blackberries and raspberries rule—they're high in fiber, packed with antioxidants and vitamins, and have a low glycemic index. For maximum health benefits, aim for one serving a day.

CURRIED CHICKEN SALAD WITH BLACKBERRIES

MAKES 4 servings **PREP** 15 minutes **COOK** 10 minutes **REFRIGERATE** 30 minutes

3	tablespoons olive oil
1	pound boneless, skinless chicken breasts
¼	teaspoon salt
⅛	teaspoon black pepper
⅓	cup light mayonnaise
2	tablespoons mango chutney
1	tablespoon lemon juice
1½	teaspoons curry powder
¼	teaspoon ground ginger
¼	cup raisins
1	celery rib, chopped
1	scallion, chopped
1½	cups blackberries
½	cup roasted salted cashews

① Heat 1 tablespoon of the olive oil in a large skillet over medium-high heat. Season chicken with salt and pepper. Sauté for 5 minutes per side or until internal temperature registers 160° on an instant-read thermometer. Cool and cut into ½-inch pieces.

② In large bowl, combine remaining 2 tablespoons olive oil, mayonnaise, mango chutney, lemon juice, curry powder and ginger. Stir in chicken, raisins, celery and scallion. Gently stir in berries. Refrigerate for at least 30 minutes. Just before serving, sprinkle with cashews.

PER SERVING 464 calories; 28 g fat (4 g sat.); 30 g protein; 26 g carbohydrate; 4 g fiber; 576 mg sodium; 73 mg cholesterol

BLUEBERRY-RASPBERRY CRISP

BLUEBERRY-RASPBERRY CRISP

MAKES 8 servings **PREP** 15 minutes
BAKE at 350° for 55 minutes

BERRY MIXTURE

4   cups blueberries
½   cup light-brown sugar
¼   cup all-purpose flour
    Juice and zest from 1 large orange
2   cups raspberries

TOPPING

¾   cup all-purpose flour
⅔   cup light-brown sugar
½   teaspoon ground cinnamon
½   cup (1 stick) cold, unsalted butter,
    cut into small pieces
½   cup rolled oats
¼   cup chopped pecans

① Heat oven to 350°.

② **Berry Mixture:** In large bowl, mix together blueberries, ½ cup light-brown sugar, flour, orange juice and zest. Place into a 6- to 8-cup baking dish. Evenly scatter raspberries over the top.

③ **Topping:** In another large bowl, whisk together flour, brown sugar and cinnamon. Cut in butter until crumbly. Stir in oats and pecans.

④ Sprinkle topping evenly over berry filling. Bake at 350° for 55 minutes, until bubbly. Allow to cool 15 minutes before serving.

PER SERVING 383 calories; 15 g fat (7 g sat.); 4 g protein; 62 g carbohydrate; 5 g fiber; 16 mg sodium; 30 mg cholesterol

To store raspberries and blackberries, place in a shallow, paper-towel-lined pan, uncovered, in the refrigerator for 2 to 3 days tops. Leave blueberries in the plastic pack or transfer to a covered bowl; use within 10 days.

SUGAR SNAP PEA & BERRY SALAD

MAKES 4 servings **PREP** 15 minutes
COOK 2 minutes **REFRIGERATE** 30 minutes

½   pound sugar snap peas, trimmed
1   cup fresh raspberries
2   tablespoons olive oil
1   tablespoon raspberry vinegar
¼   teaspoon salt
¼   teaspoon black pepper
⅛   teaspoon sugar
1   cup fresh blueberries
⅓   cup toasted walnuts
    Splash lemon juice
2   cups mixed salad greens

① Bring a large pot of water to a boil. Add snap peas; cook for 2 minutes. Drain and rinse under cold water. Set aside.

② Crush 1½ tablespoons of the raspberries through a strainer into a bowl. Discard pulp. Whisk olive oil, vinegar, salt, pepper and sugar into strained juice.

③ In large bowl, toss dressing with snap peas, remaining raspberries, blueberries, walnuts and lemon juice. Cover and chill for 30 minutes. Toss with greens and serve.

PER SERVING 202 calories; 14 g fat (2 g sat.); 4 g protein; 16 g carbohydrate; 6 g fiber; 163 mg sodium; 0 mg cholesterol

VERY RASPBERRY PIE

MAKES 8 servings **PREP** 20 minutes
COOK 2 minutes **REFRIGERATE** 3 hours

3   cups fresh raspberries
½   cup granulated sugar

4   teaspoons cornstarch
1   package (8 ounces) cream cheese, softened
1   cup whipped topping
1   cup confectioners' sugar
1   purchased graham cracker crust (9 ounces)
    Additional berries for garnish (optional)

① Mash 2 cups of the raspberries in a medium saucepan. Place over medium-high heat. Add granulated sugar, cornstarch and ¼ cup water. Bring to a boil, stirring, constantly. Cook, stirring for 2 minutes. Cool to room temperature.

② In large bowl, beat cream cheese, whipped topping and confectioners' sugar until smooth.

③ Spread cream cheese mixture evenly over bottom of prepared crust. Arrange remaining raspberries around edge of crust. Spoon cooled raspberry sauce over the top. Garnish with additional berries, if desired. Refrigerate 3 hours.

PER SERVING 412 calories; 19 g fat (9 g sat.); 4 g protein; 59 g carbohydrate; 3 g fiber; 267 mg sodium; 31 mg cholesterol

The Big Chill

Win major cool points with frozen tiramisu, banana cream pie, and icebox pudding.

FROZEN
WHOOPIE PIES,
PAGE 195

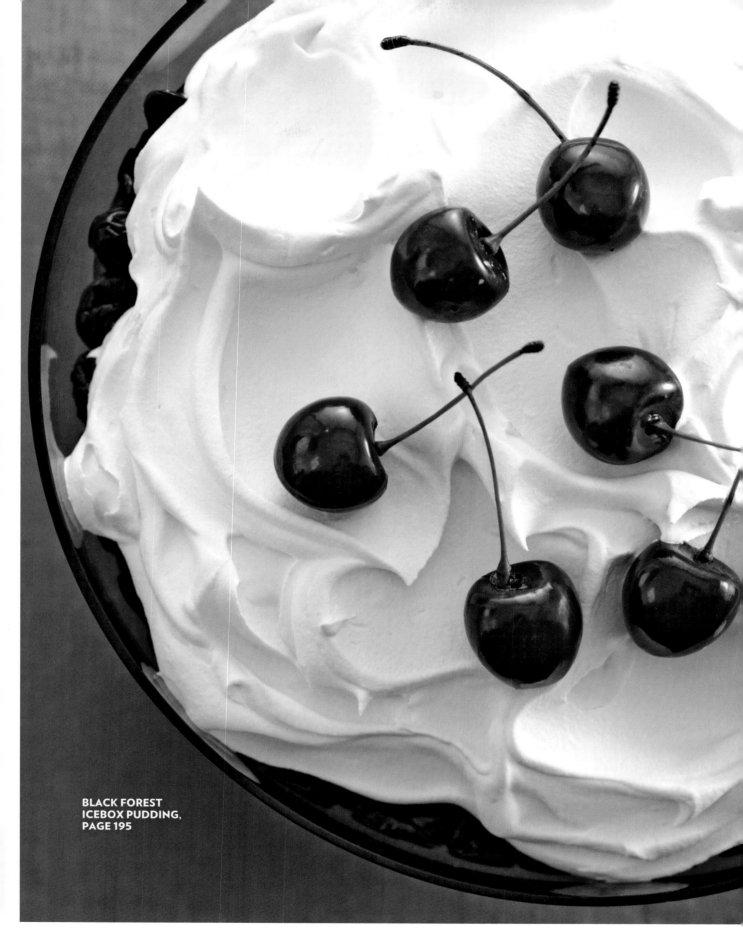

BLACK FOREST
ICEBOX PUDDING,
PAGE 195

BANANA CREAM PIE

BANANA CREAM PIE

MAKES 8 servings **PREP** 10 minutes **BAKE** at 350° for 15 minutes **MICROWAVE** 15 seconds **REFRIGERATE** 3 hours

CRUST
- 20 coconut macaroon cookies (such as Manischewitz)
- ¼ cup macadamia nuts
- 2 tablespoons unsalted butter

FILLING AND TOPPING
- 1⅓ cups low-fat milk
- 1 box (3.4 ounces) vanilla instant pudding mix
- ½ teaspoon banana extract
- 2 ripe bananas, peeled and cut into ½-inch chunks
- ½ teaspoon unflavored gelatin
- 1 cup heavy cream
- 1 tablespoon sugar
- 2 tablespoons chopped macadamia nuts (optional)

① Heat oven to 350°. Coat a 9-inch pie dish with nonstick cooking spray. **Crust:** Combine macaroons and macadamia nuts in a food processor. Pulse until ground to crumbs. Add butter; pulse until blended.

② Press crumbs into bottom and up sides of prepared pie dish. Bake at 350° for 15 minutes. Cool on wire rack.

③ **Filling and topping:** In large bowl, whisk milk, pudding mix and banana extract for 1 to 2 minutes, until mixture thickens. Fold in bananas. Pour into crust.

④ Combine 3 tablespoons water and gelatin in a glass bowl. Let stand 5 minutes. Microwave for 15 seconds or until melted. Cool to room temperature.

⑤ Beat heavy cream with mixer until it begins to thicken. Beat in gelatin mixture and then sugar. Beat to stiff peaks, then spread over top of filling. Refrigerate 3 hours, then top with chopped nuts, if desired.

PER SERVING 395 calories; 27 g fat (16 g sat.); 4 g protein; 41 g carbohydrate; 6 g fiber; 307 mg sodium; 50 mg cholesterol

FROZEN TIRAMISU

MAKES 9 servings **PREP** 10 minutes **FREEZE** 4 hours or overnight

- 1 pint coffee-flavor frozen yogurt
- 3 tablespoons chocolate sauce (such as Hershey's)
- 1 tablespoon instant coffee granules
- 1 container (8 ounces) frozen light whipped topping, thawed
- 1 package (3 ounces) soft ladyfingers
- 1 tablespoon cocoa powder

① Soften frozen yogurt on countertop for 10 minutes.

② Meanwhile, combine chocolate syrup, coffee granules and 1 tablespoon warm water in a small bowl.

③ In a large bowl, beat frozen yogurt with ⅔ cup of the whipped topping until good spreading consistency. Place half the ladyfingers on bottom of an 8 x 8 x 2-inch baking dish, spreading to cover as much as possible. Drizzle with 2 tablespoons of the chocolate mixture. Working quickly, spread with 1 cup of the frozen yogurt mixture. Top with 1 cup whipped topping. Repeat layers (ladyfingers, chocolate sauce mixture, frozen yogurt, whipped topping).

④ Dust top with cocoa; cover with plastic wrap. Freeze at least 4 hours or overnight. Let soften slightly before serving.

PER SERVING 198 calories; 5 g fat (4 g sat.); 5 g protein; 33 g carbohydrate; 0 g fiber; 93 mg sodium; 49 mg cholesterol

LEMON SEMIFREDDO

MAKES 10 servings **PREP** 10 minutes **FREEZE** 4 hours or overnight **REST** 15 minutes

1   **pint lemon ice cream (such as Häagen-Dazs)**
1   **cup heavy cream**
1   **tablespoon honey**
2   **drops yellow food coloring (optional)**
1   **package (6 ounces) fresh blueberries**
14 **lemon or shortbread cookies, coarsely crushed**

① Soften ice cream on counter for 10 minutes. Meanwhile, coat a 9 x 5 x 3-inch loaf pan with nonstick cooking spray. Line pan with plastic wrap.

② In large bowl, beat cream and honey to stiff peaks, about 3 minutes.

③ Beat ice cream mixture into whipped cream. Beat in food coloring, if using. Fold in berries and ⅔ cup of the crushed cookies.

④ Transfer ice cream mixture to pan. Tap gently on counter to release air bubbles. Press remaining cookie crumbs on top to adhere. Cover with plastic; freeze at least 4 hours or overnight. Use plastic to lift loaf from pan and invert on tray. After 15 minutes, slice and serve.

PER SERVING 238 calories; 16 g fat (9 g sat.); 3 g protein; 23 g carbohydrate; 0 g fiber; 66 mg sodium; 58 mg cholesterol

FROZEN WHOOPIE PIES

MAKES 12 servings **PREP** 10 minutes
FREEZE at least 2 hours **BAKE** at 375° for
13 minutes

ICE CREAM FILLING

½ gallon Neapolitan ice cream
(in a rectangular container)

COOKIES

2 cups all-purpose flour
2 teaspoons baking powder
2 teaspoons baking soda
½ teaspoon salt
1 cup (2 sticks) unsalted butter,
softened
1 cup packed light-brown sugar
2 eggs
1 teaspoon vanilla extract
½ cup cocoa powder
¾ cup milk

① **Ice cream:** Cut packaging from ice
cream. Slice ice cream crosswise into
6 slices, and place on two small baking
sheets. Freeze 1 hour.

② Heat oven to 375°. Line two large baking
sheets with nonstick foil. **Cookies:** Mix
flour, baking powder, baking soda and salt
in bowl. Beat butter and sugar in second
bowl until creamy. Beat in eggs and
vanilla. On low speed, beat in cocoa. Beat
in flour mixture and milk in 3 additions,
beginning and ending with flour.

③ Drop 2 heaping tablespoons batter
per cookie onto prepared sheets, spacing
3 inches apart. Spread into 2½-inch rounds
with the back of a spoon (keep size equal
since they will be sandwiched).

④ Bake at 375° for 12 to 13 minutes or until
cookies spring back when lightly touched
in center. Cool on sheets 5 minutes. Remove
cookies to rack to cool completely.

⑤ Remove one sheet of ice cream from
freezer. Working quickly, cut circles of ice
cream with 3-inch cookie cutter. Sandwich
2 cookies and 1 ice cream round. Save ice
cream scraps for snacking. Repeat with all
cookies and ice cream. Wrap in plastic and
freeze assembled whoopie pies at least
1 hour or until ready to eat.

PER SERVING 461 calories; 25 g fat (15 g sat.); 7 g
protein; 55 g carbohydrate; 2 g fiber; 466 mg
sodium; 106 mg cholesterol

BLACK FOREST ICEBOX PUDDING

MAKES 12 servings **PREP** 10 minutes
COOK 12 minutes **REFRIGERATE** 6 hours
or overnight

2 boxes (3.4 ounces each) chocolate
cook-and-serve pudding mix
½ cup semisweet chocolate chips
3¾ cups 2% milk
1 bag (6 ounces) black-and-white
sandwich cookies (15 cookies;
such as Milano)
2 cups pitted sweet cherries or
raspberries (plus more for garnish)
1 cup heavy cream
2 tablespoons sugar

① Combine pudding mix, chocolate
chips and milk in a medium-size saucepan.
Cook over medium heat, stirring, until
mixture comes to a full boil, about
12 minutes. Cool 5 minutes.

② Spoon 1 cup pudding in bottom of an
8-cup bowl. Top with 7 cookies. Spread
cookies with ¾ cup pudding. Layer with
1 cup cherries or raspberries. Top with
1 cup pudding and remaining 8 cookies.
Spread with last ¾ cup pudding and
remaining 1 cup fruit.

③ Cover bowl. Refrigerate at least 6 hours
or overnight. Remove from fridge and beat
cream with sugar to medium-stiff peaks.
Spread over pudding, leaving a small
border at edge uncovered. Garnish with
extra fruit. Serve chilled.

PER SERVING 328 calories; 17 g fat (9 g sat.); 6 g
protein; 41 g carbohydrate; 2 g fiber; 141 mg
sodium; 40 mg cholesterol

The best way to pit cherries
is to use a cherry pitter. This
kitchen tool is inexpensive
and widely available. It really
is worth the minimal
investment to save yourself
from frustration and mess.
Be sure to wear an apron or
an old shirt when pitting
cherries—they're juicy!

Slow Cooker Suppers

Chicken, pork, zingy Mexican-style rice—dig in.

LEMONY GARLIC CHICKEN THIGHS

MAKES 6 servings **PREP** 10 minutes
SLOW-COOK 3½ hours on HIGH or 5½ hours on LOW **COOK** 4 minutes

6	bone-in, skinless chicken thighs (about 2¼ pounds)
5	garlic cloves, smashed
1	tablespoon lemon zest
⅓	cup lemon juice
⅓	cup low-sodium chicken broth
1	tablespoon cornstarch
¼	teaspoon salt
¼	teaspoon black pepper
1	cup packed baby spinach, chopped
8	ounces angel hair pasta

① Trim chicken thighs of any excess fat. Place them in the slow cooker bowl and scatter garlic cloves over top.

② In a small bowl, stir together the lemon zest, juice and the chicken broth; pour half of it (about ⅓ cup) into slow cooker. Cover and cook for 3 hours on HIGH or 5 hours on LOW.

③ Remove chicken thighs to a platter and keep warm; discard garlic cloves. In a small bowl, stir together remaining ⅓ cup lemon juice mixture, cornstarch, salt and pepper. Whisk into slow cooker bowl with chopped spinach and cook another 30 minutes on HIGH or LOW.

④ Meanwhile, cook pasta according to package directions, about 4 minutes. Stir half of sauce from slow cooker bowl into pasta and serve remainder with chicken.

PER SERVING 376 calories; 8 g fat (2 g sat.); 42 g protein; 31 g carbohydrate; 2 g fiber; 301 mg sodium; 157 mg cholesterol

MEXICAN BROWN RICE CASSEROLE

MAKES 6 servings **PREP** 10 minutes **SLOW-COOK** 3 hours on HIGH or 5 hours on LOW

1	large onion, chopped
1	medium-size sweet red pepper, seeded and chopped
2	garlic cloves, minced
2	cups crushed tomatoes
¾	cup medium-grain brown rice
1½	teaspoons chili powder
1	teaspoon dried oregano
1	small jalapeño, seeded and chopped
1	package (12 ounces) chicken sausage with habaneros (such as Aidells), cut into ½-inch-thick half-moons
¼	cup chopped cilantro
6	tablespoons reduced-fat sour cream Shredded cheddar cheese (optional)

① Stir together onion, pepper, garlic, tomatoes, rice, chili powder, oregano, jalapeño, sausage and 1½ cups water in slow cooker bowl. Cover and cook on HIGH for 3 hours or LOW for 5 hours.

② Stir in cilantro; serve with sour cream and cheddar cheese, if desired.

PER SERVING 264 calories; 9 g fat (3 g sat.); 16 g protein; 30 g carbohydrate; 3 g fiber; 666 mg sodium; 46 mg cholesterol

SLOPPY JOES

MAKES 12 servings   **PREP** 15 minutes   **SLOW-COOK** 3 hours on HIGH or 6 hours on LOW

1   package (20.8 ounces) ground turkey
2   carrots, peeled and finely chopped
1   medium-size onion, finely chopped
1   rib celery, finely chopped
1   garlic clove, minced
1   can (6 ounces) tomato paste
2   tablespoons cider vinegar
2   tablespoons light-brown sugar
1   teaspoon Worcestershire sauce
¾   teaspoon paprika
½   teaspoon dry mustard
½   teaspoon salt
12 hamburger buns

① In slow cooker bowl, stir together ground turkey, carrots, onion, celery, garlic, tomato paste, vinegar, brown sugar, Worcestershire sauce, paprika and dry mustard. Cover and cook on HIGH for 3 hours or LOW for 6 hours, stirring turkey mixture halfway through cook time.

② Stir in salt. Spoon ⅓ cup turkey mixture on each bun and serve immediately.

PER SANDWICH 226 calories; 6 g fat (2 g sat.); 14 g protein; 29 g carbohydrate; 2 g fiber; 383 mg sodium; 39 mg cholesterol

PINEAPPLE-GINGER-GLAZED PORK CHOPS

MAKES 4 servings **PREP** 10 minutes
COOK 7 minutes **SLOW COOK** 3 hours on HIGH

⅓ cup crushed pineapple
3 tablespoons ketchup
3 tablespoons low-sodium soy sauce
1½ tablespoons grated fresh ginger
1 tablespoon light-brown sugar
1 tablespoon olive oil
4 bone-in pork chops, about 1 inch thick (about 2½ pounds)
¼ teaspoon salt
¼ teaspoon black pepper
1 large sweet red pepper, seeded and thinly sliced
1 tablespoon cornstarch
1½ cups fresh pineapple chunks, cut into ½-inch pieces
2 cups cooked white rice (optional)

① In a small bowl, stir together crushed pineapple, ketchup, soy sauce, ginger and brown sugar; set aside.

② Heat oil in a large nonstick skillet over medium-high heat. Sprinkle pork with salt and pepper; cook 2 to 3 minutes per side. Place chops in slow cooker; top with red pepper. Pour in ⅔ cup ketchup mixture and cover; cook for 3 hours on HIGH.

③ Remove chops to a platter. Combine remaining ketchup mixture, cornstarch and pineapple chunks. Pour liquid from slow cooker into a saucepan; bring to a boil over medium-high heat. Whisk in ketchup mixture; cook 1 minute. Serve pork with sauce, and rice, if desired.

PER SERVING 524 calories; 31 g fat (10 g sat.); 40 g protein; 19 g carbohydrate; 2 g fiber; 839 mg sodium; 135 mg cholesterol

CHEESY VEGETABLE POLENTA

MAKES 8 servings **PREP** 10 minutes **SLOW COOK** 2½ hours on HIGH or 5 hours on LOW

2 cans (14.5 ounces each) cannellini beans, rinsed and drained
¼ cup pesto
1 medium-size onion, chopped
1 medium-size green pepper, seeded and chopped
1 teaspoon Italian seasoning
1 tube (18 ounces) prepared polenta, cut into ½-inch-thick slices (about 14)
¾ cup low-sodium chicken broth
1½ cups shredded Italian-blend cheese
4 cups chopped radicchio
2 plum tomatoes, thinly sliced

① In a large bowl, stir together the beans, 2 tablespoons of the pesto, onion, green pepper and Italian seasoning. Place half of bean mixture in bottom of slow cooker. Layer half of polenta slices over top, pour ¼ cup chicken broth over polenta then sprinkle with ¾ cup cheese. Repeat layering one more time. Cover and cook for 2 hours on HIGH or 4½ hours on LOW.

② Stir together remaining 2 tablespoons pesto and remaining ¼ cup chicken broth. Pour pesto mixture into slow cooker, add radicchio and gently stir to combine. Place tomato slices on top and continue cooking for another 30 minutes on HIGH or LOW. Serve immediately.

PER SERVING 245 calories; 9 g fat (4 g sat.); 12 g protein; 29 g carbohydrate; 6 g fiber; 686 mg sodium; 18 mg cholesterol

FORTIFY THE KIDS WITH HEALTHY BACK-TO-SCHOOL SNACKS, WHIP UP A FABULOUS DINNER ON EVEN THE BUSIEST NIGHTS—AND REWARD YOURSELF WITH A SQUARE OF SOMETHING SWEET.

THAI BEEF SALAD,
PAGE 207

SEPTEMBER

212

219

221

Think Fast!

Tasty meals in 20 minutes—just what you need when there's a lot on your plate.

CRISPY BEAN & CHEESE BURRITOS

MAKES 6 servings **PREP** 10 minutes **COOK** 18 minutes

- 1   **bag (3½ ounces) boil-in-bag brown rice**
- 1   **cup salsa**
- ⅓   **cup chopped cilantro**
- 1   **ripe avocado, cut into ½-inch pieces**
- 1   **tablespoon lime juice**
- 6   **soft taco-size flour tortillas**
- 1   **cup shredded pepper Jack cheese**
- 1   **can (15.5 ounces) black beans, drained and rinsed**

① Prepare rice according to package directions, about 10 minutes. Drain and place in a medium-size bowl. Stir in salsa and cilantro; set aside. In a small bowl, gently stir together avocado pieces with lime juice; set aside.

② Place tortillas on work surface and sprinkle 2 tablespoons cheese in center of each, from left to right. Top cheese with a heaping ¼ cup black beans. Place a heaping ⅓ cup rice mixture over beans then divide avocado pieces among tortillas. Fold up like an envelope; repeat with remaining tortillas.

③ Heat a large nonstick skillet over medium-high heat. Coat top and bottom of burritos with nonstick cooking spray. Place 3 burritos in skillet, seam sides down; cook for 1 to 2 minutes or until lightly browned and crisp. Turn burritos over and cook another 2 minutes. Repeat with remaining burritos, reducing heat if they get too browned.

PER SERVING 415 calories; 15 g fat (4 g sat.); 15 g protein; 54 g carbohydrate; 7 g fiber; 761 mg sodium; 17 mg cholesterol

GREEK COUSCOUS WITH
CHICKEN & FETA,
PAGE 207

SMOKY PORK WITH
QUINOA PILAF

SMOKY PORK WITH QUINOA PILAF

MAKES 4 servings **PREP** 10 minutes
COOK 20 minutes **ROAST** at 450° for 18 minutes

- 1 pork tenderloin (1¼ pounds)
- 1 tablespoon smokehouse maple seasoning
- 1 tablespoon canola oil
- 1 onion, chopped
- 1 cup uncooked quinoa
- 1¾ cups low-sodium chicken broth
- 2 tablespoons maple syrup
- ¾ cup dried cranberries
- ½ teaspoon salt
- ¾ cup peas

① Heat oven to 450°. Season pork with 2½ teaspoons of the smokehouse seasoning. Heat 2 teaspoons of the oil in large nonstick ovensafe skillet over medium-high heat. Brown pork 2 minutes or until golden. Roast at 450° for 18 minutes or until internal temperature reaches 140° on an instant-read thermometer. Remove from oven; let stand 5 minutes.

② Meanwhile, in medium-size saucepan, heat 1 teaspoon oil over medium-high heat. Add onion and quinoa to saucepan. Stir in broth, syrup, cranberries, ½ teaspoon smokehouse seasoning and salt.

③ Bring quinoa mixture to a boil. Cover; reduce heat to medium-low. Simmer about 20 minutes or until liquid is absorbed. Stir in peas and heat through. Slice pork; serve with quinoa.

PER SERVING 529 calories; 14 g fat (3 g sat.); 38 g protein; 63 g carbohydrate; 6 g fiber; 821 mg sodium; 96 mg cholesterol

Smoky-sweet maple seasoning makes this quick-cooking pork taste like it spent a few hours over hot coals—but it cooks in less than 20 minutes in the oven.

SWEET & SPICY SHRIMP STIR-FRY

MAKES 6 servings **PREP** 10 minutes **COOK** 10 minutes

- 3 ounces cellophane noodles
- ¼ cup low-sodium soy sauce
- 3 tablespoons low-sodium chicken broth or water
- 2 tablespoons light-brown sugar
- 1 tablespoon cornstarch
- 1 teaspoon chili-garlic paste
- 1 teaspoon sesame oil
- 1 tablespoon vegetable oil
- 2 cloves garlic, minced
- 2 large sweet red peppers, seeded and chopped
- 1 large onion, chopped
- 3 cups packed baby spinach
- 1 pound medium-size shrimp, peeled and deveined
- 6 ounces snow peas, trimmed and halved diagonally

① Cover noodles with boiling water and let sit for 5 minutes. Drain and rinse under cool water, then, using scissors, snip into 6-inch lengths.

② Meanwhile, stir together soy sauce, chicken broth, brown sugar, cornstarch, chili paste and sesame oil; set aside.

③ Heat vegetable oil in a large nonstick skillet over medium-high heat. Cook garlic 1 minute. Add peppers and onion to skillet; cover and cook, stirring occasionally, for 4 minutes or until softened. Add spinach to skillet and cook 1 minute, stirring until wilted.

④ Add shrimp and snow peas to skillet and cover; cook, stirring occasionally, for 4 minutes or until shrimp is cooked through and opaque. Pour soy sauce mixture into skillet, then add noodles; stir together until well blended and serve immediately.

PER SERVING 237 calories; 5 g fat (1 g sat.); 19 g protein; 30 g carbohydrate; 3 g fiber; 438 mg sodium; 115 mg cholesterol

CHICKEN CUTLETS WITH FIG COMPOTE

MAKES 4 servings **PREP** 10 minutes **COOK** 11 minutes

½   **cup dried mission figs, chopped**
⅓   **cup chopped walnuts**
½   **teaspoon dried thyme**
2   **tablespoons unsalted butter**
4   **small boneless, skinless chicken breasts (about 1½ pounds)**
¼   **teaspoon salt**
¼   **teaspoon black pepper**
1   **medium-size onion, chopped**
⅓   **cup low-sodium chicken broth**
   Frozen roasted potatoes, prepared according to package directions (optional)

4   **cups mixed salad (optional)**

① Soak figs in hot water for 5 minutes. Meanwhile, combine walnuts and thyme in a small bowl. Drain figs and add to bowl with walnuts; stir.

② Melt the butter in a large nonstick skillet over medium-high heat. Season one side of the chicken cutlets with ⅛ teaspoon each of the salt and pepper.

③ Place chicken, seasoned side down, in skillet and cook 3 to 4 minutes. Season top side with remaining ⅛ teaspoon each salt and pepper. Flip over chicken and cook an additional 3 to 4 minutes. Remove to a serving plate and keep warm.

④ Add onion to skillet and cook 2 minutes. Add fig mixture and chicken broth to skillet and cook 1 minute. Remove skillet from heat, then spoon fig compote over chicken. Serve with roasted potatoes and salad, if desired.

PER SERVING 353 calories; 14 g fat (5 g sat.); 42 g protein; 14 g carbohydrate; 3 g fiber; 309 mg sodium; 114 mg cholesterol

THAI BEEF SALAD

MAKES 4 servings **PREP** 10 minutes **COOK** 10 minutes

1   cup cilantro leaves
¼   cup lime juice
2   tablespoons low-sodium soy sauce
1½ tablespoons fish sauce
1   tablespoon sugar
2   garlic cloves, roughly chopped
¼   teaspoon red pepper flakes
1   tablespoon canola oil
1   pound flank steak
⅛   teaspoon salt
⅛   teaspoon black pepper
1   package (8.5 ounces) precooked jasmine rice
4   cups shredded napa cabbage
1   medium-size cucumber, peeled, seeded and cut into ¼-inch-thick half-moons
4   scallions, thinly sliced
3   tablespoons chopped basil

① Pulse cilantro, lime juice, soy sauce, fish sauce, sugar, garlic and red pepper flakes in a blender until smooth; set aside.

② Heat canola oil in a large nonstick skillet over medium-high heat. Sprinkle steak with salt and pepper. Place steak in skillet and cook 4 minutes. Flip and cook an additional 4 to 6 minutes or until internal temperature reaches 135° on an instant-read thermometer, for medium-rare. Allow to rest 5 minutes. Cut against the grain into ¼-inch-thick slices.

③ Meanwhile, prepare rice according to package directions. Spoon rice onto a plate and let cool 5 minutes.

④ In a large serving bowl, combine rice, cabbage, cucumber, scallions and basil and drizzle with 6 tablespoons cilantro dressing; toss until combined. Top salad with sliced steak and drizzle with remaining dressing.

PER SERVING 338 calories; 11 g fat (3 g sat.); 29 g protein; 29 g carbohydrate; 3 g fiber; 673 mg sodium; 37 mg cholesterol

GREEK COUSCOUS WITH CHICKEN & FETA

MAKES 6 servings **PREP** 10 minutes
COOK 17½ minutes

1   tablespoon olive oil
2   cloves garlic, minced
1   onion, chopped
¾   teaspoon dried oregano
½   teaspoon salt
1½   cups Israeli pearl couscous
1¼   cups low-sodium chicken broth
6   ounces green beans, trimmed and halved
2   cups cooked, shredded chicken breast
3   plum tomatoes, seeded and chopped
1   can (13.75 ounces) artichoke hearts, drained and roughly chopped
½   cup crumbled reduced-fat feta
⅓   cup kalamata olives, halved
2   tablespoons lemon juice

① Heat oil in a medium-size nonstick saucepan over medium-high heat. Cook garlic 30 seconds, then stir in onion, oregano and ¼ teaspoon salt; cook 4 minutes.

② Stir in couscous and cook for 1 minute. Add chicken broth and 1 cup water to pot and bring to a boil; reduce heat to medium-low and cook, covered, for 12 minutes or until water is absorbed. Add green beans to pot for last 5 minutes of cook time.

③ Stir in remaining ¼ teaspoon salt, chicken, tomatoes, artichoke hearts, feta, olives and lemon juice and serve immediately.

PER SERVING 280 calories; 6 g fat (2 g sat.); 16 g protein; 42 g carbohydrate; 6 g fiber; 968 mg sodium; 19 mg cholesterol

Food For Thought

Boost your kids' brain power with these healthy snacks and light meals.

CREAMY HAM WRAPS

MAKES 4 servings **PREP** 10 minutes

2   square whole-wheat wraps
¼   cup reduced-fat vegetable cream cheese
4   ounces thinly sliced low-sodium ham (8 slices)
1   small sweet red pepper, seeded and cut into thin strips

① Place wraps on work surface; spread each with 2 tablespoons cream cheese, leaving a 1-inch border around edges.

② Place 2 slices ham on each wrap, then add red pepper strips horizontally, in lower third of wrap. Roll up, cut in half on the diagonal and serve.

PER SERVING 104 calories; 5 g fat (2 g sat.); 9 g protein; 10 g carbohydrate; 5 g fiber; 428 mg sodium; 18 mg cholesterol

CHERRY LIMEADE

MAKES 5 servings **PREP** 5 minutes

1   bottle (1 liter) lime sparkling water, chilled
½   cup lime juice
⅔   cup cherry juice
2   tablespoons superfine sugar
     Lime wedges, for garnish (optional)

① Stir together water, lime juice, cherry juice and sugar until sugar has dissolved. Pour over ice in five 8-ounce glasses and garnish with lime wedges, if desired.

PER SERVING 43 calories; 0 g fat (0 g sat.); 0 g protein; 11 g carbohydrate; 0 g fiber; 2 mg sodium; 0 mg cholesterol

MEXICAN PIZZA

MAKES 4 servings **PREP** 10 minutes **BAKE** at 350° for 17 minutes

- 4 **omega-3-enriched 10-inch whole-wheat tortillas**
- 1 **cup mild salsa**
- ½ **of a small red onion, finely chopped**
- 1⅓ **cups reduced-fat shredded Mexican-blend cheese**
- 4 **tablespoons guacamole**

① Heat oven to 350°. Place tortillas on work surface and spread each with ¼ cup salsa. Divide onion among tortillas and sprinkle each with ⅓ cup cheese.

② Place tortillas on baking sheet and bake at 350° for 17 minutes or until cheese is melted and tortillas are crisp. Remove from oven and top each with 1 tablespoon guacamole. Serve immediately.

PER PIZZA 301 calories; 14 g fat (7 g sat.); 17 g protein; 28 g carbohydrate; 3 g fiber; 941 mg sodium; 30 mg cholesterol

HUMMUS WITH PARMESAN PITA CHIPS

MAKES 1¼ cups **PREP** 10 minutes **BAKE** at 350° for 9 minutes

5   4½-inch whole-wheat pitas, split open and each side cut into fourths
¼   cup freshly grated Parmesan cheese
1   can (15.5 ounces) chickpeas, drained and rinsed
3   tablespoons lemon juice
2   tablespoons tahini
2   tablespoons extra virgin olive oil
½   teaspoon cumin
½   teaspoon salt
½   cup baby spinach, finely chopped

① Heat oven to 350°. Place pita pieces on rimmed baking sheet and coat with nonstick cooking spray. Bake at 350° for 8 minutes or until crisp. Remove from oven and divide Parmesan cheese over pitas; return to oven for 1 minute or until cheese melts.

② Meanwhile, combine chickpeas, lemon juice, tahini, olive oil, cumin and salt in a food processor bowl. Process until a smooth paste forms. Spread chickpea mixture into a serving bowl; stir in spinach. Serve with warm pita chips.

PER TABLESPOON WITH 2 CHIPS 65 calories; 2 g fat (0 g sat.); 2 g protein; 8 g carbohydrate; 2 g fiber; 179 mg sodium; 1 mg cholesterol

PEANUT BUTTER DIP

MAKES 1⅓ cups **PREP** 10 minutes

¾ cup low-fat vanilla yogurt
½ cup reduced-fat peanut butter
⅓ cup raisins
½ teaspoon cinnamon
2 apples, cored and cut into ½-inch slices
3 ribs celery, trimmed and cut into 4-inch sticks
2 cups small pretzels

① In a small serving bowl, stir together yogurt, peanut butter, raisins and cinnamon. Serve with apples, celery and pretzels.

PER TABLESPOON 43 calories; 2 g fat (0 g sat.); 2 g protein; 4 g carbohydrate; 0 g fiber; 40 mg sodium; 1 mg cholesterol

GRANOLA, YOGURT & BERRY PARFAITS

MAKES 7 servings **PREP** 10 minutes **BAKE** at 300° for 35 minutes

2½ cups old-fashioned oats
½ cup slivered almonds
⅓ cup dried cherries
½ cup maple syrup
¼ teaspoon salt
¼ teaspoon cinnamon
3½ cups mixed frozen berries, thawed
2½ cups 1% vanilla Greek yogurt

① Heat oven to 300°. Coat a large rimmed baking sheet with nonstick cooking spray.

② In a medium-size bowl, combine the oats, almonds, cherries, maple syrup, salt and cinnamon. Stir until well combined, then spread onto prepared baking sheet. Bake at 300° for about 35 minutes, stirring halfway through, or until golden brown. Remove to a wire rack and let cool completely.

③ Place ¼ cup granola in the bottom of serving glass, then top with ¼ cup berries and a scant 3 tablespoons yogurt. Repeat layering once more. Repeat with remaining glasses.

PER SERVING 348 calories; 6 g fat (0 g sat.); 12 g protein; 62 g carbohydrate; 10 g fiber; 103 mg sodium; 0 mg cholesterol

SWEET POTATO FRIES WITH ROASTED GARLIC KETCHUP

MAKES 4 servings PREP 10 minutes
BAKE at 450° for 30 minutes COOK 3 minutes

1½ pounds sweet potatoes, cut into ½-inch strips
¾ teaspoon salt
¼ teaspoon black pepper
1 tablespoon olive oil
3 cloves garlic, minced
½ of a small onion, minced
⅓ cup ketchup

① Heat oven to 450°. Cover a large rimmed baking sheet with nonstick aluminum foil; set aside.

② Place potatoes on baking sheet in a single layer and coat with nonstick cooking spray; sprinkle with salt and pepper. Bake at 450° for 30 minutes, stirring halfway through.

③ Heat oil in a small nonstick skillet over medium heat. Cook garlic and onion in skillet for 3 minutes, then stir in ketchup. Serve with fries.

PER SERVING 203 calories; 4 g fat (1 g sat.); 3 g protein; 41 g carbohydrate; 5 g fiber; 751 mg sodium; 0 mg cholesterol

GRILLED CHEESE & APPLE SANDWICH

MAKES 4 servings PREP 10 minutes COOK 6 minutes per batch

8 slices 12-grain bread
4 teaspoons honey-mustard
6 ounces 2% cheddar, shredded (about 1½ cups)
1 Granny Smith apple, cored and thinly sliced

① Spread 1 piece of bread with 1 teaspoon honey-mustard then layer ¼ cup grated cheese, 4 apple slices and another heaping tablespoon cheese. Top with another slice of bread; spritz with nonstick cooking spray.

② Heat a small nonstick skillet over medium heat. Place sandwich, cooking spray–side down, in pan and coat top slice of bread with nonstick cooking spray. Press with spatula.

③ Cook for about 2 to 3 minutes or until golden brown. Flip and cook for another 2 to 3 minutes. Repeat with remaining sandwiches.

PER SERVING 384 calories; 13 g fat (6 g sat.); 19 g protein; 48 g carbohydrate; 3 g fiber; 787 mg sodium; 31 mg cholesterol

APPLE MUFFINS

MAKES 18 servings **PREP** 15 minutes
BAKE at 400° for 20 minutes

1	cup all-purpose flour
1	cup whole-wheat flour
1	teaspoon baking soda
½	teaspoon cinnamon
½	teaspoon salt
	Pinch nutmeg
1	cup packed light-brown sugar
2	Granny Smith apples, peeled, cored and cut into ¼-inch pieces (about 3 cups)
¼	cup (½ stick) unsalted butter, softened
2	eggs
1	cup natural applesauce
1	teaspoon vanilla extract
¾	cup buttermilk

① Heat oven to 400°. Fill 18 indents of 2 muffin pans with liners; set aside.

② In a small bowl, whisk together flours, baking soda, cinnamon, salt and nutmeg. In another small bowl, stir together ¼ cup brown sugar and half of the apple pieces; set aside.

③ Beat butter and remaining ¾ cup brown sugar together on medium-high speed until well blended, about 2 minutes. Add eggs, one at a time, beating well after each. Beat in applesauce and vanilla extract.

④ Reduce speed to low and alternately add flour mixture and buttermilk, starting and ending with flour. Stir in remaining apple pieces.

⑤ Fill each muffin liner with ¼ cup batter. Sprinkle 1 tablespoon apple–brown sugar mixture on top of each muffin. Bake muffins at 400° for about 20 minutes or until toothpick inserted in center comes out clean. Cool on a rack for 15 minutes, then remove from pan and allow to cool completely.

PER SERVING 142 calories; 3 g fat (2 g sat.); 3 g protein; 26 g carbohydrate; 1 g fiber; 159 mg sodium; 31 mg cholesterol

Bar Code

Check out these crowd-pleasing brownies, blondies and more.

CHOCOLATE-CARAMEL
BARS, PAGE 219

SIMPLE LEMON BARS,
PAGE 219

CHERRY CHEESECAKE BARS

DEEP CHOCOLATE & PISTACHIO BROWNIES

APPLE CRUMB SQUARES

CHERRY CHEESECAKE BARS

MAKES 24 bars **PREP** 15 minutes **BAKE** at 350° for 50 minutes **REFRIGERATE** overnight

- 1 box (18.25 ounces) lemon cake mix
- ½ cup cornflake crumbs
- 3 eggs
- ½ cup (1 stick) unsalted butter, melted
- 2 packages (8 ounces each) cream cheese, softened
- ¼ cup sugar
- 1 teaspoon vanilla extract
- 1 cup cherry preserves
- ½ cup walnuts, coarsely chopped

① Heat oven to 350°. Coat a 13 x 9 x 2-inch baking pan with nonstick cooking spray.

② Set aside ½ cup of the cake mix. In a large bowl, stir together the remaining cake mix, cornflake crumbs, 1 egg and ¼ cup of the butter. Press into the bottom and partially up the sides of the prepared pan.

③ In another large bowl, beat cream cheese, sugar, vanilla extract and remaining 2 eggs. Spread mixture over crust. Spoon cherry preserves over the cream cheese mixture. Spread gently and evenly.

④ Sprinkle reserved cake mix over top and drizzle with the remaining ¼ cup butter. Bake at 350° for 25 minutes. Sprinkle with the walnuts and bake an additional 20 to 25 minutes or until set.

⑤ Cool completely in pan on rack. Refrigerate overnight. Cut into 24 bars; serve chilled.

PER SERVING 259 calories; 14 g fat (7 g sat.); 3 g protein; 31 g carbohydrate; 0 g fiber; 223 mg sodium; 56 mg cholesterol

Simple-to-bake bars and brownies come in an almost too-good-to-be-true array of flavors—cherry cheesecake, chocolate-pistaschio and spiced apple—to name just a few. Maybe that's why we like them so much.

DEEP CHOCOLATE & PISTACHIO BROWNIES

MAKES 16 brownies **PREP** 15 minutes
MICROWAVE 1½ minutes **BAKE** at 350° for 35 minutes

- ½ cup (1 stick) unsalted butter, cut into pieces
- 8 ounces bittersweet chocolate, chopped
- ¾ cup packed light-brown sugar
- ¾ teaspoon espresso powder
- 3 eggs
- 1 teaspoon vanilla extract
- 1¼ cups all-purpose flour
- ¼ teaspoon salt
- ½ cup mini Hershey's Kisses
- ½ cup shelled pistachios
- 2 tablespoons unsweetened cocoa
  Chopped pistachio nuts for garnish

① Heat oven to 350°. Line an 8 x 8 x 2-inch baking pan with nonstick foil.

② In a large microwave-safe bowl, combine butter and chocolate. Microwave for 1 minute. Stir and microwave for an additional 30 seconds. Stir until smooth.

③ Add sugar and espresso powder and mix until combined. Add eggs and vanilla. Stir until eggs are incorporated. Beat in flour and salt until just combined. Fold in mini Kisses and nuts.

④ Pour into prepared pan. Bake at 350° for 30 to 35 minutes or until toothpick inserted in center comes out clean. Cool 15 minutes. Use foil to lift brownie from pan; cool on a wire rack.

⑤ Cut into squares. Dust with cocoa and sprinkle with chopped nuts.

PER SERVING 271 calories; 17 g fat (9 g sat.); 5 g protein; 30 g carbohydrate; 2 g fiber; 62 mg sodium; 57 mg cholesterol

APPLE CRUMB SQUARES

MAKES 24 squares **PREP** 20 minutes
BAKE at 350° for 60 minutes

CAKE

- ¾ cup (1½ sticks) unsalted butter, softened
- 1 cup sugar
- 3 eggs
- ¾ teaspoon almond extract
- 1½ cups all-purpose flour
- ⅛ teaspoon salt
- 6 Granny Smith apples, cored, peeled, halved and thinly sliced
- ¼ cup apricot preserves, melted

CRUMB TOPPING

- 2 cups all-purpose flour
- 1 cup light-brown sugar
- 1¼ teaspoons pumpkin pie spice
- ¼ teaspoon salt
- ¾ cup (1½ sticks) unsalted butter, melted
- 2 tablespoons confectioners' sugar

① Heat oven to 350°. Coat a 15 x 10 x 1-inch pan with nonstick cooking spray.

② **Cake:** Beat together the butter and sugar until smooth, about 2 minutes. Add eggs, one at a time, beating well after each. Beat in almond extract. On low speed, beat in flour and salt until just blended. Spread evenly into prepared pan.

③ Fan apple slices over top, then brush with preserves. Bake at 350° for 25 minutes.

④ **Crumb Topping:** Whisk together the flour, brown sugar, pumpkin pie spice and salt. Stir in the butter until mixture is moistened and clumps together. Sprinkle evenly over cake. Bake for an additional 35 minutes. Remove pan to wire rack; cool completely.

⑤ Dust with confectioners' sugar and cut into 24 squares.

PER SERVING 269 calories; 12 g fat (7 g sat.); 3 g protein; 38 g carbohydrate; 1 g fiber; 51 mg sodium; 57 mg cholesterol

HAZELNUT BLONDIES

SIMPLE LEMON BARS

MAKES 24 bars **PREP** 15 minutes **BAKE** at 350°
for 45 minutes

CRUST
1   cup (2 sticks) unsalted butter, softened
½   cup confectioners' sugar
⅛   teaspoon salt
2   cups all-purpose flour

FILLING
1¾   cups granulated sugar
¼   cup all-purpose flour
4   eggs
6   tablespoons fresh lemon juice
2   tablespoons confectioners' sugar

① Heat oven to 350°. Line a 13 x 9 x 2-inch baking pan with nonstick foil.

② **Crust:** In a large bowl, blend butter, confectioners' sugar and salt until well combined and smooth. Stir in flour until blended. Scrape into the prepared baking pan and press evenly into the bottom.

③ Bake at 350° for 20 minutes or until crust is golden brown. Remove from oven and set aside.

④ **Filling:** In a large bowl, beat granulated sugar, flour, eggs and lemon juice until completely smooth. Pour over crust.

⑤ Bake at 350° for 25 minutes or until no imprint remains in the filling when lightly touched in the center. Remove from oven to a wire rack and cool completely. Dust lightly with confectioners' sugar. Cut into 24 bars and serve.

PER SERVING 191 calories; 9 g fat (5 g sat.); 2 g protein; 27 g carbohydrate; 0 g fiber; 25 mg sodium; 55 mg cholesterol

CHOCOLATE-CARAMEL BARS

MAKES 16 bars **PREP** 15 minutes **BAKE** at 350°
for 23 minutes **REFRIGERATE** overnight

1   package (9 ounces) Famous chocolate wafers, finely crushed
10   tablespoons (1¼ sticks) unsalted butter, melted
1   bag (7 ounces) shredded coconut
1   cup semi-sweet chocolate baking bits
1   cup white chocolate pieces
1   cup pecans, chopped
24   caramel-filled Hershey's Kisses, halved

① Heat oven to 350°. Line a 13 x 9 x 2-inch baking pan with nonstick foil.

② Stir together crushed wafers and butter. Press evenly into prepared pan. Bake at 350° for 5 minutes. Cool slightly on wire rack.

③ In a large bowl, combine coconut, chocolate bits, white chocolate and pecans. Evenly distribute over cookie crust. Scatter the halved Kisses over top. Bake at 350° for 18 minutes. Cool completely.

④ Refrigerate overnight. Cut into 16 bars with a large knife using a gentle rocking motion.

PER SERVING 382 calories; 26 g fat (14 g sat.); 4 g protein; 37 g carbohydrate; 3 g fiber; 173 mg sodium; 25 mg cholesterol

HAZELNUT BLONDIES

MAKES 16 blondies **PREP** 10 minutes
BAKE at 325° for 40 minutes
MICROWAVE 30 seconds

¾   cup (1½ sticks) unsalted butter, softened
1   cup packed light-brown sugar
1   egg
1   teaspoon vanilla extract
2   tablespoons hazelnut liqueur (such as Frangelico)
2   cups all-purpose flour
1   cup hazelnuts, chopped
½   teaspoon salt
1   ounce white chocolate

① Heat oven to 325°. Coat an 8 x 8 x 2-inch baking pan with nonstick cooking spray.

② In a large bowl, beat butter and sugar together until completely smooth. Next, beat in egg, vanilla extract and hazelnut liqueur. On low speed, stir in flour, hazelnuts and salt. Press evenly into bottom of prepared baking pan.

③ Bake at 325° for 35 to 40 minutes or until center is firm to the touch. Cool completely on a wire rack.

④ Place white chocolate in a small plastic food storage bag. Leave top open and microwave for 30 seconds. Press to soften. Snip off one corner of bag and drizzle chocolate over blondies. Cut into 16 squares.

PER SERVING 251 calories; 14 g fat (6 g sat.); 3 g protein; 28 g carbohydrate; 1 g fiber; 86 mg sodium; 36 mg cholesterol

Slow Cooker Suppers

Surprising (think lasagna!), savory dishes that conveniently cook in your slow cooker.

**CURRIED CHICKPEAS
WITH COUSCOUS**

CURRIED CHICKPEAS WITH COUSCOUS

MAKES 6 servings **PREP** 10 minutes
SLOW-COOK 3 hours on HIGH or 6 hours on LOW

- 3 medium-size carrots, finely chopped
- 4 cups cauliflower florets (about ¾ pound)
- 2 cans (15 ounces each) chickpeas, drained and rinsed
- 1 cup frozen peas
- 1 medium-size onion, chopped
- 3 garlic cloves, minced
- 2½ teaspoons curry powder
- ¾ teaspoon ground coriander
- ¼ teaspoon crushed red pepper flakes
- 1 cup vegetable broth
- ¾ cup coconut milk
- ¼ cup chopped fresh basil
- ¾ teaspoon salt
- 1 cup dry couscous (optional)

① In slow cooker bowl, stir together carrots, cauliflower, chickpeas, peas, onion, garlic, curry powder, coriander and red pepper flakes. Pour vegetable broth and coconut milk over top.

② Cover slow cooker bowl and cook for 3 hours on HIGH or for 6 hours on LOW. Remove 2 cups chickpea mixture to a small bowl and mash with a potato masher; stir in basil and salt and return mashed chickpea mixture to slow cooker bowl. Stir until well combined and heated through.

③ If using couscous, prepare according to package directions, about 5 minutes; serve with chickpea curry.

PER SERVING 360 calories; 8 g fat (5 g sat.); 15 g protein; 58 g carbohydrate; 13 g fiber; 782 mg sodium; 0 mg cholesterol

SAUSAGE & TORTELLINI STEW

MAKES 6 servings **PREP** 10 minutes **SLOW-COOK** 3 hours on HIGH or 6 hours on LOW

- 4 sweet Italian turkey sausage links, casings removed
- 1 can (28 ounces) crushed tomatoes with basil, garlic and oregano
- 1 package (9 ounces) frozen cut green beans
- 1 large onion, chopped
- ½ teaspoon Italian seasoning
- 1 package (9 ounces) refrigerated cheese tortellini (such as Buitoni)
- 1 tablespoon chopped fresh oregano

① Crumble sausages into a bowl and stir together with tomatoes, green beans, onion and Italian seasoning; place mixture in slow cooker. Cover slow cooker bowl and cook 3 hours on HIGH or 6 hours on LOW.

② When there is 20 minutes remaining, stir in tortellini, oregano and 1 cup water; continue cooking. Serve immediately.

PER SERVING 305 calories; 10 g fat (2 g sat.); 19 g protein; 34 g carbohydrate; 5 g fiber; 709 mg sodium; 57 mg cholesterol

LATIN-STYLE PORK

MAKES 8 servings **PREP** 10 minutes **SLOW COOK** 3 hours on HIGH or 6 hours on LOW

1	boneless pork loin roast (about 3 pounds), trimmed and cut in half lengthwise
2	large yellow peppers, seeded and sliced
1	medium-size onion, thinly sliced
1	can (14.5 ounces) diced tomatoes
1	tablespoon capers, drained
1	tablespoon ground cumin
½	teaspoon cinnamon
3	garlic cloves, sliced
1	tablespoon sliced pickled jalapeños
½	teaspoon salt
4	cups cooked white rice (optional)

① Place pork in slow cooker bowl with peppers, onion, tomatoes, capers, cumin, cinnamon, garlic and jalapeños; stir to combine. Cover and cook on HIGH for 3 hours or LOW for 6 hours.

② Remove pork from slow cooker. When cool enough to handle, shred pork into bite-size pieces; discard any excess fat. Combine pork with tomato mixture in slow cooker bowl; stir in salt. Serve with rice, if desired.

PER SERVING 283 calories; 13 g fat (5 g sat.); 34 g protein; 9 g carbohydrate; 2 g fiber; 911 mg sodium; 83 mg cholesterol

CHICKEN & PESTO LASAGNA

MAKES 6 servings **PREP** 10 minutes **COOK** 7 minutes **SLOW COOK** 3 hours on HIGH or 5½ hours on LOW

- 1 tablespoon canola oil
- 1 medium-size onion, chopped
- 2 garlic cloves, minced
- 1 pound ground chicken
- 1 package (10 ounces) frozen chopped spinach, thawed and squeezed dry
- ¼ cup reduced-fat pesto
- ½ teaspoon salt
- ¼ teaspoon black pepper
- 1 cup part-skim ricotta
- ¾ cup Italian-blend shredded cheese
- 10 lasagna noodles, broken in half

① Heat oil in a large nonstick skillet over medium-high heat. Add onion and garlic to skillet and cook for 3 minutes or until softened. Add chicken to skillet and cook, stirring frequently, for about 4 minutes or until no longer pink. Add spinach, pesto, salt and pepper to skillet and stir until well blended; set aside.

② In a small bowl, combine ricotta and ½ cup of the Italian shredded cheese.

③ Coat slow cooker bowl with nonstick cooking spray, then layer one-third of the uncooked noodles, overlapping as necessary. Spread one-third of the chicken mixture over noodles, then top with ¼ cup water. Dollop one-third of the ricotta mixture on top, and continue layering with remaining noodles, meat, an additional ¼ cup water and ricotta mixture.

④ Cover and cook on HIGH for 3 hours or LOW for 5½ hours. Sprinkle remaining ¼ cup of Italian cheese on top for last 15 minutes of cook time or until melted.

PER SERVING 394 calories; 19 g fat (8 g sat.); 28 g protein; 29 g carbohydrate; 3 g fiber; 547 mg sodium; 144 mg cholesterol

BAKED POTATO SOUP

MAKES 8 servings **PREP** 10 minutes
SLOW COOK 3 hours on HIGH or 6 hours on LOW

- 3½ pounds potatoes, peeled and cut into ¾-inch pieces
- 1 small sweet red pepper, seeded and chopped
- 1 package (10 ounces) frozen chopped broccoli
- 4 cups low-sodium chicken broth
- ⅓ cup half-and-half
- ⅓ cup reduced-fat sour cream, plus additional for garnish
- 1 tablespoon cornstarch
- 1¼ teaspoons salt
- ½ teaspoon black pepper
- 4 scallions, trimmed and thinly sliced
- 4 slices bacon, cooked and crumbled Shredded cheddar cheese (optional)

① Combine potatoes, red pepper and broccoli in slow cooker bowl. Pour broth over top; cover and cook 3 hours on HIGH or 6 hours on LOW or until potatoes are tender.

② In a small bowl, stir together half-and-half, ⅓ cup sour cream, cornstarch, salt and pepper. Remove cover and mash potatoes slightly. Stir in half-and-half mixture and scallions. Spoon soup into bowls.

③ Divide bacon among bowls and dollop each with sour cream. Sprinkle with cheddar cheese, if desired.

PER SERVING 195 calories; 4 g fat (2 g sat.); 9 g protein; 30 g carbohydrate; 5 g fiber; 764 mg sodium; 16 mg cholesterol

WHEN THE WEATHER TURNS CHILLY, TUCK INTO COMFORT-FOOD FAVORITES SUCH AS MACARONI AND CHEESE, HOMEMADE PIZZA AND WARMING APPLE DESSERTS.

CARAMEL APPLES,
PAGE 255

OCTOBER

231

247

265

Wok & Roll

Our healthy, homemade versions of Chinese takeout really deliver.

**MOO SHU VEGETABLES,
PAGE 231**

CANTONESE SHRIMP,
PAGE 231

PORK FRIED RICE

PORK FRIED RICE

MAKES 6 servings **PREP** 15 minutes
BROIL 8 minutes **COOK** 12 minutes

- ½ cup reduced-sodium chicken broth
- ¼ cup light soy sauce
- 1 tablespoon oyster sauce
- ½ teaspoon ground ginger
- ¼ teaspoon red pepper flakes
- 1 pound boneless pork chops, about ½ inch thick
- 2 eggs, lightly beaten
- 1 tablespoon canola oil
- 1 large onion, peeled and chopped
- 1 large red sweet pepper, cored, seeded and thinly sliced
- 3 cups cooked brown rice
- 4 scallions, sliced
- 1 cup frozen peas, thawed
- 1 tablespoon sesame oil

① In a small bowl, mix together broth, soy sauce, oyster sauce, ginger and pepper flakes. Set aside.

② Heat broiler. Broil pork chops for 4 minutes per side. Dice and reserve.

③ Heat a medium nonstick skillet over medium heat. Coat with cooking spray. Add eggs and cook for 2 minutes, until set. Remove to a plate and cut into ½-inch strips. Reserve.

④ Heat oil in a large nonstick skillet or wok. Add onion and red pepper and stir-fry for 5 to 6 minutes, until softened. Stir in broth mixture and rice. Stir-fry 2 minutes. Add reserved pork, egg strips, scallions, peas and sesame oil. Stir gently to combine and heat through, about 2 minutes.

PER SERVING 339 calories; 11 g fat (2 g sat.); 24 g protein; 36 g carbohydrate; 5 g fiber; 653 mg sodium; 117 mg cholesterol

SICHUAN CHICKEN

MAKES 6 servings **PREP** 15 minutes **COOK** 15 minutes

- ½ cup low-sodium chicken broth
- 2 tablespoons light soy sauce
- 2 tablespoons rice vinegar
- 2 teaspoons cornstarch
- 1 teaspoon sugar
- 1 to 2 teaspoons Sriracha (Thai chile and garlic sauce)
- 1 tablespoon canola oil
- 1½ pounds boneless, skinless chicken breast, cut into 1-inch chunks
- 8 ounces sliced white mushrooms
- 1 sweet red pepper, seeded and chopped
- 1 medium onion, peeled and chopped
- 3 ribs celery, chopped
- 1 can (8 ounces) diced water chestnuts, drained
- ¼ cup chopped peanuts
- 3 cups cooked white rice

① In a medium bowl, mix together broth, soy sauce, vinegar, cornstarch, sugar and Sriracha sauce. Set aside.

② Heat oil in a large nonstick skillet or wok over medium-high heat. Add chicken and stir-fry for 6 to 7 minutes, until no longer pink inside. Remove to a plate and keep warm. Add mushrooms, red pepper, onion and celery to skillet and stir-fry for 6 minutes until vegetables are crisp-tender. Stir in reserved broth and soy sauce mixture, water chestnuts and cooked chicken. Simmer for 2 minutes, stirring occasionally, until thickened and water chestnuts and chicken are heated through.

③ Sprinkle with chopped peanuts and serve with cooked white rice.

PER SERVING 373 calories; 8 g fat (1 g sat.); 33 g protein; 42 g carbohydrate; 5 g fiber; 339 mg sodium; 68 mg cholesterol

PEPPER STEAK

MAKES 6 servings **PREP** 15 minutes **COOK** 15 minutes

1 tablespoon canola oil
1½ pounds boneless sirloin, sliced against the grain ¾ inch thick
¼ teaspoon salt
2 large onions, peeled, halved and cut into ½-inch-thick slices
3 green peppers, cored, seeded and cut into ¾-inch-thick slices
3 cloves garlic, sliced
½ cup reduced-sodium beef broth
3 tablespoons light soy sauce
1 tablespoon rice vinegar

1 teaspoon cornstarch
½ teaspoon Chinese five-spice powder
1 can (14½ ounces) no-salt-added stewed tomatoes, drained
3 cups cooked brown rice

① Heat oil in a large nonstick skillet or wok over medium-high heat. Season steak with the salt and cook 4 to 5 minutes, turning after 2 minutes. Remove to a plate and keep warm.

② Add onions, peppers and garlic to skillet and stir-fry 8 minutes, stirring occasionally. Mix together broth, soy sauce, vinegar, cornstarch and Chinese five-spice powder. Add to skillet; stir in the tomatoes. Simmer for 2 minutes. Add in the steak along with any accumulated juices. Heat through. Serve with cooked brown rice.

PER SERVING 351 calories; 8 g fat (2 g sat.); 28 g protein; 42 g carbohydrate; 5 g fiber; 685 mg sodium; 42 mg cholesterol

PEANUT NOODLES & CHICKEN

MAKES 4 servings (6 cups) **PREP** 15 minutes
COOK about 10 minutes

½   pound linguine
2   tablespoons light soy sauce
2   tablespoons lemon juice
½   teaspoon cornstarch
⅓   cup reduced-fat peanut butter
2   cloves garlic, finely chopped
½   teaspoon sugar
¼   teaspoon red pepper flakes
1   teaspoon sesame oil
1   pound cooked chicken, shredded
½   cucumber, peeled and cut into 2-inch matchsticks
½   cup bean sprouts

① Cook linguine following package directions. Drain and rinse under cold water.

② Mix together the soy sauce, lemon juice and cornstarch. In a medium-size saucepan, combine peanut butter, garlic, sugar, red pepper flakes and ½ cup hot water. Whisk in the soy sauce mixture and bring to a simmer. Whisk until smooth. Remove from heat; stir in the sesame oil.

③ In a large bowl, toss together linguine, chicken and peanut butter mixture. Scatter cucumber and bean sprouts over the top and serve at room temperature.

PER SERVING 487 calories; 11 g fat (2 g sat.); 40 g protein; 56 g carbohydrate; 4 g fiber; 547 mg sodium; 66 mg cholesterol

MOO SHU VEGETABLES

MAKES 10 wraps **PREP** 15 minutes
GRILL 6 minutes **COOK** 10 minutes, 30 seconds

1   package (8 ounces) firm tofu, cut into 6 slices
2   tablespoons smoky spicy grilling sauce
1   tablespoon canola oil
2   cloves garlic, peeled and chopped
2   tablespoons gingerroot, peeled and chopped
1   bag (10 ounces) coleslaw mix
1   bag (8 ounces) shredded carrots
4   ounces sliced mixed mushrooms
1   cup bean sprouts
½   cup vegetable broth
¼   cup hoisin sauce
3   tablespoons light soy sauce
6   scallions, sliced
1   teaspoon sesame oil
10 whole-wheat flour tortillas

① Heat a grill pan over medium heat. Coat with cooking spray. Brush both sides of the tofu slices with the grilling sauce and grill for 3 minutes per side. Remove to a plate and cut into small cubes. Keep warm.

② In a large nonstick skillet or wok, heat oil over medium-high heat. Add garlic and ginger and cook 30 seconds. Add coleslaw mix, carrots, mushrooms, bean sprouts and ¼ cup of the broth. Cook, stirring frequently, for 8 minutes.

③ Stir together remaining ¼ cup broth, hoisin sauce and soy sauce. Add to skillet and cook 2 minutes, stirring occasionally. Stir in the scallions, sesame oil and reserved tofu.

④ Serve with slightly warmed tortillas.

PER WRAP 221 calories; 6 g fat (2 g sat.); 8 g protein; 32 g carbohydrate; 5 g fiber; 843 mg sodium; 0 mg cholesterol

CANTONESE SHRIMP

MAKES 6 servings **PREP** 15 minutes
COOK about 9 minutes

1   cup vegetable broth
2   tablespoons light soy sauce
1   tablespoon cornstarch
1   tablespoon oyster sauce
2   tablespoons canola oil
1¾   pounds extra-large shrimp, shelled and deveined
½   pound snow peas
2   tablespoons gingerroot, finely chopped
1   can (8 ounces) bamboo shoots, drained
1   can (8 ounces) baby corn, drained
1   package (13.75 ounces) whole-grain thin spaghetti, cooked following package directions

① In a small bowl, stir together broth, soy sauce, cornstarch and oyster sauce. Set aside.

② Heat 1 tablespoon of the oil in a large nonstick skillet or wok over medium-high heat. Add shrimp and cook for 4 minutes, turning after 2 minutes. Remove shrimp to a plate and keep warm.

③ Add remaining tablespoon oil to skillet and add snow peas and ginger. Stir-fry for 2 minutes. Add bamboo shoots, corn, broth and soy sauce mixture. Simmer for 2 minutes, until thickened. Stir in shrimp and cook until heated through, about 1 minute. Serve over cooked spaghetti.

PER SERVING 466 calories; 9 g fat (1 g sat.); 36 g protein; 60 g carbohydrate; 12 g fiber; 807 mg sodium; 172 mg cholesterol

High Five

5 ingredients + 30 minutes = delicious dinners.

CHICKEN & BROCCOLI ALFREDO

MAKES 4 servings **PREP** 10 minutes **COOK** 14 minutes

WHAT YOU NEED:

1 pound boneless, skinless chicken breast, cut into 1-inch pieces
1 large onion, chopped
4 cups broccoli florets
1 can (14.5 ounces) petite diced tomatoes, drained
¼ cup reduced-fat scallion and chive cream cheese

FROM THE PANTRY:

1 tablespoon plus 1 teaspoon olive oil
½ teaspoon salt
¼ teaspoon black pepper

1 tablespoon flour
½ teaspoon dried thyme

① Heat 1 tablespoon oil in a large nonstick skillet over medium-high heat. Add chicken to pan and cook for 4 minutes or until browned. Remove chicken from skillet.

② Reduce heat to medium and add 1 teaspoon oil, onion and ¼ teaspoon each salt and pepper to skillet and cook for 5 minutes or until softened. Add flour to skillet and cook 1 minute, stirring. Add broccoli, thyme and ½ cup water to skillet.

Cover; cook for 4 minutes or until broccoli is crisp-tender.

③ Remove cover and add chicken, remaining ¼ teaspoon salt, tomatoes and cream cheese to pan; stir until well blended.

PER SERVING 272 calories; 9 g fat (3 g sat.); 32 g protein; 15 g carbohydrate; 4 g fiber; 621 mg sodium; 73 mg cholesterol

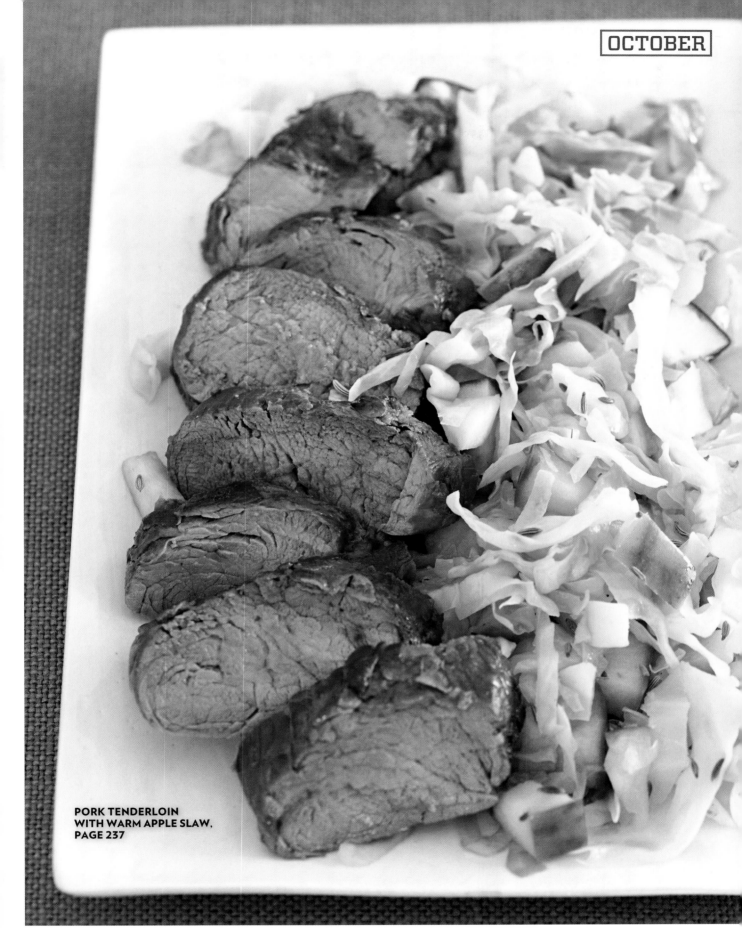

**PORK TENDERLOIN
WITH WARM APPLE SLAW,
PAGE 237**

PHILLY CHEESESTEAKS,
PAGE 237

PASTA WITH HAM & PEAS

MAKES 6 servings **PREP** 10 minutes **COOK** 13 minutes

WHAT YOU NEED:

1 box (13.25 ounces) whole-wheat rotini pasta

1 package (10 ounces) frozen peas, thawed

2 packages (4.4 ounces each) reduced-fat herbed soft cheese

¼ cup grated Parmesan (optional)

8 ounces sliced low-sodium ham, cut into ½-inch-wide ribbons

① Bring a large pot of salted water to a boil. Add pasta; cook 13 minutes or until tender. When there is 1 minute cook time remaining, add peas to pasta water.

② Drain pasta mixture, setting aside 1 cup pasta water. Return pasta and peas to pot and stir in cheeses and ham. Stir until well blended, adding pasta water by the tablespoonful if mixture appears dry.

PER SERVING 371 calories; 7 g fat (3 g sat.); 22 g protein; 55 g carbohydrate; 8 g fiber; 604 mg sodium; 27 mg cholesterol

GREEK SHRIMP & GREEN BEANS

MAKES 6 servings **PREP** 10 minutes **COOK** 12 minutes

WHAT YOU NEED:

- 1¼ pounds large raw shrimp, peeled and deveined
- ½ pound green beans, trimmed and halved
- ¼ cup reduced-fat red wine vinaigrette
- 2 cups yellow and red cherry tomatoes, halved
- ¼ cup chopped fresh parsley

FROM THE PANTRY:

- 1 tablespoon Greek seasoning
- 2 tablespoons olive oil

① In a medium bowl, stir together shrimp and Greek seasoning; set aside.

② Bring a large pot of lightly salted water to a boil. Add green beans to boiling water and simmer for 5 minutes or until crisp-tender; drain and set aside.

③ Heat the olive oil in a large nonstick skillet over medium-high heat. Add shrimp in a single layer; cook for about 2 to 3 minutes per side or until cooked through. Reduce heat to medium and add red wine vinaigrette, tomatoes and parsley to skillet and cook 1 minute or until warmed through. Remove shrimp mixture from heat and stir in green beans until well combined; serve immediately.

PER SERVING 149 calories; 7 g fat (1 g sat.); 16 g protein; 6 g carbohydrate; 2 g fiber; 272 mg sodium; 140 mg cholesterol

GNOCCHI WITH TOMATO SAUCE

MAKES 4 servings **PREP** 10 minutes
COOK 5 minutes

WHAT YOU NEED:

1   package (17.5 ounces) prepared gnocchi
1   bag (6 ounces) baby spinach
1   can (14.5 ounces) diced tomatoes with basil and oregano
½   cup shredded part-skim mozzarella
¼   cup chopped fresh basil

FROM THE PANTRY:

1   tablespoon olive oil
¼   teaspoon crushed red pepper flakes
½   teaspoon salt

① Bring a large pot of salted water to a boil. Add gnocchi to pot and cook according to package directions, removing them from the pot with a slotted spoon as they come to the surface. Once all of the gnocchi are removed, add baby spinach to the water and boil 1 minute; remove with slotted spoon and drain well.

② Meanwhile, place tomatoes in a food processor; process until almost smooth; set aside. Heat oil in a large nonstick skillet over medium-high heat. Add pepper flakes to pan and cook, stirring, for 1 minute. Stir tomatoes and salt into pan. Cook 4 minutes or until thickened.

③ Stir gnocchi and spinach into tomato sauce. Divide gnocchi mixture among 4 bowls and top each with 2 tablespoons mozzarella cheese and 1 tablespoon basil.

PER SERVING 210 calories; 9 g fat (4 g sat.); 7 g protein; 25 g carbohydrate; 3 g fiber; 720 mg sodium; 55 mg cholesterol

PORK TENDERLOIN WITH WARM APPLE SLAW

MAKES 4 servings **PREP** 10 minutes **ROAST** at 400° for 30 minutes **COOK** 12 minutes

WHAT YOU NEED:

1   pork tenderloin (about 1½ pounds)
3   teaspoons honey
½   head green cabbage, thinly sliced (about 8 cups)
2   Gala apples (about 4 ounces each), cored and cut into ¼-inch pieces
1   teaspoon caraway seeds

FROM THE PANTRY:

½   teaspoon salt
½   teaspoon black pepper
2   tablespoons olive oil

① Heat oven to 400°. Rub pork with 1 teaspoon honey and ¼ teaspoon each salt and pepper; place in a roasting pan. Roast at 400° for 25 to 30 minutes, turning halfway through, or until internal temperature registers 155° on an instant-read thermometer.

② Meanwhile, heat oil in a large nonstick skillet over medium-high heat. Add cabbage and cook, covered, for 6 minutes. Reduce heat to medium; stir in remaining 2 teaspoons honey, apple, caraway seeds and remaining ¼ teaspoon each salt and pepper. Cook for 6 minutes, uncovered, stirring, until cabbage is tender.

③ Cut pork into 1-inch slices and serve with slaw.

PER SERVING 346 calories; 15 g fat (4 g sat.); 31 g protein; 22 g carbohydrate; 4 g fiber; 537 mg sodium; 94 mg cholesterol

PHILLY CHEESESTEAKS

MAKES 8 servings **PREP** 10 minutes
COOK 11 minutes **BROIL** 1 minute

WHAT YOU NEED:

1   medium onion, thinly sliced
1   large green pepper, seeded and thinly sliced
¾   pound top round steak, trimmed and cut into ½ x 3-inch strips
½   pound sliced reduced-fat provolone cheese (about 8 slices)
8   white whole-wheat hot dog rolls

FROM THE PANTRY:

1   tablespoon olive oil
¼   teaspoon salt
¼   teaspoon black pepper
2   teaspoons Worcestershire sauce

① Heat oil in a large nonstick skillet over medium-high heat. Add onion and green pepper to pan and cook, stirring often, for 7 minutes or until softened.

② Sprinkle beef with salt and pepper. Add beef to pan and cook 3 minutes, stirring occasionally, or until cooked through. Stir in Worcestershire sauce; cook 1 minute.

③ Heat broiler. Tuck 1 slice provolone into rolls and top with a scant ½ cup beef mixture. Arrange rolls on a baking sheet and put under broiler for 1 minute or until cheese has melted.

PER SERVING 230 calories; 9 g fat (4 g sat.); 20 g protein; 21 g carbohydrate; 2 g fiber; 360 mg sodium; 25 mg cholesterol

Easy As Pie

These delicious homemade pizzas are fun to make and will save you some dough.

SICILIAN-STYLE PEPPERONI PIZZA, PAGE 243

SMOKY VEGETABLE PIZZA

MAKES 8 slices **PREP** 15 minutes
COOK 4 minutes **BAKE** at 500° for 20 minutes

- 2 tablespoons olive oil
- 3 cloves chopped garlic
- ½ bunch broccoli rabe, cut into 1-inch pieces
- ½ sweet red pepper, seeded and sliced
- ½ red onion, thinly sliced
- 4 ounces cremini mushrooms, sliced
- ¼ teaspoon salt
- ¼ teaspoon black pepper
- 1 pound pizza dough, at room temperature, or 1 batch Basic Pizza Dough (recipe, page 243)
- 1 cup marinara sauce
- ½ pound smoked mozzarella, shredded

① Heat oven to 500°. Coat a 14-inch pizza pan with nonstick cooking spray.

② Heat olive oil in a large nonstick skillet over medium-high heat. Stir in garlic, broccoli rabe, red pepper, onion, mushrooms, salt and pepper. Cook for 4 minutes, stirring occasionally.

③ On a lightly floured surface, roll out dough into a 14-inch circle. Gently roll up onto a lightly floured rolling pin and unroll onto prepared pizza pan.

④ Spread sauce over dough to within ½ inch of edge. Sprinkle 1½ cups of cheese over sauce. Evenly spoon the vegetables over cheese. Scatter the remaining cheese over vegetables. Bake at 500° for 18 to 20 minutes or until nicely browned on bottom.

⑤ Cool slightly and cut into 8 slices; serve.

PER SLICE 275 calories; 13 g fat (4 g sat.); 12 g protein; 31 g carbohydrate; 2 g fiber; 644 mg sodium; 22 mg cholesterol

MEAT LOVER'S DEEP DISH,
PAGE 245

FOUR CHEESE
WHITE PIZZA,
PAGE 245

CLASSIC MARGHERITA

BASIC PIZZA DOUGH

MAKES 8 servings **PREP** 5 minutes
RISE 2 hours

1 cup warm water (about 110°)
1 package (.25 ounce) dry active yeast
2¾ cups all-purpose flour
1 teaspoon sugar
1 teaspoon salt
2 tablespoons olive oil

① Place water in a small bowl and stir in yeast. Let stand 5 minutes.

② In a large bowl, whisk together 2½ cups of the flour, sugar and salt. Make well in the center and add the yeast mixture and olive oil. Stir until dough comes together and forms a ball. Turn out onto a well-floured surface and knead for 5 minutes, adding as much of the remaining ¼ cup flour as needed. Form into a disk and place in a bowl that has been lightly coated with olive oil. Turn disk over and cover bowl with plastic wrap. Allow to rise in a warm place for 2 hours.

③ Remove dough from bowl and punch down. Roll out into desired diameter.

PER SERVING 191 calories; 4 g fat (1 g sat.); 5 g protein; 34 g carbohydrate; 1 g fiber; 294 mg sodium; 0 mg cholesterol

MARINARA SAUCE

MAKES 2 cups **PREP** 5 minutes
COOK 31 minutes

2 tablespoons olive oil
4 cloves garlic, finely chopped
1 can (28 ounces) San Marzano tomatoes, crushed by hand

1 teaspoon sugar
½ teaspoon dried oregano
½ teaspoon dried basil
¼ teaspoon salt

① In a medium saucepan, heat oil over medium heat. Add garlic; cook 1 minute, stirring so garlic does not burn. Stir in tomatoes, sugar, oregano, basil and salt. Bring to a boil. Cook, with lid ajar, for 30 minutes over medium-low heat, stirring occasionally.

PER CUP 221 calories; 14 g fat (2 g sat.); 4 g protein; 18 g carbohydrate; 4 g fiber; 1,014 mg sodium; 0 mg cholesterol

SICILIAN-STYLE PEPPERONI PIZZA

MAKES 12 slices **PREP** 10 minutes
BAKE at 500° for 20 minutes

1 pound pizza dough, at room temperature, or 1 batch Basic Pizza Dough
1 cup marinara sauce
½ teaspoon dried oregano
2 cups shredded mozzarella cheese
2 ounces sliced pepperoni (about ⅓ cup)

① Heat oven to 500°. Coat a 15 x 10 x 1-inch baking pan with nonstick cooking spray.

② On a lightly floured surface, roll dough into a 15 x 10-inch rectangle. Gently roll up onto a lightly floured rolling pin and unroll onto prepared pan. Push dough into corners.

③ Spread sauce evenly over dough to within ½ inch of edge. Sprinkle oregano over sauce. Scatter cheese over top. Place pepperoni slices over cheese. Bake at 500° for 18 to 20 minutes or until nicely browned on bottom. Remove from oven.

④ Cool slightly and cut into 12 slices; serve.

PER SLICE 255 calories; 10 g fat (4 g sat.); 10 g protein; 35 g carbohydrate; 1 g fiber; 582 mg sodium; 21 mg cholesterol

CLASSIC MARGHERITA

MAKES 8 slices **PREP** 10 minutes
BAKE at 500° for 13 minutes

1 pound pizza dough, at room temperature, or 1 batch Basic Pizza Dough
¾ cup marinara sauce
¼ teaspoon dried oregano
6 ounces fresh mozzarella cheese, thinly sliced
1 tablespoon grated Parmesan cheese
8 fresh basil leaves

① Heat oven to 500°. Coat a 14-inch pizza pan with nonstick cooking spray.

② On a lightly floured surface, roll out dough into a 14-inch circle. Gently roll up onto a lightly floured rolling pin and unroll onto prepared pizza pan.

③ Spread sauce evenly over dough to within ½ inch of edge. Sprinkle oregano over the sauce. Arrange mozzarella over the top and sprinkle with Parmesan. Bake at 500° for 12 to 13 minutes or until nicely browned on bottom. Remove from oven.

④ Garnish with basil. Cool slightly and cut into 8 slices; serve.

PER SLICE 207 calories; 9 g fat (4 g sat.); 9 g protein; 27 g carbohydrate; 1 g fiber; 495 mg sodium; 16 mg cholesterol

SWEET & SOUR
GRILLED CHICKEN PIZZA

⑤ To serve, scatter pine nuts over the top and cut into 8 slices.

PER SLICE 308 calories; 17 g fat (7 g sat.); 14 g protein; 29 g carbohydrate; 2 g fiber; 449 mg sodium; 32 mg cholesterol

SWEET & SOUR GRILLED CHICKEN PIZZA

MAKES 8 slices **PREP** 10 minutes
GRILL 6 minutes **BAKE** at 500° for 18 minutes

¾   **pound thin-cut boneless, skinless chicken breasts**
6   **tablespoons Lawry's Szechuan Sweet & Sour BBQ Marinade**
1   **pound pizza dough, at room temperature, or 1 batch Basic Pizza Dough (recipe page 243)**
2   **cups shredded cheddar and Jack cheese blend**
½   **small red onion, peeled, halved and sliced**
1   **cup pineapple tidbits, drained**

① Coat chicken with 2 tablespoons of the marinade. Heat a grill pan over medium-high heat. Grill chicken for 5 to 6 minutes, turning after 3 minutes. Place chicken on a cutting board and slice into strips. Set aside.

② Heat oven to 500°. Lightly coat a 14-inch pizza pan with nonstick cooking spray.

③ On a lightly floured surface, roll out dough into a 14-inch circle. Gently roll up onto a lightly floured rolling pin and unroll onto prepared pizza pan.

④ Scatter 1½ cups of the cheese evenly over the dough. Scatter the chicken slices, onion and pineapple over the cheese. Drizzle the remaining 4 tablespoons of marinade over the top and sprinkle on the remaining ½ cup of cheese. Bake at 500° for 15 to 18 minutes or until nicely browned on bottom. Remove from oven.

⑤ Cool slightly and cut into 8 slices before serving.

PER SLICE 326 calories; 12 g fat (6 g sat.); 21 g protein; 35 g carbohydrate; 1 g fiber; 732 mg sodium; 54 mg cholesterol

MEAT LOVER'S DEEP DISH

MAKES 8 slices **PREP** 10 minutes
COOK 5 minutes **BAKE** at 450° for 30 minutes

1   **tablespoon olive oil**
½   **pound ground beef**
½   **pound sweet or hot Italian pork sausage**
½   **teaspoon dried Italian seasoning**
1   **pound pizza dough, at room temperature, or 1 batch Basic Pizza Dough (recipe page 243)**
2   **cups shredded mozzarella cheese**
½   **green pepper, seeded and thinly sliced**
1   **cup marinara sauce**
2   **tablespoons grated Parmesan cheese**

① Heat oven to 450°. Lightly coat a 10-inch deep dish pizza pan with olive oil.

② Heat oil in a large nonstick skillet over medium-high heat. Crumble in the ground beef and sausage; season with the Italian seasoning and cook for 4 to 5 minutes or until meat is no longer pink. Set aside.

③ On a lightly floured surface, roll out the dough to form a circle slightly larger than the pan. Place dough in prepared pan, pressing excess dough to the sides.

④ Layer 1½ cups mozzarella cheese, reserved meat mixture, pepper and sauce onto dough. Bake at 450° for 15 minutes. Top with the remaining ½ cup mozzarella and Parmesan cheese. Bake an additional 15 minutes. Remove from oven and allow to cool slightly.

⑤ Use a sharp knife to cut into 8 slices, then remove with pie server or spatula.

PER SLICE 350 calories; 19 g fat (7 g sat.); 19 g protein; 29 g carbohydrate; 1 g fiber; 768 mg sodium; 49 mg cholesterol

FOUR CHEESE WHITE PIZZA

MAKES 8 slices **PREP** 10 minutes
COOK 2½ minutes **BAKE** at 500° for 15 minutes

2   **tablespoons olive oil**
4   **cloves garlic, coarsely chopped**
1   **bag (6 ounces) baby spinach**
1   **pound pizza dough, at room temperature, or 1 batch Basic Pizza Dough (recipe page 243)**
1   **cup shredded mozzarella cheese**
½   **cup shredded provolone cheese**
½   **cup shredded Asiago cheese**
¾   **cup ricotta cheese**
2   **tablespoons toasted pine nuts**

① Heat oven to 500°. Coat a 14-inch pizza pan with nonstick cooking spray.

② Heat 1 tablespoon of the oil in a medium-size nonstick skillet over medium-high heat. Add garlic and cook 30 seconds. Gradually add spinach and cook until wilted, about 2 minutes. Remove from heat.

③ On a lightly floured surface, roll out dough into a 14-inch circle. Gently roll up onto a lightly floured rolling pin and unroll onto prepared pizza pan.

④ In a medium bowl, mix together mozzarella, provolone and Asiago cheeses. Sprinkle half of the cheese mixture over the dough. Evenly spoon the spinach over the cheese. Drizzle any oil and garlic from the skillet over the spinach. Sprinkle the remaining cheese mixture over the spinach. Dollop tablespoons of the ricotta cheese over top. Drizzle remaining tablespoon olive oil over the pizza. Bake at 500° for 14 to 15 minutes or until nicely browned on bottom. Remove from oven.

Macaroni and Cheese

The only thing better than one fantastic recipe? Five of them.

FOUR CHEESE WITH BACON

MAKES 10 cups (12 servings) **PREP** 10 minutes **COOK** 10 minutes **BAKE** at 350° for 20 minutes **BROIL** 3 minutes

- 1   box (1 pound) cavatappi
- 6   slices bacon, diced
- 1   tablespoon unsalted butter
- 3   tablespoons all-purpose flour
- 2   cups 2% milk
- ½   teaspoon onion flakes
- ¼   teaspoon salt
- ¼   teaspoon pepper
- ½   pound sharp cheddar cheese, shredded
- 1   cup shredded colby-Jack cheese (4 ounces)
- 1   cup shredded mozzarella cheese (4 ounces)
- 8   slices Kraft Deli Deluxe American cheese (6 ounces)

① Heat oven to 350°. Coat a 3-quart broiler-safe baking dish with nonstick cooking spray. Bring a large pot of lightly salted water to boiling.

② Cook cavatappi 8 minutes in boiling water, then drain. Meanwhile, in medium-size saucepan, cook bacon over medium heat until crisp, 6 minutes. Transfer to paper towels. Carefully pour off drippings, returning 2 tablespoons to pan. Add butter.

③ Whisk in flour until smooth. In a thin stream, whisk in milk. Stir in onion flakes, salt and pepper. Bring to a boil over medium-high heat, then reduce heat and simmer 2 minutes. In large bowl, toss together cheddar, colby-Jack and mozzarella.

④ Remove milk mixture from heat; whisk in American cheese and 1¼ cups of the cheddar mixture. Toss bacon pieces with remaining shredded cheese.

⑤ In pasta pot, combine cooked pasta and cheese sauce. Pour half into prepared dish. Sprinkle with a generous cup of the bacon-cheese mixture. Repeat layering.

⑥ Bake at 350° for 20 minutes. Increase oven temperature to broil and broil 3 minutes, until top is lightly browned. Cool slightly before serving.

PER SERVING 404 calories; 21 g fat (11 g sat.); 20 g protein; 33 g carbohydrate; 2 g fiber; 616 mg sodium; 63 mg cholesterol

CHEESEBURGER MAC & CHEESE

MAKES 8 servings **PREP** 10 minutes
COOK 10 minutes **BAKE** at 350° for 20 minutes
BROIL 2 minutes

1	box (1 pound) elbow macaroni or rotini
1	pound ground sirloin
½	teaspoon salt
¼	teaspoon black pepper
¼	cup ketchup
2	tablespoons yellow mustard
1	tablespoon unsalted butter
1	tablespoon all-purpose flour
1	can (12 ounces) evaporated milk
3	cups shredded cheddar cheese
2	medium tomatoes, cored and thinly sliced
2	tablespoons seasoned bread crumbs

① Heat oven to 350°. Coat a 2-quart oval baking dish with nonstick cooking spray.

② Bring a large pot of lightly salted water to boiling. Add pasta and cook 10 minutes according to package directions. Drain.

③ While pasta cooks, heat a large nonstick skillet over medium-high heat. Add sirloin, breaking apart with a wooden spoon. Cook 6 minutes, until no longer pink. Season with ¼ teaspoon of the salt and the pepper. Remove from heat and stir in ketchup and mustard. Transfer to a bowl.

④ Return skillet to medium heat and add butter. Once melted, whisk in flour, then add milk in a thin stream. Bring to a simmer and cook 2 minutes. Remove from heat and whisk in remaining ¼ teaspoon salt and 2 cups of the cheese. Stir in pasta. Pour into prepared dish. Top with meat mixture, remaining cheese, sliced tomatoes and bread crumbs. Spritz with nonstick cooking spray.

⑤ Bake at 350° for 20 minutes. Increase heat to broil and broil for 2 minutes.

PER SERVING 554 calories; 23 g fat (13 g sat.); 34 g protein; 53 g carbohydrate; 3 g fiber; 653 mg sodium; 92 mg cholesterol

CHICKEN TACO MAC

BROCCOLI
SHELLS & CHEESE

TOMATO BASIL RIGATONI

MAKES 6 servings **PREP** 10 minutes
LET STAND 5 minutes **COOK** 14 minutes

½   cup dry-packed sun-dried tomatoes
      (about 3 ounces)
1   box (16 ounces) rigatoni pasta
1½   cups milk
¼   cup tomato-basil-flavor cream
      cheese (such as Philadelphia)
4   ounces (4 to 6 slices) provolone
      cheese, chopped
1   cup shredded part-skim mozzarella
      cheese
2   teaspoons cornstarch mixed with
      1 tablespoon water
½   cup fresh basil leaves, cut into
      thin strips
      Freshly ground black pepper
      Pinch of salt
      Shredded Parmesan (optional)

① Heat a large pot of lightly salted water to boiling. Carefully scoop out 1 cup and pour over sun-dried tomatoes in a small heatproof bowl. Let stand 5 minutes.

② Meanwhile, cook rigatoni as per package directions, 14 minutes. Drain.

③ While pasta cooks, heat milk over medium heat until bubbly. Remove from heat and whisk in cream cheese, provolone

and mozzarella until melted (mixture will be a little stringy). Stir in cornstarch-water mixture and return pan to heat. Bring to a simmer, stirring until smooth.

④ Drain and finely chop sun-dried tomatoes. Stir into pasta, along with sauce and basil. Top with a little freshly ground black pepper, a pinch of salt, and Parmesan, if desired.

PER SERVING 493 calories; 14 g fat (8 g sat.); 23 g protein; 67 g carbohydrate; 3 g fiber; 637 mg sodium; 40 mg cholesterol

CHICKEN TACO MAC

MAKES 6 servings **PREP** 10 minutes
COOK 21 minutes

1   pound boneless chicken breast
      halves, cut in half horizontally if
      large
1   box (12 ounces) garden radiatore or
      rotini pasta (such as Ronzoni)
1   sweet red pepper, cored and diced
      (about 1 cup)
1   tablespoon unsalted butter
1   tablespoon all-purpose flour
1½   teaspoons chili powder
½   teaspoon salt
1¼   cups milk
8   ounces pepper-Jack cheese,
      shredded (about 2 cups)
3   scallions, trimmed and sliced
1½   cups crushed lime-flavor
      tortilla chips

① Bring a large pot of water just to boiling. Add chicken breast and reduce heat to a gentle simmer. Cook chicken in barely simmering water for 12 minutes. Remove to cutting board; return water to boiling; add a little salt to the water.

② Add pasta to boiling water and cook as per package directions, 9 minutes. Add pepper during last minute of cook time. Drain.

③ Meanwhile, melt butter in a medium saucepan over medium heat. Whisk in flour, chili powder and salt. Add milk in a thin stream, whisking constantly. Bring to a simmer over medium-high heat; simmer 2 minutes. Remove from heat and whisk in shredded cheese.

④ With 2 forks or your hands, shred chicken into bite-size pieces. In large bowl, combine pasta and pepper, chicken, scallions and cheese sauce. Stir until blended; top with crushed chips and serve.

PER SERVING 557 calories; 22 g fat (10 g sat.); 35 g protein; 56 g carbohydrate; 5 g fiber; 558 mg sodium; 94 mg cholesterol

BROCCOLI SHELLS & CHEESE

MAKES 6 servings **PREP** 10 minutes
COOK 7 minutes **LET STAND** 5 minutes

1   box (13.25 ounces) whole-wheat
      medium pasta shells
½   pound broccoli florets, cut into
      bite-size pieces
1   cup milk
12   slices Kraft Deli Deluxe American
      cheese (or ½ pound sliced American
      from deli counter)

① Heat a large pot of lightly salted water to boiling. Add pasta and cook 4 minutes. Stir in broccoli, return to a boil and cook for 3 minutes. Drain.

② Meanwhile, in a small saucepan, heat milk just until bubbles begin to burst at edge of pan. Add cheese slices one by one, whisking until smooth. Simmer 3 minutes.

③ Transfer pasta and broccoli to a large bowl. Add cheese sauce and stir to combine. Let stand 5 minutes before serving.

PER SERVING 447 calories; 20 g fat (11 g sat.); 22 g protein; 49 g carbohydrate; 6 g fiber; 952 mg sodium; 64 mg cholesterol

Cooking the pasta until tender—just past the al dente stage—is essential to making a great mac & cheese.

No Tricks. Just Treats

Cookies, brownies and a pie so good, it's scary.

**CARAMEL APPLES,
PAGE 255**

BLACK & WHITE
BROWNIES, PAGE 255

S'MORES BARS

MAKES 24 bars **PREP** 25 minutes **MICROWAVE** 1 minute **BAKE** at 350° for 33 minutes

CRUST

- 14 **whole graham cracker boards, crushed (2¼ cups crumbs)**
- 3 **tablespoons sugar**
- ¼ **teaspoon salt**
- 6 **tablespoons (¾ stick) unsalted butter, melted**

BROWNIE

- 6 **ounces bittersweet chocolate, chopped**
- ¾ **cup (1½ sticks) unsalted butter**
- 3 **eggs**
- 1¼ **cups sugar**
- 1 **cup all-purpose flour**
- 1 **teaspoon salt**
- 2 **teaspoons vanilla extract**

TOPPING

- 1 **jar (7.5 ounces) marshmallow cream (about 1½ cups)**
- 2 **tablespoons milk**
- 1 **cup mini chocolate Kisses**
- 3 **whole graham cracker boards, broken up**

① Heat oven to 350°.

② **Crust.** In a small bowl, combine the graham cracker crumbs, sugar, salt and melted butter until evenly moistened. Transfer crumb mixture to a 13 x 9 x 2-inch baking pan; press over bottom and up sides of pan. Refrigerate until chilled and set.

③ **Brownie.** Combine the bittersweet chocolate and butter in a microwave-safe glass bowl. Microwave chocolate mixture 1 minute. Stir the chocolate mixture until smooth. If necessary, microwave another 15 seconds to melt.

④ In a large bowl, beat together the eggs and sugar on medium-high speed until well blended. Reduce the speed to medium and gradually add the melted chocolate mixture; beat until smooth.

⑤ Stir the flour and salt into the egg mixture; stir in vanilla until smooth. Scrape the brownie mixture into the crust-lined baking pan; smooth the top level.

⑥ Bake at 350° for 30 minutes or until toothpick inserted in center tests clean.

⑦ **Topping.** Meanwhile, whisk together the marshmallow cream and the milk until well blended and smooth.

⑧ Pour the marshmallow topping mixture over the brownie layer. Tilt the pan to level the topping or spread it, covering the brownie layer completely.

⑨ Sprinkle the mini chocolate Kisses evenly over the marshmallow topping, then scatter the broken graham crackers over the top. Bake at 350° for 3 minutes or until the chocolate Kisses are glossy and the marshmallow topping is set. Let cool completely in the pan on a wire rack. Cut into 24 bars.

PER BAR 300 calories; 15 g fat (8 g sat.); 3 g protein; 40 g carbohydrate; 1 g fiber; 218 mg sodium; 51 mg cholesterol

SPIDERWEB COOKIES

MAKES 14 cookies **PREP** 20 minutes **BAKE** at 350° for 15 minutes per batch

COOKIES

2⅔ cups all-purpose flour
1   teaspoon baking soda
¾   teaspoon salt
½   teaspoon ground allspice
¾   cup canned solid-pack pumpkin
¼   cup milk
1   cup granulated sugar
¼   cup (½ stick) unsalted butter, softened
2   eggs

ICING

3   cups confectioners' sugar
3   tablespoons light corn syrup
½   teaspoon vanilla extract
3   tablespoons plus 4 teaspoons milk
2   tablespoons unsweetened cocoa powder

① Cookies. Heat oven to 350°. Coat 2 baking sheets with nonstick cooking spray. Combine flour, baking soda, salt and allspice. In small bowl, stir together the pumpkin and milk. In large bowl, beat sugar and butter until blended, 1 minute. Beat in eggs. On low speed, alternately beat in flour

mixture and pumpkin mixture, ending with flour mixture.

② Drop ¼-cupfuls of dough onto prepared sheets, spacing 2 inches apart. Spread slightly with spatula.

③ Bake 1 sheet at a time at 350° for 13 to 15 minutes, until toothpick inserted in center tests clean. Remove to rack to cool.

④ Icing. Blend confectioners' sugar, corn syrup, vanilla and 3 tablespoons plus 2 teaspoons milk until smooth. Remove ⅓ cup icing to small bowl and stir in cocoa and remaining 2 teaspoons milk. Transfer chocolate icing to plastic bag; snip off corner.

⑤ Turn cookies flat side up. Spread white icing over one cookie. Beginning in center, pipe a spiral of chocolate icing. Starting in center, drag a knife through spiral for spiderweb pattern. Repeat with all cookies. Let stand until set.

PER COOKIE 273 calories; 5 g fat (3 g sat.); 4 g protein; 57 g carbohydrate; 1 g fiber; 230 mg sodium; 40 mg cholesterol

CHOCOLATE PEANUT BUTTER PIE

MAKES 10 servings **PREP** 20 minutes
BAKE at 375° for 40 minutes **CHILL** 2 hours

1   refrigerated rolled piecrust (from 15-ounce package)
3   eggs
1   cup light corn syrup
½   cup sugar
⅓   cup chunky peanut butter
½   teaspoon vanilla extract
½   cup semisweet chocolate chips, plus additional for garnish (optional)
    Frozen whipped topping (such as Cool Whip), thawed (optional)
    Chopped peanuts (optional)

① Heat oven to 375°. Fit piecrust into a 9-inch pie plate. Flute if desired. Refrigerate while preparing filling.

② In a small bowl, lightly beat eggs with a fork. Stir in corn syrup, sugar, peanut butter and vanilla extract; mix until completely blended.

③ Remove piecrust from refrigerator and sprinkle with chocolate chips, then pour peanut butter mixture over top. Cover edges of pie with aluminum foil.

④ Bake pie at 375° for 20 minutes; remove foil. Bake an additional 15 to 20 minutes more or until knife inserted near center comes out clean. Cover and chill for 2 hours. Garnish with whipped topping, remaining chocolate chips and chopped peanuts, if desired.

PER SLICE 360 calories; 15 g fat (3 g sat.); 6 g protein; 53 g carbohydrate; 1 g fiber; 143 mg sodium; 64 mg cholesterol

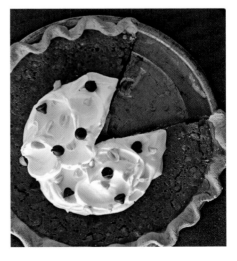

PUMPKIN BUNDT CAKE

MAKES 16 slices **PREP** 10 minutes **BAKE** at 350° for 57 minutes

CAKE

3   cups cake flour (not self-rising)
3   teaspoons baking powder
2½ teaspoons pumpkin pie spice
1   cup (2 sticks) unsalted butter, softened
1½ cups granulated sugar
1¼ cups solid-pack pumpkin

PUREE

3   eggs
1   teaspoon vanilla extract
1   cup milk

GLAZE

4   ounces reduced-fat cream cheese
½   cup sifted confectioners' sugar
4   tablespoons milk
1   teaspoon grated lemon zest
¼   teaspoon fresh lemon juice
¼   teaspoon vanilla extract

① Cake. Heat oven to 350°. Lightly coat 12-cup Bundt pan with nonstick cooking spray.

② In a medium-size bowl, stir together flour, baking powder and pumpkin pie spice.

③ Beat together the butter and sugar in a large bowl until light and fluffy. Beat in the pumpkin, eggs and vanilla.

④ Into pumpkin mixture, alternately beat in flour mixture and milk. Pour into prepared pan.

⑤ Bake at 350° for 57 minutes or until toothpick inserted in the center of the cake tests clean. Cool the cake in the pan on a wire rack for 10 minutes. Remove cake to wire rack to cool completely.

⑥ Glaze. Beat together the cream cheese, confectioners' sugar, milk, lemon zest, lemon juice and vanilla in a medium bowl until well blended and a good glazing consistency. Pour the glaze over top of the cake, letting it drip down the sides.

PER SLICE 312 calories; 15 g fat (9 g sat.); 5 g protein; 41 g carbohydrate; 1 g fiber; 129 mg sodium; 77 mg cholesterol

CARAMEL APPLES

MAKES 12 apples **PREP** 15 minutes
COOK 15 minutes **MICROWAVE** 1 minute
CHILL 30 minutes

- 12 **small McIntosh apples (about 3 pounds)**
- 12 **wooden ice cream sticks**
- 2 **packages (14 ounces each) soft caramels**
- ¼ **cup shelled pistachios, coarsely chopped; or ¼ cup peanuts, coarsely chopped; or 3 tablespoons chocolate sprinkles; or 3 tablespoons vanilla sprinkles**
- 1 **ounce semisweet chocolate, broken up**
- ½ **teaspoon solid vegetable shortening**

① Line a large baking sheet with nonstick foil. Coat foil with nonstick cooking spray.

② Remove stems from apples; wash and dry apples. Insert wooden stick into stem end of each apple.

③ Place unwrapped caramels in medium-size saucepan. Add 3 tablespoons water; heat over medium-low heat, stirring occasionally, until caramels are melted and smooth.

④ Working quickly with one apple at a time, and keeping caramel over low heat, dip the apple into the caramel, turning to

coat the apple completely (tilt pot slightly for easier dipping). Remove apple from caramel, letting excess caramel drip back into saucepan. Scrape bottom of apple on edge of pan, and transfer to prepared baking sheet. Repeat with remaining apples.

⑤ Press pistachios, peanuts or sprinkles onto bottom of apples and 1 inch up the sides. Refrigerate for 10 minutes or until caramel is cool.

⑥ Meanwhile, microwave chocolate and shortening in a small microwave-safe bowl for 1 minute. Stir until smooth. Transfer to a small plastic bag; snip off corner. Drizzle over apples. Refrigerate until hardened, about 20 minutes. Store in refrigerator.

PER APPLE 378 calories; 9 g fat (5 g sat.); 5 g protein; 74 g carbohydrate; 4 g fiber; 182 mg sodium; 5 mg cholesterol

BLACK & WHITE BROWNIES

MAKES 16 brownies **PREP** 25 minutes
MICROWAVE 1 minute **BAKE** at 350° for 30 minutes

BROWNIE
- 1¾ **cups all-purpose flour**
- ¾ **teaspoon baking powder**

- ¾ **teaspoon salt**
- ½ **cup (1 stick) unsalted butter**
- 4 **ounces unsweetened chocolate, chopped**
- 1½ **cups sugar**
- 4 **eggs**
- 1 **teaspoon vanilla extract**

CHEESECAKE DIMPLES
- 6 **ounces cream cheese, softened**
- ⅓ **cup all-purpose flour**
- ½ **cup sugar**
- ½ **teaspoon vanilla extract**
- 2 **tablespoons milk**

① Heat oven to 350°. Line a 13 x 9 x 2-inch baking pan with nonstick aluminum foil.

② **Brownie.** Whisk together flour, baking powder and salt until blended.

③ In large microwave-safe bowl, combine butter and chocolate. Microwave for 1 minute; stir until smooth.

④ Stir sugar into chocolate mixture. Add eggs and vanilla; stir until smooth. Stir in flour mixture until smooth. Spoon into prepared pan; spread and level top.

⑤ **Cheesecake Dimples.** Beat cream cheese on medium speed until smooth. On low speed, beat in flour, sugar and vanilla until blended. Add milk; beat until smooth.

⑥ With a tablespoon, make a depression in top of brownie batter. With another tablespoon, drop a dollop of cream cheese mixture into the dimple. Continue to make and fill dimples over the top in an uneven pattern.

⑦ Bake at 350° for 30 minutes or until toothpick inserted in center tests clean. Remove to wire rack for 15 minutes. Using foil, remove brownie from pan to rack. Let cool completely. Cut into 16 squares.

PER BROWNIE 302 calories; 15 g fat (9 g sat.); 5 g protein; 40 g carbohydrate; 2 g fiber; 177 mg sodium; 81 mg cholesterol

Comfort Desserts

A pie, crumble, tart and more—take your pick from our favorite apple treats.

CARAMEL-SPICED
APPLES, PAGE 261

CRANBERRY-APPLE CRISP,
PAGE 261

CLASSIC APPLE PIE

MAKES 10 servings **PREP** 30 minutes **COOK** 10 minutes **BAKE** at 400° for 20 minutes, then at 350° for 25 minutes

- 1 **15-ounce package rolled refrigerated piecrust (2 crusts)**
- ½ **cup plus 1 teaspoon granulated sugar**
- ½ **cup packed brown sugar**
- 3 **tablespoons cornstarch**
- ½ **teaspoon ground cinnamon**
- ¼ **teaspoon salt**
   Pinch ground cloves
- 2 **pounds Granny Smith apples, peeled and cored**
- 2 **pounds Fuji apples, peeled and cored**
- 2 **tablespoons unsalted butter**
- 2 **tablespoons lemon juice**
- 1 **large egg, beaten with 1 tablespoon water**

① Heat oven to 400°. Unroll 1 piecrust onto a work surface. Roll out to 12-inch circle. Fit into bottom and up sides of a 9-inch deep-dish pie plate. Prick bottom of crust with a fork; refrigerate.

② In small bowl, blend ½ cup of the granulated sugar, the brown sugar, cornstarch, cinnamon, salt and cloves.

③ Cut apples into ½-inch pieces. Melt butter in a large skillet over medium heat. Add apples, lemon juice and sugar mixture. Cook 10 minutes, stirring, until pan juices thicken. Set aside to cool.

④ Pour cooled apple mixture into crust. Unroll second crust and roll out to 12-inch circle. Cut vent hole in center of dough. Transfer to pie, centering over filling. Crimp edge together.

⑤ Brush pie with egg mixture; sprinkle with remaining teaspoon granulated sugar. Bake at 400° for 20 minutes, then at 350° for 25 minutes. Cover pie with foil if it browns too quickly. Cool at least 1 hour before slicing and serving.

PER SERVING 395 calories; 14 g fat (6 g sat.); 2 g protein; 68 g carbohydrate; 4 g fiber; 228 mg sodium; 25 mg cholesterol

GINGER-APPLE TART

MAKES 12 servings **PREP** 25 minutes
BAKE at 400° for 25 minutes

1   egg, lightly beaten
½   17.3-ounce package frozen puff pastry sheets (1 sheet), thawed
2   tablespoons coarse or granulated sugar
2   tablespoons finely chopped crystallized ginger
2   small baking apples, cored, halved and thinly sliced

(1) Heat oven to 400°. In a small bowl, combine egg and 1 tablespoon water; set aside. Line a large baking sheet with parchment paper; set aside. Unfold pastry onto a lightly floured surface. Roll into a 12-inch square. Using a pizza cutter, cut a ½-inch strip from each side of the square. Brush edges of pastry square with egg wash. Transfer pastry to prepared baking sheet. Attach a pastry strip to each side of square to form an edge; brush with egg mixture. Prick pastry with a fork.

(2) In small bowl, stir together sugar and ginger. Arrange apple slices over pastry, overlapping. Sprinkle with sugar mixture.

(3) Bake at 400° for 20 to 25 minutes or until pastry is deep golden brown and crisp. Cool on baking sheet on a wire rack.

PER SERVING 120 calories; 7 g fat (0 g sat.); 1 g protein; 14 g carbohydrate; 1 g fiber; 83 mg sodium; 18 mg cholesterol

SINGLE-CRUST APPLE BAKE

MAKES 6 servings **PREP** 30 minutes **BAKE** at 400° for 20 minutes

½   15-ounce package rolled refrigerated piecrust (1 crust)
6   small Jonathan apples (2½ to 3 ounces each), cored and quartered
2   tablespoons lemon juice
2   tablespoons honey
4   teaspoons finely chopped crystallized ginger
    Coarsely ground black pepper
2   tablespoons milk
1   tablespoon sugar
    Whipped cream (optional)

(1) Let piecrust stand at room temperature 15 minutes. Heat oven to 400°. Arrange apple quarters in six 6-ounce custard cups.

In a small bowl, stir together lemon juice, honey and ginger. Drizzle over apples. Sprinkle lightly with coarsely ground pepper; set aside.

(2) Unroll piecrust. Brush lightly with milk. Sprinkle sugar evenly over piecrust. Cut into 12 wedges. Drape 2 pastry wedges over apples in each cup, allowing corners to hang over edge of cup. Place cups in a 15 x 10 x 1-inch baking pan. Bake for 20 minutes or until crust is golden brown. Serve warm with whipped cream, if desired.

PER SERVING 285 calories; 10 g fat (4 g sat.); 1 g protein; 51 g carbohydrate; 5 g fiber; 135 mg sodium; 7 mg cholesterol

CARAMELIZED APPLE CAKE

CARAMEL-SPICED APPLES

MAKES 10 servings **PREP** 20 minutes
SLOW COOK 3 hours on LOW

1 teaspoon ground cinnamon
⅛ teaspoon ground cloves
5 medium red-skinned cooking apples (such as Rome or Jonathan), cored and halved
½ cup apple juice or apple cider
1 tablespoon lemon juice
⅔ cup sugar-free caramel ice cream topping
½ cup toasted, chopped pecans

① In small bowl, combine cinnamon and cloves. Place half of the apple halves in a 4-quart slow cooker. Sprinkle evenly with half of the cinnamon mixture. Add remaining apples and sprinkle with remaining cinnamon mixture. Pour apple juice and lemon juice over apples. Stir to coat apples evenly.

② Cover and cook on LOW for 2½ to 3 hours, stirring gently halfway through cooking time. Spoon apples and cooking liquid into individual serving dishes. Drizzle with caramel topping and sprinkle with pecans.

PER SERVING 128 calories; 4 g fat (0 g sat.); 1 g protein; 25 g carbohydrate; 2 g fiber; 33 mg sodium; 0 mg cholesterol

CRANBERRY-APPLE CRISP

MAKES 8 servings **PREP** 15 minutes
BAKE at 350° for 45 minutes

3 Granny Smith apples (unpeeled), cored and cut into 1-inch pieces (about 4 cups)
2 cups whole fresh cranberries
¾ cup sugar
1½ cups old-fashioned oats (not quick-cook)
½ cup packed light-brown sugar
⅓ cup all-purpose flour
½ cup chopped pecans
½ cup (1 stick) unsalted butter, melted
Vanilla ice cream (optional)

① Heat oven to 350°. Butter a 2-quart baking dish.

② In a large bowl, mix together apples, cranberries and sugar. Spoon into prepared baking dish.

③ In the same bowl, mix together oats, brown sugar, flour and pecans. Stir in melted butter.

④ Sprinkle oatmeal mixture evenly over the top of the apples. Bake at 350° for 45 minutes, until bubbly and apples are tender. Serve warm or cold with a scoop of ice cream, if desired.

PER SERVING 389 calories; 18 g fat (8 g sat.); 4 g protein; 58 g carbohydrate; 5 g fiber; 10 mg sodium; 30 mg cholesterol

CARAMELIZED APPLE CAKE

MAKES 10 servings **PREP** 10 minutes
COOK 12 minutes **BAKE** at 375° for 30 minutes

1½ cups flour
1½ teaspoons baking powder
½ teaspoon salt
½ cup (1 stick) plus 5 tablespoons unsalted butter, softened
⅔ cup granulated sugar
2 eggs
1 teaspoon vanilla extract
½ cup sour cream
½ cup packed dark-brown sugar
2 large Granny Smith apples, peeled, cored, cut into ¼-inch slices

① Heat oven to 375°.

② Mix flour, baking powder and salt in a medium bowl; set aside. Using an electric mixer on high speed, beat ½ cup of the butter in a large bowl for 1 minute or until creamy. Add granulated sugar and continue to beat until light and fluffy.

③ Add eggs and vanilla, and beat until blended. Reduce speed to low. Gradually blend in flour mixture, then sour cream.

④ Melt remaining 5 tablespoons butter in an ovenproof 10-inch nonstick skillet. Add brown sugar; stir 2 minutes.

⑤ Add apple slices to the pan and reduce heat to medium-low. Cook for about 10 minutes or until tender. Let cool for 5 minutes.

⑥ Spoon batter over apples and spread to edge of pan. Bake at 375° for 30 minutes or until golden brown. Cool on rack for 20 minutes. Run knife around edge. Carefully invert onto a plate.

PER SERVING 345 calories; 19 g fat (11 g sat.); 4 g protein; 42 g carbohydrate; 1 g fiber; 119 mg sodium; 88 mg cholesterol

Slow Cooker Suppers

Here's chili 5 ways—tuck into a bowl of this hearty and heartwarming dish.

ALL-AMERICAN CHILI

MAKES 6 servings **PREP** 10 minutes
SLOW COOK 4 hours on HIGH or 6 hours on LOW

- 1½ pounds lean ground beef
- 2 onions, chopped
- 1 yellow bell pepper, seeded and chopped
- 2 garlic cloves, minced
- 2 cans (15.5 ounces each) kidney beans, rinsed and drained
- 1 can (14.5 ounces) diced tomatoes, drained
- 1 can (8 ounces) no-salt-added tomato sauce
- 1 cup low-sodium chicken broth
- 3 tablespoons chili powder
- 1 teaspoon ground cumin
- 1 teaspoon dried oregano
- ½ teaspoon salt
- 1 box (8.5 ounces) cornbread mix, prepared according to package directions (optional)

① Combine beef, onions, pepper, garlic, beans, tomatoes, tomato sauce, broth, 2 tablespoons of the chili powder, and ½ teaspoon *each* of the cumin and the oregano in slow cooker. Cover and cook on HIGH for 4 hours or LOW for 6 hours.

② Remove cover and stir in remaining 1 tablespoon chili powder, ½ teaspoon each cumin and oregano, and salt. Serve with corn bread, if desired.

PER SERVING 353 calories; 7 g fat (3 g sat.); 35 g protein; 37 g carbohydrate; 13 g fiber; 710 mg sodium; 71 mg cholesterol

Whether you like your chili with beans or without, meaty or meatless, red or white, the spicy smell of this all-American stew bubbling away in the slow cooker is sure to make mouths water.

CHILI CON CARNE

MAKES 6 servings **PREP** 10 minutes **COOK** 11 minutes
SLOW COOK 4 hours on HIGH or 6 hours on LOW

- 1 tablespoon plus 1 teaspoon olive oil
- 2 pounds boneless beef round steak, trimmed and cut into ½-inch cubes
- 3 cloves garlic, minced
- 1 large onion, finely chopped
- 3 tablespoons plus 1 teaspoon chili powder
- 3½ teaspoons ground cumin
- 1 teaspoon salt
- ½ teaspoon cayenne pepper
- 1 package (10 ounces) frozen corn
- 3 tablespoons finely ground cornmeal
   Sour cream, sliced avocado and cilantro for garnish (optional)

① Heat 1 tablespoon of the oil in a large nonstick skillet over medium-high heat. Add beef to skillet and cook, stirring occasionally, for 8 minutes, draining any accumulated fat. Remove beef to slow cooker; reduce heat to medium. Add 1 teaspoon oil to skillet; add garlic and onion and cook, stirring, for 2 minutes. Stir in 3 tablespoons chili powder, 2 teaspoons cumin, ½ teaspoon salt and ¼ teaspoon cayenne; cook 1 minute, stirring constantly.

② Scrape skillet contents into slow cooker and add corn and 3¾ cups water (enough to cover by 1 inch). Cover and cook on HIGH for 4 hours or on LOW for 6 hours.

③ When there is 1 hour cook time remaining, stir together cornmeal and 3 tablespoons water. Stir in cornmeal paste, remaining 1 teaspoon chili powder, 1½ teaspoons cumin, ½ teaspoon salt and ¼ teaspoon cayenne; cook for 1 more hour or until thickened. Garnish with sour cream, avocado and cilantro, if desired.

PER SERVING 374 calories; 17 g fat (5 g sat.); 36 g protein; 21 g carbohydrate; 4 g fiber; 536 mg sodium; 60 mg cholesterol

MEDITERRANEAN ROASTED VEGETABLE & CHICKEN CHILI

MAKES 6 servings **PREP** 10 minutes **SLOW COOK** 4 hours 15 minutes on HIGH or 6 hours 15 minutes on LOW **ROAST** at 425° for 35 minutes

- 2 **pounds bone-in chicken breasts, skin removed**
- 2 **cans (15.5 ounces each) Great Northern beans, drained and rinsed**
- 1 **can (14.5 ounces) diced tomatoes, drained**
- 3 **tablespoons Greek seasoning**
- 2 **teaspoons paprika**
- 1 **cup low-sodium chicken broth**
- 2 **zucchini, cut into ½-inch pieces**
- 1 **red onion, thinly sliced**
- 1 **fennel bulb, trimmed, cored and sliced**
- 3 **cloves garlic, minced**
- 2 **tablespoons olive oil**

- 2 **tablespoons lemon juice**
- 1 **tablespoon chopped fresh oregano**
- 1 **teaspoon lemon zest**
- ¼ **teaspoon salt**
- ⅓ **cup crumbled feta cheese (optional)**

① Combine chicken, beans, tomatoes, 2 tablespoons of the Greek seasoning and 1 teaspoon of the paprika in slow cooker; add broth and 1 cup water. Cover; cook on HIGH for 4 hours or LOW for 6 hours.

② When there is 1 hour cook time remaining, heat oven to 425°. In a large roasting pan, toss together 2 teaspoons of the Greek seasoning, 1 teaspoon paprika, zucchini, onion, fennel, garlic and olive oil. Roast at 425° for 35 minutes, stirring twice. Stir in lemon juice, oregano and zest.

③ Remove chicken; shred into bite-size pieces. Discard bones and stir chicken back into slow cooker. Stir in vegetables, remaining 1 teaspoon Greek seasoning and salt; cook an additional 15 minutes. Sprinkle with feta cheese, if desired.

PER SERVING 300 calories; 6 g fat (1 g sat.); 37 g protein; 29 g carbohydrate; 9 g fiber; 619 mg sodium; 71 mg cholesterol

3-BEAN CHILI

MAKES 8 servings **SOAK** overnight **PREP** 10 minutes **SLOW COOK** 7½ hours on LOW

- 1 **cup (about 6 ounces) dried black beans, picked over**
- 1 **cup (about 6 ounces) dried pinto beans, picked over**
- 6 **cups (about 6 ounces) dried kidney beans, picked over**
- 1 **bay leaf**
- 2 **tablespoons ancho chile powder**
- 1 **tablespoon ground cumin**
- 1 **teaspoon oregano**
- 1 **medium onion, chopped**
- 1 **medium green pepper, seeded and chopped**
- 3 **garlic cloves, minced**
- 1 **can (14.5 ounces) diced tomatoes, drained**
- 1 **package (12 ounces) soy crumbles (such as Smart Ground)**
- ¼ **cup ketchup**
- ¼ **cup cornmeal**
- 1 **teaspoon salt**
- ½ **teaspoon black pepper**

Monterey Jack cheese and cilantro for garnish (optional)

① Soak beans overnight. Drain beans and place in slow cooker bowl. Add the bay leaf and 2 teaspoons chile powder and cover with 5 cups water. Cover; cook on LOW for 7 hours or until beans are tender.

② Stir in remaining 1 tablespoon plus 1 teaspoon chile powder, cumin, oregano, onion, green pepper, garlic, tomatoes, soy crumbles, ketchup, cornmeal, salt and pepper; cook an additional 30 minutes.

③ Top with cheese and cilantro, if desired.

PER SERVING 349 calories; 2 g fat (0 g sat.); 26 g protein; 57 g carbohydrate; 18 g fiber; 902 mg sodium; 0 mg cholesterol

WHITE TURKEY CHILI

MAKES 6 servings **PREP** 10 minutes
SLOW COOK 4 hours on HIGH or 6 hours on LOW

- 2 **cans (15.5 ounces each) small white beans, drained and rinsed**
- 1 **package (20.8 ounces) ground turkey breast**
- 2 **jalapeño peppers, seeded and minced**
- 2 **green peppers, seeded and chopped**
- 1 **poblano pepper, seeded and chopped**
- 1 **large onion, chopped**
- 4 **garlic cloves, minced**
- 2½ **teaspoons ground cumin**
- ¾ **teaspoon ground coriander**
- 2 **cups low-sodium chicken broth**
- 3 **tablespoons fresh lime juice**
- ¼ **cup chopped cilantro**
- ½ **teaspoon salt**
- 4 **scallions, thinly sliced**

① Set aside 1 cup of the beans. Combine remaining beans, turkey, jalapeños, green peppers, poblano, onion, garlic, 2 teaspoons cumin, ½ teaspoon coriander and broth in slow cooker. Cover and cook on HIGH for 4 hours or LOW for 6 hours, stirring once halfway through.

② Mash reserved beans. Stir in mashed beans, ½ teaspoon cumin, ¼ teaspoon coriander, lime juice, cilantro and salt. Sprinkle with scallions and serve immediately.

PER SERVING 241 calories; 2 g fat (0 g sat.); 35 g protein; 31 g carbohydrate; 9 g fiber; 581 mg sodium; 41 mg cholesterol

THE OFFICIAL FEASTING SEASON BEGINS.
ASSEMBLE A THANKSGIVING MENU THAT
SUITS YOUR STYLE WITH FRESH RECIPES
FOR TURKEY AND ALL THE FIXINGS.

NOVEMBER

281

287

293

The Ultimate Thanksgiving Feast

The classics, plus dozens of new ideas that bring a little something extra to the table.

TURKEY WITH PAN GRAVY

→ CLASSIC
TURKEY WITH PAN GRAVY

MAKES 12 servings **PREP** 15 minutes
ROAST at 350° for 3½ to 4 hours
COOK 3 minutes

① Position rack in lowest third of oven. Heat to 350°. Prep a 14-pound turkey per "Talking Turkey." Rub with 1 tbsp. vegetable oil.

② Spread 4 cups onions, coarsely chopped, in a large roasting pan. Place turkey on top.

③ Roast at 350° for 30 minutes. Add 1 cup chicken broth. Roast 3 to 3½ hours. Tent with foil if browning too quickly. Remove to platter.

④ **Gravy.** Strain drippings into bowl. Skim fat. Melt 2 tbsp. butter in saucepan. Stir in ¼ cup flour. Whisk in 2 cups strained pan juices and 2 cups chicken broth. Add ½ cup dry white wine and ½ tsp. salt; simmer, stirring, until thickened, 2 to 3 minutes.

→ HEALTHY
HERITAGE TURKEY WITH CRAN-ORANGE GLAZE

MAKES 12 servings **PREP** 15 minutes
ROAST at 350° for 2¾ to 3 hours

① Heat oven to 350°. Prep a 12- to 13-pound heritage turkey (see Note) per "Talking Turkey." Season all over and inside cavity with 1 tsp. each salt and pepper. Stuff with 1 each quartered onion and orange, 4 sprigs each fresh sage and thyme.

② Roast on a rack in a roasting pan at 350° for 2¾ to 3 hours.

③ Melt 1 can (8 ounces) jellied cranberry sauce, ¼ cup orange marmalade, 2 tbsp. honey, 1 tbsp. lemon juice and ½ tsp. fresh thyme in a pan. Brush on turkey during last hour of cooking.

Note: Heritage turkeys are purebred, pasture-raised and free-range (which makes them more flavorful).

→ TEX-MEX
SPICE-RUB TURKEY

MAKES 12 servings **PREP** 15 minutes
ROAST at 350° for 2¾ hours **COOK** 3 minutes

① Heat oven to 350°. Rub ¼ cup taco seasoning (from 1.25-oz. packet) under and over skin of 13.5-pound turkey.

② Peel and quarter 1 large onion. Place 2 quarters in cavity and 2 under loose flap of skin near wings. Tie legs, then transfer turkey to a rack in a large roasting pan. Pour in ½ cup water. Bake at 350° for 2¾ hours.

③ **Gravy.** Remove turkey from pan to platter. Pour pan juices into fat separator. Skim off fat, returning 3 tbsp. to pan. Over medium heat, whisk in 3 tbsp. flour. Carefully whisk in ½ cup strained pan juices and 1½ cups low-sodium chicken broth. Cook 3 minutes, until thickened.

→ INDULGENT
DEEP-FRIED TURKEY

MAKES 8 servings **PREP** 15 minutes
COOK 40 minutes

① Prep a 10-pound turkey. Dry well. Coat turkey all over with 2 tbsp. turkey rub (such as McCormick). Allow to sit at room temperature for about 45 minutes. Place turkey in fry basket.

② Heat 3 to 5 gallons peanut oil in a turkey fryer or a very large stockpot to 350°. Carefully lower fry basket into oil, making sure turkey is fully submerged. Fry for 40 minutes or 4 minutes per pound.

③ Remove turkey from oil; let rest for 10 minutes on paper towels.

→ SPEEDY
LEMONY TURKEY BREAST & GRAVY

MAKES 8 servings **PREP** 15 minutes
ROAST at 425° for 30 minutes, then 325° for 50 minutes **COOK** 24 minutes

① Heat oven to 425°. Blend 3 tbsp. butter, 3 tsp. lemon zest, 2 tsp. dried thyme, ¾ tsp. salt and ¼ tsp. black pepper. Rub half under skin of a 5-pound bone-in turkey breast and other half on outside of skin.

② Place turkey on rack in roasting pan and pour in 1 cup water.

③ Roast turkey at 425° for 30 minutes. Reduce oven to 325°; roast 50 minutes or until breast registers 160°on an instant-read thermometer. Rest 20 minutes.

④ Pulse 1 each carrot, celery stalk and small onion, halved, in a food processor until finely chopped.

⑤ Melt 4 tbsp. unsalted butter over medium-high heat. Add veggies; cook 7 minutes. Add ¼ cup flour; cook, stirring, 4 minutes. Lower heat to medium. Whisk in 3 cups low-sodium chicken broth, 1 tbsp. lemon juice, ½ tsp. salt and ⅛ tsp. pepper; simmer for 13 minutes; strain well.

PER SERVING OF ANY VARIETY WITH SKIN (APPROX.) 493 calories; 16 g fat (5 g sat.); 78 g protein; 4 g carbohydrate; 0 g fiber; 347 mg sodium; 326 mg cholesterol

TALKING TURKEY

Plan on about 1 pound per person. If frozen, thaw in its packaging on a tray in the refrigerator; it will take 24 hours for each 4 pounds (figure 3 to 4 days for a 15-pound bird). When thawed, unwrap and remove giblets and neck; rinse inside and out with cold water. Dry turkey, including both cavities. Tuck wings under, if desired. Season as recipe recommends. For roasting: Roast at 350° for 12 to 15 minutes per pound or until instant-read thermometer inserted in thickest part of the thigh registers 180°, 160° in the breast. Transfer to platter; let rest 20 minutes before carving.

FRESH SAGE STUFFING

→ CLASSIC
FRESH SAGE STUFFING

MAKES 8 servings **PREP** 15 minutes
COOK 5 minutes **BAKE** at 350° for 45 minutes

① Heat oven to 350°. Coat a 13 x 9 x 2-inch baking dish with nonstick spray.

② Heat 2 tbsp. butter in a large skillet. Add 1½ cups each finely chopped onion and celery; cook until softened, 5 minutes.

③ Mix 8 cups toasted bread cubes, 3 tbsp. chopped sage, ½ cup chopped parsley, 1 tsp. salt and ½ tsp. pepper in large bowl. Add onion mixture and 6 tbsp. melted butter. Add ½ to 1 cup chicken broth, a little at a time, tossing. Add only enough to moisten; too much will make stuffing mushy.

④ Bake at 350° in prepared dish, covered, 30 minutes. Uncover. Bake for 15 minutes or until browned.

PER SERVING 243 calories; 13 g fat (7 g sat.); 5 g protein; 27 g carbohydrate; 2 g fiber; 649 mg sodium; 31 mg cholesterol

→ HEALTHY
BULGUR STUFFING

MAKES 10 servings **PREP** 15 minutes
COOK 21 minutes **MICROWAVE** 2 minutes

① Heat 1 tbsp. oil in large pot. Add 3 cups chopped onion, 1 cup chopped celery and 2 cloves chopped garlic; cook over medium heat 6 minutes, stirring.

② Add 2 cups bulgur, 3 cups low-sodium chicken broth, ½ tsp. poultry seasoning and ¼ tsp. salt; cover. Simmer 15 minutes, until bulgur is tender.

③ In small bowl, microwave ⅔ cup dried cranberries and ¼ cup orange juice, covered, 2 minutes. Stir into bulgur with ⅔ cup chopped toasted walnuts, ¼ cup chopped parsley and ¼ tsp. pepper.

PER SERVING 215 calories; 7 g fat (1 g sat.); 6 g protein; 35 g carbohydrate; 7 fiber; 256 mg sodium; 2 mg cholesterol

→ TEX-MEX
ZESTY CORNBREAD STUFFING

MAKES 10 servings **PREP** 15 minutes
BAKE at 400° for 20 minutes; 350° for 1 hour

① Heat oven to 400°. Prepare 2 boxes (8.5 oz. each) cornbread mix (such as Jiffy) per package directions.

② Bake at 400° for 20 minutes or until toothpick inserted in center comes out clean.

③ Cool completely on wire rack.

④ Reduce oven heat to 350°. Coat a 2-quart baking dish with nonstick cooking spray.

⑤ Cut cornbread into ½-inch cubes (10 cups). Place in bowl with 1 can (11 oz.) Mexicorn, drained; 6 thinly sliced scallions; 2 cups low-sodium chicken broth; 1 cup shredded pepper Jack cheese; 1 tbsp. dried oregano; and ¾ tsp. cumin; stir until blended.

⑥ Pour mixture into dish; bake at 350° for 50 minutes. Top with ¼ cup shredded pepper Jack cheese; bake 10 minutes.

PER SERVING 314 calories; 12 g fat (6 g sat.); 9 g protein; 43 g carbohydrate; 1 g fiber; 735 mg sodium; 61 mg cholesterol

→ INDULGENT
SAUSAGE, APPLE & LEEK STUFFING

MAKES 8 servings **PREP** 15 minutes
COOK 22 minutes **BAKE** at 350° for 50 minutes

① Heat oven to 350°. Coat a 13 x 9 x 2-inch baking pan with nonstick spray.

② Place a large nonstick skillet over medium-high heat. Remove casings from ¾ pound sausage and crumble into skillet. Cook 7 minutes or until no longer pink. Remove sausage to a large bowl with a slotted spoon.

③ Add 2 tbsp. unsalted butter to skillet. Add 3 leeks, trimmed, washed and cut into ½-inch half-moons; 2 celery stalks, finely chopped; and ¼ tsp. each salt and black pepper. Cover. Cook, stirring occasionally, for about 10 minutes or until softened.

④ Stir in 2 Granny Smith apples, cored, peeled and cut into ½-inch pieces; ½ tsp. dried thyme; and ¼ tsp. each salt and pepper; cook 5 minutes, stirring occasionally.

⑤ Add to sausage. Stir in 8 cups cubed stale white bread, 1½ cups low-sodium chicken broth, ½ cup half-and-half and ¼ cup chopped parsley.

⑥ Pour mixture into prepared pan and bake at 350° for 50 minutes or until lightly browned on top.

PER SERVING 423 calories; 20 g fat (8 g sat.); 13 g protein; 48 g carbohydrate; 3 g fiber; 1,081 mg sodium; 48 mg cholesterol

→ SPEEDY
CARROT & BACON STUFFING

MAKES 8 servings **PREP** 15 minutes
COOK 5 minutes

① Bring 2 cups water, ½ cup golden raisins and 2 tbsp. unsalted butter to a boil.

② Stir in 4 cups herb stuffing mix and 1 cup grated carrot; cover, remove from heat and let sit 5 minutes. Remove cover and stir in 8 slices cooked bacon, crumbled; serve immediately.

PER SERVING 279 calories; 14 g fat (5 g sat.); 6 g protein; 32 g carbohydrate; 3 g fiber; 600 mg sodium; 23 mg cholesterol

There's something here for everyone who thinks the stuffing is the best part of the Thanksgiving spread—a classic, as well as versions that are zippy, fast, healthy and indulgent.

GREEN BEAN BAKE

→ CLASSIC
GREEN BEAN BAKE

MAKES 6 servings **PREP** 15 minutes
BAKE at 350° for 30 minutes

① Heat oven to 350°. Coat a 1½-quart casserole dish with nonstick cooking spray.

② Mix 1 can (10¾ oz.) cream of mushroom soup, ½ cup milk, 1 tsp. soy sauce and a pinch black pepper. Stir in 2 packages (9 oz. each) frozen green beans, cooked and drained; and 1 can (2.8 oz.) French-fried onions. Bake at 350° for 20 minutes. Stir well. Top with another can (2.8 oz.) French-fried onions. Bake for 10 minutes.

PER SERVING 256 calories; 17 g fat (5 g sat.); 2 g protein; 21 g carbohydrate; 3 g fiber; 648 mg sodium; 4 mg cholesterol

→ HEALTHY
GREEN BEAN & SHIITAKE CASSEROLE

MAKES 8 servings **PREP** 15 minutes
COOK 14 minutes **BAKE** at 350° for 14 minutes

① Heat oven to 350°. Cook 2 pounds green beans in boiling water for 7 minutes or until tender. Drain and place in a greased 13 x 9-inch baking dish.

② In a large skillet, melt 2 tbsp. butter; cook 1 pound sliced shiitake mushrooms and 4 cloves chopped garlic for 5 minutes, stirring occasionally. Sprinkle on ¼ cup flour, ¾ tsp. salt, ¼ tsp. pepper and ⅛ tsp. dried thyme.

③ Gradually stir in 3 cups 2% milk and simmer 2 minutes. Pour sauce over beans; scatter 1 cup Seneca crisp onions over top. Bake at 350° for 14 minutes.

PER SERVING 211 calories; 10 g fat (3 g sat.); 7 g protein; 25 g carbohydrate; 4 g fiber; 337 mg sodium; 15 mg cholesterol

→ TEX-MEX
3-BEAN SALAD

MAKES 8 servings **PREP** 15 minutes
COOK 5 minutes

① In a small bowl, whisk together ¼ cup lime juice, 2 tbsp. rice vinegar, 2 tsp. lime zest, 1 tsp. cumin and ¼ tsp. each salt and black pepper. Slowly drizzle in ¼ cup olive oil and whisk until combined; set aside.

② Bring a large pot of lightly salted water to a boil. Add 1½ pounds green beans, trimmed and cut into 1-inch pieces, to pot and cook 5 minutes; drain and place in a large serving bowl.

③ Add 1 can (15.5 oz.) drained and rinsed black beans and 1 can (15.5 oz.) drained and rinsed kidney beans to serving bowl. Drizzle with lime dressing and stir until well coated.

PER SERVING 187 calories; 7 g fat (1 g sat.); 8 g protein; 27 g carbohydrate; 10 g fiber; 299 mg sodium; 0 mg cholesterol

→ INDULGENT
HARICOT VERTS WITH BACON & BRUSSELS SPROUTS

MAKES 8 servings **PREP** 15 minutes
COOK 20 minutes

① Bring a pot of lightly salted water to a boil. Cook 1 pound trimmed haricot verts about 5 minutes; drain and set aside.

② Cook 6 slices bacon, cut crosswise into ¼-inch slices, in a large nonstick skillet over medium-high heat for 8 minutes or until crisp. Remove to a paper towel–lined plate with a slotted spoon.

③ Melt 1 tbsp. unsalted butter in skillet. Add 1½ pounds Brussels sprouts, trimmed and cut from top to bottom into ¼-inch slices, to skillet and sprinkle with ¼ tsp. each salt and pepper. Cook, stirring, for 5 minutes or until lightly browned. Stir in haricot verts and bacon, and cook until warmed through, about 2 minutes. Sprinkle with additional salt, if desired.

PER SERVING 145 calories; 9 g fat (4 g sat.); 6 g protein; 12 g carbohydrate; 5 g fiber; 239 mg sodium; 15 mg cholesterol

→ SPEEDY
GREEN BEAN & SHALLOT SAUTÉ

MAKES 8 servings **PREP** 10 minutes
MICROWAVE 11 minutes
COOK 4 minutes, 30 seconds

① Microwave 2 bags (12 oz. each) steam-in-bag green beans separately for 4 minutes each, then let sit 2 minutes before removing from microwave; drain beans and set aside.

② Place ¼ cup pine nuts on a plate and microwave for 3 minutes, stirring halfway through, or until lightly toasted; set aside.

③ Heat 1 tbsp. canola oil in a large nonstick skillet over medium-high heat and cook 2 garlic cloves, minced, 30 seconds. Add 3 shallots, thinly sliced, to pan and cook 2 minutes. Stir in green beans, ¼ tsp. each salt and black pepper, and cook 2 minutes or until heated through.

④ Remove from heat and stir in ¼ cup reduced-fat red wine vinaigrette; sprinkle with pine nuts and serve immediately.

PER SERVING 382 calories; 7 g fat (1 g sat.); 22 g protein; 62 g carbohydrate; 14 g fiber; 166 mg sodium; 0 mg cholesterol

Some version of this tried-and-true casserole appears on thousands of tables across America every Thanksgiving. If yours is one of them, consider putting a new spin on this beloved dish.

WHIPPED POTATO
CASSEROLE

→ CLASSIC
WHIPPED POTATO CASSEROLE

MAKES 12 servings **PREP** 15 minutes
COOK 20 minutes **BAKE** at 350° for 45 minutes

① Heat oven to 350°. Coat a 2-quart baking dish with nonstick cooking spray.

② Place 5 pounds peeled, quartered all-purpose potatoes in a large pot. Add enough water to cover. Lightly salt and bring to a boil. Lower heat; simmer for 15 to 20 minutes or until fork-tender. Drain.

③ In large bowl, mash potatoes with hand mixer. Add ½ cup softened butter, 1¼ cups half-and-half, 1 tub (8 oz.) cream cheese with chives, 1 tsp. garlic salt and ¼ tsp. nutmeg. Beat potatoes on medium-high speed until very smooth. Spoon into prepared dish.

④ Bake at 350° for 30 minutes. Sprinkle with 1 cup sliced almonds; bake 15 minutes more, until lightly browned. Let stand 15 minutes before serving.

PER SERVING 364 calories; 21 g fat (11 g sat.); 8 g protein; 37 g carbohydrate; 4 g fiber; 232 mg sodium; 54 mg cholesterol

→ HEALTHY
SCALLOPED POTATOES

MAKES 6 servings **PREP** 15 minutes
COOK 2 minutes **BAKE** at 375° for 50 minutes

① Heat 1 tbsp. olive oil in a large saucepan over medium heat. Whisk in 2 tbsp. flour; cook 1 minute.

② Whisk in 1 cup fat-free half-and-half, ¾ cup 2% milk, 3 cloves chopped garlic, ¾ tsp. salt and ⅛ tsp. dried thyme. Add 1½ pounds thinly sliced baking potatoes and bring to simmer. Cook 1 minute.

③ Spoon into greased 8 x 8 x 2-inch baking dish and cover with foil. Bake at 375° for 40 minutes. Uncover and bake 10 minutes. Cool slightly. Garnish with chopped parsley.

PER SERVING 158 calories; 3 fat (1 g sat.); 5 g protein; 28 g carbohydrate; 2 g fiber; 344 mg sodium; 2 mg cholesterol

→ TEX-MEX
ROASTED POTATOES & PEPPERS

MAKES 10 servings **PREP** 10 minutes
ROAST at 400° for 35 minutes

① Heat oven to 400°. Cut 2½ pounds golden potatoes (unpeeled and scrubbed) into 1-inch pieces. Toss in a large bowl with 1 each orange, red and yellow sweet peppers, cored and cut into pieces; 2 tbsp. olive oil; 2 tsp. taco seasoning (from a 1.25-oz. packet); and 1 tsp. oregano. Spread onto large rimmed baking sheet. Roast at 400° for 35 minutes, until tender.

PER SERVING 134 calories; 3 g fat (0 g sat.); 3 g protein; 24 g carbohydrate; 2 g fiber; 38 mg sodium; 0 mg cholesterol

→ INDULGENT
POTATO GRATIN WITH WILD MUSHROOMS

MAKES 8 servings **PREP** 25 minutes
COOK 3 minutes, 30 seconds
BAKE at 350° for 1 hour

① Heat oven to 350°. Coat a 2-quart oval baking dish with nonstick cooking spray. Combine 2.5 oz. dried porcini mushrooms with 1½ cups boiling water; soak 20 minutes, then drain and chop.

② Blend ¾ cup finely grated Parmesan, ¾ cup mascarpone, 1 cup half-and-half and a pinch of nutmeg; set aside.

③ Heat 1 tbsp. butter and 1 tbsp. canola oil in a large nonstick skillet over medium-high heat. Cook 2 minced garlic cloves 30 seconds, then add mushrooms. Cook 3 minutes.

④ Carefully slice 2½ pounds all-purpose potatoes into ⅛-inch-thick slices using a mandoline or V-slicer.

⑤ Spread ¼ of the potato slices over bottom of prepared dish, overlapping as necessary, then sprinkle with ¼ tsp. salt. Sprinkle with ¼ of the mushrooms. Repeat layer, then top with half of the cheese mixture. Repeat with remaining potatoes

and mushrooms, forming 2 layers, then finish with remaining cheese mixture. Sprinkle with 2 tbsp. Gruyère cheese.

⑥ Bake at 350° for 1 hour or until top is browned and bubbly.

PER SERVING 425 calories; 29 g fat (15 g sat.); 13 g protein; 31 g carbohydrate; 3 g fiber; 234 mg sodium; 80 mg cholesterol

→ SPEEDY
BUTTERMILK-CHIVE MASHED POTATOES

MAKES 8 servings **PREP** 15 minutes
MICROWAVE 20 minutes

① Microwave 2 bags (24 oz. each) microwavable potato chunks (such as Ore-Ida Steam n' Mash) for 10 minutes each, then let sit for 2 minutes before removing from microwave. Pour potatoes into serving bowl.

② Add ½ cup buttermilk, ¼ cup whipped chive cream cheese and 3 tsp. dried chives; mash until blended.

PER SERVING 167 calories; 2 g fat (1 g sat.); 4 g protein; 31 g carbohydrate; 4 g fiber; 514 mg sodium; 6 mg cholesterol

Scalloped, whipped, mashed or all dressed up in a cheesy gratin, the humble potato is far more than an excuse to eat gravy.

Whatever form the cranberries take—in a
tangy-sweet sauce or crisp salsa, they
provide a light and refreshing counterpoint
to the richness of the rest of the meal.

→ CLASSIC
CRANBERRY SAUCE

MAKES 8 servings **PREP** 5 minutes
COOK 18 minutes

① Combine 1 bag (12 oz.) fresh or frozen cranberries, 1¾ cups sugar, ¾ cup water, 1 orange slice and 1 tsp. freshly grated orange peel in medium saucepan. Stir over high heat 3 minutes, until sugar melts and water starts to boil. Reduce heat; simmer until thickened, 15 minutes. Discard orange. Pour into serving bowl; cool completely.

PER SERVING 153 calories; 0 g fat; 0 g protein; 40 g carbohydrate; 1 g fiber; 1 mg sodium; 0 mg cholesterol

→ HEALTHY
CRANBERRY-APPLE RELISH

MAKES 8 servings **PREP** 10 minutes
COOK 10 minutes

① Combine 1 bag (12 oz.) cranberries; 1 Granny Smith apple, cored, peeled and chopped; 1 cup water; ¾ cup sugar; 3 tbsp. currants; and ⅛ tsp. ground cloves in a medium saucepan.

② Bring to a boil. Reduce heat to medium-low and simmer 10 minutes. Cool before serving.

PER SERVING 110 calories; 0 g fat; 0 g protein; 29 g carbohydrate; 3 g fiber; 1 mg sodium; 0 mg cholesterol

→ TEX-MEX
CRAN-PINEAPPLE SALSA

MAKES 12 servings **PREP** 5 minutes

① Combine 1 package (12 oz.) fresh cranberries (thawed if frozen); 2 cups fresh pineapple chunks; ½ cup sugar; ½ red onion, chopped; 1 jalapeño, seeded; 2 tbsp. lime juice; and ½ tsp. salt in food processor. Pulse until evenly chopped and serve.

PER SERVING 60 calories; 0 g fat; 0 g protein; 16 g carbohydrate; 2 g fiber; 98 mg sodium; 0 mg cholesterol

→ INDULGENT
CRANBERRY, BLOOD ORANGE & PEARL ONION RELISH

MAKES 8 servings **PREP** 15 minutes

① Peel 6 blood oranges and cut away the white pith, then cut orange segments between membranes; roughly chop and set aside.

② Place 2 bags (12 oz. each) cranberries, 1⅓ cups sugar, 2 tbsp. cider vinegar and ½ tsp. allspice in a large bowl; place half of mixture in food processor and pulse until roughly chopped. Remove to serving bowl. Repeat with remaining half of cranberry mixture, adding to mixture in serving bowl. Add 1 bag (16 oz.) frozen pearl onions, thawed to room temperature, to food processor and pulse 2 to 3 times or until very roughly chopped. Add to mixture in serving bowl and stir in chopped blood oranges.

PER SERVING 243 calories; 0 g fat; 2 g protein; 61 g carbohydrate; 7 g fiber; 4 mg sodium; 0 mg cholesterol

→ SPEEDY
QUICKIE CRANBERRY SAUCE WITH ORANGE

MAKES 8 servings **PREP** 15 minutes

① Peel 2 oranges and cut away the white pith, then cut orange segments between membranes. Squeeze juice from orange membranes into serving bowl. Roughly chop segments and add to serving bowl.

② Stir together 2 cans (14 oz. each) whole-berry cranberry sauce and ½ cup red currant jam into oranges in serving bowl.

PER SERVING 209 calories; 0 g fat; 0 g protein; 54 g carbohydrate; 2 g fiber; 22 mg sodium; 0 mg cholesterol

MENUS

→ **CLASSIC**
Turkey with Pan Gravy
Fresh Sage Stuffing
Green Bean Casserole
Whipped Potato Casserole
Cranberry Sauce

→ **HEALTHY**
Heritage Turkey
with Cran-Orange Glaze
Bulgur Stuffing
Green Bean & Shiitake Casserole
Scalloped Potatoes
Cranberry-Apple Relish

→ **TEX-MEX**
Spice-Rub Turkey
Zesty Cornbread Stuffing
3-Bean Salad
Roasted Potatoes & Peppers
Cran-Pineapple Salsa

→ **INDULGENT**
Deep-Fried Turkey
Sausage, Apple & Leek Stuffing
Haricot Verts with Bacon
& Brussels Sprouts
Potato Gratin with
Wild Mushrooms
Cranberry, Blood Orange
& Pearl Onion Relish

→ **SPEEDY**
Lemony Turkey Breast & Gravy
Carrot & Bacon Stuffing
Green Bean & Shallot Sauté
Buttermilk-Chive Mashed Potatoes
Quickie Cranberry Sauce with Orange

Full Speed Ahead

6 simple recipes to get dinner on the table fast.

**HARVEST PORK ROAST
& VEGETABLES,
PAGE 283**

MAHOGANY ROASTED CHICKEN THIGHS

MAKES 6 servings **PREP** 10 minutes **BAKE** at 450° for 40 minutes **COOK** 10 minutes

¼ **cup reduced-sodium soy sauce**
¼ **cup honey**
¼ **cup orange juice**
2 **tablespoons ketchup**
½ **teaspoon hot sauce**
6 **large skinless chicken thighs, about 2¼ pounds total**
2 **cups reduced-sodium chicken broth**
1 **tablespoon dried onion flakes**
2 **cups tricolor couscous**
1 **pound frozen shelled edamame, cooked following package directions**

① Heat oven to 450°. Coat a roasting pan with nonstick cooking spray.

② In a medium bowl, whisk soy sauce, honey, orange juice, ketchup and hot sauce. Set aside half for basting, half for serving.

③ Place chicken, skinned side up, in pan. Brush generously with soy mixture for basting. Roast at 450° for 40 minutes, brushing every 10 minutes with sauce. Remove from oven when internal temperature registers 160° on an instant-read thermometer.

④ Combine chicken broth and onion flakes in a saucepan. Bring to a simmer; stir in couscous, cover and remove from heat. Let stand 5 minutes. Fluff with a fork.

⑤ Serve the chicken with the reserved sauce, couscous and edamame.

PER SERVING 392 calories; 13 g fat (2 g sat.); 43 g protein; 29 g carbohydrate; 4 g fiber; 754 mg sodium; 166 mg cholesterol

PEPPERY CUBE STEAK

MAKES 6 servings **PREP** 10 minutes **BAKE** at 450° for 20 minutes **COOK** 4 minutes

TOMATO SALAD

2	pounds beefsteak or plum tomatoes, seeds squeezed out, chopped
6	cloves garlic, thinly sliced
1	tablespoon olive oil
1	tablespoon red wine vinegar
¼	teaspoon salt
⅛	teaspoon black pepper
3	tablespoons shredded basil

POTATOES AND STEAK

2½	pounds fingerling potatoes, larger potatoes cut in half
2	tablespoons olive oil
¼	teaspoon salt
¼	teaspoon black pepper
6	beef cube steaks, about 4 ounces each
¾	teaspoon Montreal steak seasoning

① **Tomato Salad.** In a medium bowl, combine tomatoes, garlic, olive oil, vinegar, salt, pepper and basil. Cover and refrigerate for 20 minutes.

② **Potatoes and Steak.** Heat oven to 450°. Coat a 15 x 10 x 1-inch baking pan with nonstick cooking spray. Place potatoes in the baking pan and toss with 1 tablespoon of the olive oil. Season with salt and pepper. Bake at 450° for 20 minutes, stirring once, or until fork-tender.

③ Heat remaining tablespoon olive oil in a large nonstick skillet over medium-high heat. Season both sides of steaks with Montreal steak seasoning. Sauté meat in batches, for 2 minutes, then turn and sauté for an additional 1 to 2 minutes, until medium-rare.

④ Serve steaks immediately with roasted potatoes and tomato salad.

PER SERVING 408 calories; 15 g fat (4 g sat.); 31 g protein; 40 g carbohydrate; 4 g fiber; 321 mg sodium; 48 mg cholesterol

SAVORY MEAT LOAF & MUSHROOM GRAVY

MAKES two 6-serving meals   **PREP** 30 minutes   **BAKE** at 400° for 70 minutes   **COOK** 9 minutes

MEAT LOAF

2	tablespoons canola oil
3	pounds ground turkey
2	cups chopped onion
2	cups chopped carrot
1	cup unseasoned whole-wheat bread crumbs mixed with 1 cup 1% milk
½	cup grated Parmesan cheese
¼	cup ketchup
4	eggs, lightly beaten
1	teaspoon salt
1	teaspoon poultry seasoning
1	teaspoon garlic-pepper blend (such as McCormick)

GRAVY AND SIDES

1	tablespoon canola oil
½	pound sliced mixed mushrooms
¼	cup all-purpose flour
3	cups low-sodium chicken broth
½	cup dry white wine
½	teaspoon poultry seasoning
¼	teaspoon salt
3	cups cooked mashed potatoes (optional)
3	cups cooked wide noodles (optional)

① **Meat Loaf.** Heat oven to 400°. Coat a large roasting pan with canola oil.

② In large bowl, mix turkey, onion, carrot, bread crumb mixture, Parmesan, ketchup, eggs, salt, poultry seasoning and garlic-pepper. Divide in half; form into 2 loaf shapes. Place each in prepared pan. Bake at 400° for 60 to 70 minutes or until internal temperature registers 160° on an instant-read thermometer.

③ **Gravy and Sides.** Heat oil in a large skillet over medium heat. Add mushrooms. Cook 5 minutes. Stir in flour; cook 1 minute. Gradually whisk in broth, wine, poultry seasoning and salt. Simmer 3 minutes.

④ If desired, serve 1 meat loaf with half the gravy and the mashed potatoes. Refrigerate second loaf and remaining gravy for a second meal with noodles.

PER SERVING 332 calories; 17 g fat (4 g sat.); 27 g protein; 16 g carbohydrate; 2 g fiber; 750 mg sodium; 165 mg cholesterol

SHRIMP FAJITAS

MAKES 8 fajitas **PREP** 10 minutes **COOK** 11 minutes

- **2** tablespoons canola oil
- **1½** pounds large shrimp, shelled and deveined
- **2** pounds presliced peppers and onions, about 6 cups
- **1** tablespoon preminced garlic
- **½** package (1.2 ounces) fajita seasoning mix
- **8** whole-wheat fajita-size tortillas
  Reduced-fat sour cream, salsa, refrigerated guacamole, microwavable rice and salad, for serving (optional)

① Heat 1 tablespoon oil in a large stainless steel skillet. Add shrimp and cook 3 to 4 minutes, turning once, until cooked through. Remove to a plate and reserve.

② Add remaining tablespoon oil and peppers and onions to the skillet. Cook for 5 minutes, stirring occasionally, scraping up any browned bits from bottom of pan. Add garlic after 4 minutes. Stir in ¼ cup water and seasoning mix. Cook for 2 minutes, stirring occasionally. Return shrimp to skillet and heat through.

③ Serve with warm tortillas. If desired, accompany with sour cream, salsa, guacamole, rice and salad.

PER FAJITA 263 calories; 7 g fat (2 g sat.); 19 g protein; 29 g carbohydrate; 5 g fiber; 834 mg sodium; 126 mg cholesterol

GOAT CHEESE–STUFFED CHICKEN BREASTS

MAKES 6 servings **PREP** 15 minutes
COOK 7 minutes **BAKE** at 350° for 25 minutes

- 3 ounces (about ⅓ cup) herbed goat cheese
- 7 sun-dried tomatoes packed in oil, chopped
- 6 boneless, skinless chicken breasts (5 to 6 ounces each)
- 2 cups whole milk
- 1 teaspoon garlic salt
- 6 teaspoons cornstarch
- 1 tablespoon canola oil
- 2 tablespoons snipped chives
- ¾ pound angel hair pasta, cooked following package directions
  Steamed green beans (optional)

① In a small bowl, blend goat cheese and 2 tablespoons of the chopped tomatoes. Place chicken breasts on a cutting board. Make a slit about 2 inches long and 1½ inches deep in the thickest part, forming a pocket. Fill each breast with about 1 tablespoon of the goat cheese mixture. Place chicken in a container and freeze.

② In a small freezer-safe container, combine milk, garlic salt, cornstarch and remaining 3 tablespoons chopped tomatoes. Freeze.

③ Thaw chicken and sauce in refrigerator overnight.

④ Heat oven to 350°. In a large ovenproof stainless skillet, heat oil over medium-high heat. Place chicken, skinned side down, in skillet and cook for 4 minutes. Turn chicken and transfer skillet to oven. Bake at 350° for 20 to 25 minutes or until internal temperature registers 160° on an instant-read thermometer. Remove chicken to a serving platter and keep warm.

⑤ Whisk the sauce into the skillet and cook over medium heat for 3 minutes, until thickened, scraping up any browned bits from the bottom of the pan. Stir in chives.

⑥ Serve chicken with the sauce and angel hair pasta. Accompany with green beans, if desired.

PER SERVING 497 calories; 12 g fat (5 g sat.); 46 g protein; 50 g carbohydrate; 3 g fiber; 366 mg sodium; 97 mg cholesterol

HARVEST PORK ROAST & VEGETABLES

MAKES 6 servings **PREP** 20 minutes
MARINATE overnight **ROAST** at 450° for 15 minutes, then at 400° for 55 minutes

PORK ROAST

- 2 tablespoons olive oil
- 1 tablespoon lemon juice
- 1 teaspoon lemon zest
- 1 teaspoon Dijon mustard
- 1 teaspoon chopped rosemary
- 4 cloves garlic, chopped
- ¼ teaspoon salt
- ⅛ teaspoon black pepper
- 1 boneless center-cut pork roast, about 2½ pounds
- 1 tablespoon canola oil

VEGETABLES

- 6 cups cauliflower florets (about ½ large cauliflower)
- 1 large butternut squash, peeled and cut into 1-inch pieces (about 4 cups)
- 2 sweet peppers, cored, seeded and cut into 1-inch pieces
- 1 large sweet onion, peeled and cut into 10 wedges
- 4 tablespoons olive oil
- 4 cloves garlic, smashed
  Squeeze of lemon juice
  Leaves of 1 rosemary branch
- ½ teaspoon salt
- ½ teaspoon black pepper

① **Pork.** In small bowl, blend olive oil, lemon juice, zest, mustard, rosemary, garlic, salt and pepper. Rub pork with olive oil mixture. Place in a resealable plastic bag and refrigerate overnight.

② **Vegetables.** Place cauliflower, squash, peppers and onion in a large bowl and toss with olive oil, garlic, lemon juice and rosemary. Place in a resealable plastic bag and refrigerate overnight.

③ Heat oven to 450°. Brush large roasting pan with canola oil. Add pork. Arrange vegetables on a second large greased baking pan and season with salt and pepper. Place both pans in the oven and roast at 450° for 15 minutes. Reduce heat to 400° and continue roasting for 50 to 55 minutes or until pork's internal temperature registers 160° on an instant-read thermometer.

④ Thinly slice pork, place on platter and surround with vegetables.

PER SERVING 508 calories; 26 g fat (6 g sat.); 46 g protein; 24 g carbohydrate; 7 g fiber; 446 mg sodium; 104 mg cholesterol

Comfort Zone

Delicious casseroles, baked until bubbly. Life is good.

JULIE'S NOODLE CASSEROLE, PAGE 289

SHEPHERD'S PIE,
PAGE 289

BROCCOLI, CHEDDAR
& HAM STRATA,
PAGE 289

BAKED ZITI

Instead of Parmesan, sprinkle the ziti with Pecorino Romano—its stronger flavor stands up well to the rich sausage and tangy tomatoes.

BAKED ZITI

MAKES 8 servings **PREP** 15 minutes **COOK** 25 minutes **BAKE** at 375° for 25 minutes

SAUCE

2	tablespoons olive oil
1	medium onion, chopped
3	cloves garlic, sliced
1	can (28 ounces) whole tomatoes
1	can (15 ounces) tomato sauce
2	tablespoons tomato paste
2	teaspoons sugar
¼	teaspoon salt
¼	teaspoon black pepper
1	can (14.5 ounces) basil-and-oregano diced tomatoes, drained
½	cup fresh basil leaves, chopped

ZITI AND CHEESE

1	box (16 ounces) ziti
1	bag (8 ounces) shredded part-skim mozzarella cheese
¼	cup grated Parmesan or Pecorino Romano cheese

① Heat oven to 375°. Coat a 13 x 9 x 2-inch baking dish with nonstick cooking spray.

② **Sauce.** Heat oil in a 3-quart saucepan over medium heat. Add onion and cook 4 minutes. Add garlic and cook another minute. Stir in whole tomatoes and their juice, breaking tomatoes apart with your hands or a wooden spoon. Stir in tomato sauce, tomato paste, sugar, salt and pepper. Simmer, stirring occasionally, for 20 minutes.

③ Remove pan from heat. Stir in diced tomatoes and basil.

④ **Ziti and Cheese.** Bring a large pot of lightly salted water to boiling. Add ziti; boil 10 minutes, stirring. Drain and transfer to a large bowl. Add half the sauce to bowl with ziti. Stir to coat. Pour ziti mixture into prepared dish. Top with remaining sauce and then sprinkle with the cheeses.

⑤ Bake at 375° for 20 to 25 minutes, until bubbly and lightly browned. Cool 10 minutes.

PER SERVING 379 calories; 10 g fat (4 g sat.); 18 g protein; 55 g carbohydrate; 4 g fiber; 985 mg sodium; 20 mg cholesterol

SAUSAGE VARIATION (10 SERVINGS):

① **Sauce.** Crumble 1 pound sweet Italian sausage in a 3-quart saucepan over medium heat. Cook 8 minutes, or until no longer pink. Remove from pot with a slotted spoon. Add onion to pot; cook 4 minutes. Add garlic and cook another minute. Stir in whole tomatoes and their juice, breaking tomatoes apart with a wooden spoon. Stir in tomato sauce, tomato paste, sugar, salt and pepper. Simmer, stirring occasionally, for 20 minutes.

② Remove pan from heat. Stir in sausage, diced tomatoes and basil. Continue with Step 4 of the recipe.

PER SERVING 383 calories; 14 g fat (5 g sat.); 19 g protein; 45 g carbohydrate; 3 g fiber; 1,009 mg sodium; 29 mg cholesterol

SHRIMP SCAMPI BAKE

MAKES 4 servings **PREP** 20 minutes
COOK 24 minutes **BAKE** at 375° for 20 minutes

1	cup uncooked white rice
½	teaspoon salt
1	package (9 ounces) frozen asparagus cuts, thawed
2	tablespoons unsalted butter
4	cloves garlic, chopped
½	cup dry white wine
1	tablespoon fresh lemon juice
1	teaspoon cornstarch
1	pound fresh or frozen cleaned shrimp, thawed if frozen
	Pinch of black pepper
2	tablespoons seasoned dry bread crumbs

① Heat oven to 375°. Coat four 16-ounce baking dishes (or one 2-quart dish) with nonstick cooking spray.

② In medium saucepan, combine rice, 2¼ cups water and ¼ teaspoon of the salt. Bring to a boil over high heat, then cover and reduce heat to medium-low. Cook 20 minutes. Uncover and stir in asparagus pieces. Cover and set aside.

③ Melt butter in medium saucepan over medium heat. Add garlic and cook, stirring, 2 minutes. Meanwhile, whisk wine, lemon juice and cornstarch together in a measuring cup or bowl. Add to saucepan and cook 2 minutes, until thickened and bubbly. Stir in shrimp, remaining ¼ teaspoon salt and the pepper. Remove from heat.

④ Divide rice mixture among prepared dishes. Top with shrimp mixture. Sprinkle each dish with ½ tablespoon of the bread crumbs. Spritz bread crumbs with nonstick spray. Bake at 375° for 15 to 20 minutes or until shrimp are cooked through.

PER SERVING 406 calories; 8 g fat (4 g sat.); 29 g protein; 48 g carbohydrate; 1 g fiber; 528 mg sodium; 187 mg cholesterol

REUBEN CASSEROLE

MAKES 8 servings **PREP** 20 minutes
COOK 6 minutes **BAKE** at 375° for 1 hour

2 tablespoons unsalted butter

1 medium onion, halved and sliced

1 can (14.5 ounces) sauerkraut, drained

1 teaspoon caraway seeds

1 cup dry white wine

1½ pounds all-purpose potatoes

1 package (14 ounces) light or turkey kielbasa, sliced on the diagonal

1 bag (8 ounces) shredded Swiss cheese

2 teaspoons cornstarch

① Heat oven to 375°. Coat a 10 x 10 x 2-inch baking dish with nonstick cooking spray.

② Melt butter in a medium nonstick skillet over medium heat. Add onion and cook 5 minutes. Remove from heat and transfer to a bowl with a slotted spoon. Stir sauerkraut and caraway seeds into onion and toss to mix. Return skillet to heat and add wine. Heat through, 1 minute.

③ Thinly slice potatoes with a food processor, V-slicer or mandoline. Begin layering: Spread a layer of potatoes (one-third of the slices) on the bottom of prepared dish, overlapping slightly. Top with half of the sauerkraut mixture and half of the kielbasa.

④ In a medium bowl, toss Swiss cheese with cornstarch. Pour half of the wine over the kielbasa, then top with half the cheese. Add a second layer of potatoes, and the remaining sauerkraut and kielbasa. Pour remaining wine over kielbasa, then fan remaining potatoes over kielbasa. Sprinkle with remaining cheese.

⑤ Coat a sheet of foil with nonstick spray and cover dish. Bake, covered, at 375° for 40 minutes. Uncover and bake an additional 20 minutes, or until potatoes are tender.

PER SERVING 296 calories; 15 g fat (8 g sat.); 18 g protein; 22 g carbohydrate; 4 g fiber; 838 mg sodium; 66 mg cholesterol

JULIE'S NOODLE CASSEROLE

MAKES 6 servings **PREP** 20 minutes

COOK 10 minutes **BAKE** at 350° for 30 minutes

1   bag (12 ounces) whole-wheat wide noodles
1   pound lean ground beef
1   container (15 ounces) refrigerated marinara sauce
1   container (16 ounces) 2% cottage cheese
1   package (10 ounces) frozen chopped spinach, thawed and squeezed dry
2   cups shredded cheddar cheese
1   large egg
3   scallions, chopped
¼   teaspoon salt
¼   teaspoon black pepper

① Heat oven to 350°. Coat a deep 2-quart casserole dish with nonstick cooking spray.

② Bring a large pot of salted water to boiling. Add noodles and cook 5 minutes. Drain.

③ Crumble beef into empty pasta pot. Cook over medium-high heat for 5 minutes, until no longer pink. Drain off excess fat. Remove from heat and stir in marinara sauce.

④ In large bowl, combine noodles, cottage cheese, spinach, ¾ cup of the cheddar cheese, egg, scallions, salt and pepper.

⑤ Transfer noodle mixture to prepared dish. Top with beef and sprinkle with remaining cheese. Bake at 350° for 30 minutes. Cool slightly before serving.

PER SERVING 520 calories; 18 g fat (9 g sat.); 43 g protein; 53 g carbohydrate; 10 g fiber; 954 mg sodium; 111 mg cholesterol

SHEPHERD'S PIE

MAKES 6 servings **PREP** 15 minutes

COOK 13 minutes **MICROWAVE** 10 minutes

BAKE at 350° for 15 minutes

FILLING

2   tablespoons vegetable oil
2   pounds boneless, skinless chicken thighs, cut into bite-size pieces
1   medium onion, chopped
2   ribs celery, diced
1   cup baby carrots, sliced
1   cup chicken broth
2   tablespoons all-purpose flour
¼   teaspoon salt
¼   teaspoon black pepper
2   tablespoons chopped fresh dill (or 2 teaspoons dried)
1   cup frozen peas, thawed

TOPPING

1   package (24 ounces) Ore-Ida Steam n' Mash potatoes
⅔   cup milk
2   tablespoons unsalted butter
1   tablespoon chopped fresh dill (or 1 teaspoon dried)
½   teaspoon salt

① Heat oven to 350°. **Filling.** Heat oil in a flame-proof casserole over medium-high heat. Add chicken pieces and cook, stirring, 5 minutes. Stir in onion, celery and carrots. Cook 5 minutes.

② In a small bowl or measuring cup, whisk broth, flour, salt and pepper. Pour into dish and bring to a simmer. Simmer 1 to 2 minutes, until thickened. Stir in dill and peas; cook 1 more minute.

③ **Topping.** Meanwhile, microwave potatoes for 10 minutes, as per package directions. Carefully transfer to a large bowl and add milk, butter, dill and salt. Mash until smooth. Dollop onto filling and gently spread to dish edges.

④ Transfer to oven and bake at 350° for 15 minutes, or until bubbly. Cool slightly before serving.

PER SERVING 423 calories; 18 g fat (6 g sat.); 35 g protein; 31 g carbohydrate; 5 g fiber; 915 mg sodium; 160 mg cholesterol

BROCCOLI, CHEDDAR & HAM STRATA

MAKES 8 servings **PREP** 15 minutes

COOK 8 minutes **BAKE** at 375° for 45 minutes

1   tablespoon olive oil
1   medium sweet onion, diced
1   bag (1 pound) frozen chopped broccoli, thawed
1   loaf Italian bread (14 ounces), cut into cubes
½   pound sliced low-sodium deli ham, chopped
6   large eggs
1½ cups 2% milk
2   tablespoons chopped fresh or freeze-dried chives
1   tablespoon Dijon mustard
½   teaspoon salt
¼   teaspoon black pepper
1½ cups shredded cheddar cheese

① Heat oven to 375°. Coat a 2-quart oval baking dish with nonstick spray.

② Heat oil in a large nonstick skillet over medium heat. Add onion and cook 5 minutes. Add broccoli and cook another 3 minutes.

③ Place bread cubes in a large bowl. Stir in broccoli-onion mixture and the ham.

④ In a medium bowl, whisk together the eggs, milk, chives, mustard, salt and pepper. Pour over bread mixture, stirring to mix. Transfer to prepared dish, and top evenly with cheese.

⑤ Bake at 375° for 40 to 45 minutes, or until strata registers 160° on an instant-read thermometer.

PER SERVING 365 calories; 16 g fat (7 g sat.); 23 g protein; 33 g carbohydrate; 3 g fiber; 890 mg sodium; 197 mg cholesterol

Save Room for Dessert

End your meal on a sweet note with these irresistible cakes, pies, even a spiced compote.

**SIMPLY PECAN PIE,
PAGE 293**

**WREATH SPICE CAKE
& FALL FRUIT COMPOTE,
PAGE 295**

APPLE CHERRY LATTICE

EASY PUMPKIN PIE

APPLE CHERRY LATTICE

MAKES 8 servings **PREP** 25 minutes
BAKE at 400° for 60 minutes

1. package (15 ounces) refrigerated piecrusts or 1 batch Double Piecrust, rolled out
2½ pounds Granny Smith apples, peeled, cored and cut into ¼-inch-thick slices
¾ cup dried tart cherries
⅔ cup plus 1 tablespoon sugar
⅓ cup frozen apple juice concentrate, thawed
3 tablespoons cornstarch
2 tablespoons lemon juice
¼ teaspoon cinnamon
⅛ teaspoon ground nutmeg
⅛ teaspoon salt
1 egg beaten with 1 tablespoon water

① Heat oven to 400°. Fit one piecrust into 9-inch pie plate. Set aside.

② Place second piecrust on a cutting board. Cut into 1-inch-wide strips.

③ In a large bowl, combine apples, cherries, ⅔ cup of the sugar, apple juice concentrate, cornstarch, lemon juice, cinnamon, nutmeg and salt. Pour apple filling into crust in pie plate.

④ With pastry strips, weave a lattice over top of pie. Crimp ends of strips under edge of crust.

⑤ Brush egg mixture over lattice. Sprinkle with remaining tablespoon sugar.

⑥ Bake at 400° for 50 to 60 minutes, until apples are tender. Cover edge with foil after 25 minutes if browning too quickly. Cool on wire rack.

PER SERVING 438 calories; 14 g fat (6 g sat.); 3 g protein; 77 g carbohydrate; 6 g fiber; 243 mg sodium; 23 mg cholesterol

EASY PUMPKIN PIE

MAKES 8 servings **PREP** 20 minutes
BAKE at 425° for 15 minutes, then at 350° for 45 minutes **REFRIGERATE** overnight

1 package (15 ounces) refrigerated piecrusts or 1 batch Double Piecrust, rolled out
1 can (30 ounces) pumpkin pie filling
2 large eggs
⅓ cup sweetened condensed milk
1 egg beaten with 1 tablespoon water
1 teaspoon sugar

① Heat oven to 425°. Fit one piecrust into a 9-inch pie plate. Set aside.

② Using a 1-inch star-shaped cookie cutter, cut out 50 stars from second crust; place on a baking sheet and refrigerate until ready to use.

③ In a large bowl, beat pumpkin pie filling, eggs and condensed milk until smooth. Spoon into piecrust.

④ Brush edge of pie with egg mixture. Overlap pastry stars around edge. Brush with egg mixture; sprinkle with sugar.

⑤ Bake at 425° for 15 minutes. Reduce oven to 350° and cover edge with foil. Bake for an additional 45 minutes.

⑥ Cool pie completely on wire rack. Refrigerate overnight or until chilled. Serve with Brandied Whipped Cream, if desired.

PER SERVING 416 calories; 17 g fat (7 g sat.); 6 g protein; 59 g carbohydrate; 3 g fiber; 377 mg sodium; 79 mg cholesterol

SIMPLY PECAN PIE

MAKES 12 servings **PREP** 10 minutes
BAKE at 350° for 55 minutes

1 piecrust (from a 15-ounce package of refrigerated piecrusts) or ½ batch Double Piecrust, rolled out
4 large eggs
1 cup light corn syrup
½ cup granulated sugar
½ cup packed dark-brown sugar
1 teaspoon vanilla extract
2 cups pecan halves
⅓ cup mini chocolate chips

① Heat oven to 350°. Fit piecrust into a 9-inch pie plate.

② In a large bowl, lightly beat eggs. Stir in corn syrup, granulated and dark-brown sugar and vanilla until combined. Stir in 1½ cups of the pecans and the chocolate chips. Pour into pie shell and scatter the remaining ½ cup pecans over the top.

③ Bake at 350° for 55 minutes or until knife inserted between center and rim tests clean. Cool on rack to room temperature. Serve with Brandied Whipped Cream, if desired.

PER SERVING 397 calories; 21 g fat (4 g sat.); 5 g protein; 53 g carbohydrate; 2 g fiber; 111 mg sodium; 74 mg cholesterol

BRANDIED WHIPPED CREAM

In a large bowl, beat 1 cup of heavy cream on medium-high speed until foamy. Add in 2 tablespoons sugar and beat until soft peaks form. Beat in 1 tablespoon brandy.

DOUBLE PIECRUST

MAKES two 9-inch piecrusts **PREP** 15 minutes
CHILL 1 hour

2½ cups all-purpose flour
1 teaspoon salt
½ cup (1 stick) cold unsalted butter, cut into small pieces
½ cup solid vegetable shortening, chilled
6 to 8 tablespoons cold water

① Stir flour and salt in a bowl. Cut in butter and shortening with a pastry blender until mixture resembles coarse meal. Sprinkle with cold water, 1 tablespoon at a time, tossing with fork after each addition, until pastry is just moist enough to hold together.

② Divide pastry in half; shape each half into a disk. Wrap in plastic wrap. Chill for 1 hour or up to 2 days.

KAHLUA CHEESECAKE

MAKES 16 servings **PREP** 20 minutes
BAKE at 350° for 70 minutes
REFRIGERATE overnight

CRUST

12 cinnamon honey graham
    cracker boards
1   tablespoon sugar
½   cup (1 stick) unsalted butter, melted

FILLING

2   packages (8 ounces each) cream
    cheese, softened
2   packages (8 ounces each) reduced-
    fat cream cheese, softened
1¼ cups sugar
3   tablespoons cornstarch
4   eggs
¼   cup coffee liqueur (such as Kahlua)
1   teaspoon vanilla extract

TOPPING

½   cup heavy cream
1   tablespoon sugar
    Chocolate-covered coffee beans,
    optional
1   tablespoon cocoa powder for
    dusting, optional

① Heat oven to 350°.

② **Crust.** In food processor, pulse graham crackers until fine crumbs are formed (about 3 cups). Add sugar and butter; pulse until crumbs are moist. Press into bottom and up sides of a 9-inch springform pan. Wrap foil around bottom and up side. Chill.

③ **Filling.** In a large bowl, beat cream cheese until smooth, about 1 minute. Add sugar and cornstarch; beat 2 to 3 minutes on medium-high speed until creamy. Add eggs, one at a time, beating well after each addition. Beat in Kahlua and vanilla. Pour filling into crust.

④ Place springform pan into large baking pan; place on oven rack and pour in hot water halfway up sides of springform pan (about 6 cups).

⑤ Bake at 350° for 60 to 70 minutes or until center of cheesecake is set. Remove pan from water bath. Run knife around edge of cake and remove foil. Place on wire rack and cool completely. Cover and refrigerate overnight.

⑥ Remove side of pan. **Topping.** Whip cream and sugar to stiff peaks. Garnish cheesecake with whipped cream. Scatter top with coffee beans and dust with cocoa powder, if desired.

PER SERVING 405 calories; 27 g fat (16 g sat.); 8 g protein; 31 g carbohydrate; 0 g fiber; 289 mg sodium; 128 mg cholesterol

FALL FRUIT COMPOTE

MAKES 4 cups **PREP** 15 minutes
COOK 12 minutes

2   tablespoons unsalted butter
3   McIntosh apples, cored, peeled and
    cut into bite-size chunks
3   pears, cored, peeled and cut into
    bite-size chunks
½   cup dried apricots, sliced
½   cup dried mixed fruit, thinly sliced
½   cup sugar
2   tablespoons lemon juice
½   teaspoon pumpkin pie spice
½   teaspoon vanilla extract

① In a large nonstick skillet, melt butter over medium-high heat. Add apples, pears, apricots, mixed fruit, sugar, lemon juice and pumpkin pie spice. Stir to combine. Simmer 10 to 12 minutes, stirring occasionally, until fruit is tender.

② Stir in vanilla and cool. Serve at room temperature or slightly warm with vanilla ice cream or Brandied Whipped Cream, page 293.

PER CUP 376 calories; 6 g fat (4 g sat.); 2 g protein; 84 g carbohydrate; 9 g fiber; 32 mg sodium; 15 mg cholesterol

WREATH SPICE CAKE

MAKES 16 servings **PREP** 20 minutes
BAKE at 350° for 45 minutes

3   cups all-purpose flour
1   tablespoon ground cinnamon
1   tablespoon ground ginger
2¼ teaspoons baking powder
½   teaspoon salt
½   teaspoon ground cloves
¾   cup (1½ sticks) unsalted butter,
    softened
⅔   cup granulated sugar
⅔   cup packed light-brown sugar
¼   cup molasses
2   teaspoons vanilla extract
3   large eggs
⅔   cup 2% milk
    Confectioners' sugar (optional)

① Heat oven to 350°. Coat a 10-cup wreath-shape pan with nonstick cooking spray.

② In a bowl, blend flour, cinnamon, ginger, baking powder, salt and cloves.

③ In large bowl, beat butter until smooth. Add sugars, molasses and vanilla; beat 1 minute. Beat in eggs, one at a time. On low speed, alternately beat in flour mixture and milk, ending with flour. Spoon into prepared pan.

④ Bake at 350° for 40 to 45 minutes or until toothpick inserted in center comes out clean. Cool in pan on wire rack for 25 minutes. Invert onto wire rack and cool completely. Lightly dust with confectioners' sugar, if desired.

PER SERVING 264 calories; 10 g fat (6 g sat.); 4 g protein; 40 g carbohydrate; 1 g fiber; 154 mg sodium; 63 mg cholesterol

Pass the Pudding

There's nothing better than these classic crowd-pleasers.

Whether it's custard, bread, or rice—served warm or chilled—creamy and comforting pudding is a simple but special treat.

BITTERSWEET ALMOND CHOCOLATE PUDDING

MAKES 4 servings **PREP** 5 minutes
MICROWAVE 8½ minutes
REFRIGERATE 4 hours

2   cups milk
⅓   cup sugar
2   eggs
2   tablespoons cornstarch
    Pinch of salt
3   ounces bittersweet chocolate, chopped
½   teaspoon almond extract
¼   cup sliced almonds
¼   teaspoon olive oil
½   cup frozen whipped topping, thawed

1 In a large microwave-safe bowl, combine milk, sugar, eggs, cornstarch and salt. Whisk until well blended.

2 Microwave, uncovered, for 5 minutes. Whisk until smooth.

3 In second bowl, melt chocolate in microwave for 1 minute. Stir. Microwave another 30 seconds. Stir until smooth. Whisk chocolate and almond extract into milk mixture until smooth.

4 Spoon into 4 serving dishes, cover and refrigerate for at least 4 hours.

5 Just before serving, toast almonds: Place nuts in a glass pie plate. Toss with olive oil. Microwave, uncovered, for 1 minute. Stir. Microwave an additional minute or until lightly toasted. Garnish puddings with whipped topping, then sprinkle with toasted nuts. Serve immediately.

PER SERVING 358 calories; 20 g fat (9 g sat.); 10 g protein; 40 g carbohydrate; 2 g fiber; 84 mg sodium; 118 mg cholesterol

BUTTERSCOTCH PUDDING

MAKES 6 servings **PREP** 5 minutes **COOK** 20 minutes **REFRIGERATE** at least 2 hours, 10 minutes

3   cups milk
½   cup granulated sugar
½   cup packed dark-brown sugar
3   tablespoons cornstarch
¼   teaspoon ground nutmeg
3   egg yolks
¼   teaspoon salt
2   tablespoons unsalted butter, cut into pieces
2   teaspoons vanilla extract
    Whipped cream, to garnish

1 Stir together 2½ cups of the milk and the granulated sugar in a large saucepan. Heat until just steaming. Remove from heat; set aside.

2 Meanwhile, in a medium bowl, mix together dark-brown sugar, cornstarch and nutmeg until evenly blended. Whisk in egg yolks, remaining ½ cup milk and salt. Stir a little of the hot milk mixture into the brown sugar mixture to warm egg yolks, then stir brown sugar mixture back into milk mixture in saucepan. Cook, stirring constantly with wooden spoon, over medium-low heat until thickened and it registers 160° on an instant-read thermometer, 20 minutes. Remove from heat. Add butter and vanilla; stir until smooth.

3 Pour mixture through strainer into 6 dishes. Cool 10 minutes. Cover surface directly with plastic; refrigerate at least 2 hours. Garnish with whipped cream.

PER SERVING 313 calories; 13 g fat (7 g sat.); 5 g protein; 44 g carbohydrate; 0 g fiber; 161 mg sodium; 135 mg cholesterol

COCONUT CROISSANT BREAD PUDDING

MAKES 12 servings **PREP** 20 minutes
LET STAND 30 minutes **BAKE** at 350° for
90 minutes

8	egg yolks
4	whole eggs
2½	cups milk
1	can (13½ ounces) coconut milk
1	cup sugar
1	teaspoon coconut extract
1	teaspoon vanilla extract
½	teaspoon salt
5	large croissant pastries
1	cup semisweet chocolate chips
1	cup sweetened flake coconut
1	tablespoon confectioners' sugar, for dusting, (optional)

① Whisk together egg yolks, whole eggs, milk, coconut milk, sugar, coconut extract, vanilla and salt.

② Coat a 2½-quart baking dish with cooking spray. Cut croissants in half horizontally. Place bottom halves, cut side up, in prepared dish. Sprinkle with chocolate chips and coconut. Cover with top halves of croissants, cut side down. Pour egg mixture over top. Top with baking sheet weighted down with cans so croissants get pressed into and submerged in liquid. Let stand 30 minutes.

③ Heat oven to 350°. Remove baking sheet used as weight.

④ Cover pudding loosely with foil. Place pudding pan in a larger pan on oven rack. Pour hot water into larger pan to fill to a depth of 1 inch.

⑤ Bake at 350° for 1 hour. Remove foil; bake an additional 30 minutes or until temperature registers 160° on an instant-read thermometer. Carefully remove dish to wire rack; cool slightly. Dust with confectioners' sugar before serving, if desired.

PER SERVING 398 calories; 27 g fat (15 g sat.); 10 g protein; 31 g carbohydrate; 2 g fiber; 466 mg sodium; 212 mg cholesterol

RICE PUDDING WITH RAISINS

MAKES 8 servings **PREP** 5 minutes **COOK** 45 minutes

4	cups milk
1	cup long-grain white rice (not converted)
⅔	cup sugar
¼	teaspoon salt
¾	cup golden raisins
¼	teaspoon ground allspice, plus more for dusting

① In a heavy-bottomed saucepan, mix milk, rice, sugar and salt. Bring to a simmer over high heat. Reduce heat to low; cover and simmer, stirring occasionally, 20 minutes.

② Add raisins and allspice. Continue to cook, covered, stirring occasionally, for about 25 minutes, until rice and raisins are tender.

③ Divide pudding among 8 dishes, about ½ cup each. Top with a sprinkling of allspice; serve warm.

PER SERVING 271 calories; 4 g fat (2 g sat.); 6 g protein; 53 g carbohydrate; 1 g fiber; 124 mg sodium; 12 mg cholesterol

Slow Cooker Suppers

When the weather chills your bones, nothing warms the body like soup or stew.

PORK & HOMINY STEW

MAKES 6 servings **PREP** 10 minutes
SLOW COOK 4 hours, 15 minutes on HIGH or
6 hours, 45 minutes on LOW

- 2½ pounds boneless pork shoulder,
  well-trimmed and cut into 1-inch
  chunks
- ¼ teaspoon salt
- ¼ teaspoon black pepper
- 2 green peppers, seeded and chopped
- 2 onions, chopped
- 4 garlic cloves, minced
- 2 teaspoons chili powder
- 1 teaspoon dried oregano
- 1¼ cups low-sodium chicken broth
- ⅔ cup salsa verde
- 3 tablespoons finely ground cornmeal
- 2 tablespoons chopped cilantro
- 1 can (15 ounces) white hominy,
  rinsed and drained

① Sprinkle pork with salt and pepper.
Place pork in slow cooker with peppers,
onions, garlic, chili powder, oregano and
broth. Cover; cook on HIGH for 4 hours or
LOW for 6½ hours.

② Stir together salsa, cornmeal and
cilantro. Remove cover and stir in salsa
mixture and hominy. Cook an additional
15 minutes or until thickened and warmed
through.

PER SERVING 347 calories; 11 g fat (4 g sat.); 39 g
protein; 23 g carbohydrate; 4 g fiber; 749 mg
sodium; 114 mg cholesterol

Paired with a green salad
and bread, even light
vegetable-based soups—
such as this gorgeous
butternut squash puree—
make a satisfying meal.

GINGERY BUTTERNUT SQUASH SOUP

MAKES 6 servings **PREP** 10 minutes **SLOW COOK** 3½ hours on HIGH or 5½ hours on LOW
COOK 6 minutes **BAKE** at 350° for 15 minutes

- 1 small butternut squash (about
  3 pounds), seeded, peeled and cut
  into 2-inch cubes
- 2 cloves garlic, crushed
- 1 tablespoon canola oil
- 1 large onion, chopped
- 1 tablespoon grated ginger
- 3 cups vegetable broth
- 1 teaspoon salt
- 1 teaspoon sugar
- ¼ teaspoon black pepper
- 6 slices French bread (optional)
- 6 teaspoons shredded cheddar cheese
  (optional)

① Place squash cubes and garlic in slow
cooker with ¼ cup water. Cover and cook
on HIGH for 3 hours or on LOW for 5 hours
or until squash is tender.

② Meanwhile, heat oil in a medium
nonstick skillet over medium-high heat.
Cook onion in skillet for 5 minutes or
until softened. Stir ginger into skillet and
cook 1 minute.

③ Heat oven to 350°. Remove squash
from slow cooker using a slotted spoon
and discard garlic and remaining liquid in
slow cooker. Puree half of squash in
blender or food processor with half of
onion mixture and 2 cups of the broth until
completely smooth; pour into slow cooker
and repeat with remaining squash, onion
mixture, 1 cup broth and ¾ cup water. Stir
in salt and pepper, then cover soup and
cook an additional 30 minutes or until hot.

④ While soup is heating up, if desired,
place bread slices on a baking sheet and
top each with 1 teaspoon cheese. Bake at
350° for 15 minutes or until lightly browned.
Place 1 bread slice on top of soup in each
serving bowl.

PER SERVING 143 calories; 3 g fat (0 g sat.); 3 g
protein; 31 g carbohydrate; 5 g fiber; 868 mg
sodium; 0 mg cholesterol

SAUSAGE & LENTIL SOUP

MAKES 6 servings **PREP** 10 minutes **SLOW COOK** 2 hours on HIGH or 4 hours on LOW

2 medium carrots, cut into ¼-inch pieces
1 large onion, chopped
1 celery stalk, cut into ¼-inch pieces
2 garlic cloves, minced
7 ounces turkey kielbasa, cut into ½-inch pieces
1¼ cups (from a 1-pound bag) lentils, rinsed and picked over

2 cups low-sodium beef broth
3 loosely packed cups baby spinach
½ teaspoon salt
¼ teaspoon black pepper

① Combine carrots, onion, celery, garlic, kielbasa and lentils in slow cooker bowl. Pour in beef broth and 2½ cups water.

② Cover and cook on HIGH for 2 hours or LOW for 4 hours. Stir in baby spinach, salt and pepper before serving.

PER SERVING 236 calories; 3 g fat (1 g sat.); 20 g protein; 35 g carbohydrate; 7 g fiber; 559 mg sodium; 22 mg cholesterol

BEEF STEW WITH POTATO DUMPLINGS

MAKES 6 servings **PREP** 10 minutes
SLOW COOK 5½ hours on HIGH or 7½ hours on LOW

- 1   pound chuck steak, trimmed and cut into 1-inch pieces
- 3   tablespoons flour
- ½   teaspoon salt
- ¼   teaspoon black pepper
- 3   medium carrots, cut into ¼-inch-thick coins
- 1   package (10 ounces) cremini mushrooms, cleaned and quartered
- 2   cloves garlic, minced
- 1   package (1 pound) frozen pearl onions
- 1½   cups low-sodium beef broth
- ¾   cup dry red wine
- ¾   teaspoon dried thyme
- 1   package (17.5 ounces) gnocchi

① In large bowl, toss together steak, flour and ¼ teaspoon each salt and pepper. Place steak in slow cooker with carrots, mushrooms, garlic, onions, broth, red wine and ½ teaspoon thyme. Cover and cook on HIGH for 5 hours or LOW for 7 hours.

② Remove lid and stir in remaining ¼ teaspoon each salt and dried thyme and the gnocchi. Cover and cook an additional 30 minutes or until gnocchi is tender.

PER SERVING 322 calories; 4 g fat (1 g sat.); 20 g protein; 45 g carbohydrate; 4 g fiber; 604 mg sodium; 44 mg cholesterol

TERIYAKI CHICKEN STEW

MAKES 6 servings **PREP** 10 minutes **SLOW COOK** 3 hours on HIGH or 5½ hours on LOW

- 1½   pounds boneless, skinless chicken thighs, trimmed and cut into 1-inch pieces
- 1   bag (16 ounces) frozen Asian stir-fry vegetable blend
- 2   cups halved baby carrots
- ½   cup low-sodium chicken broth
- ½   cup low-sodium teriyaki sauce
- 2   tablespoons cornstarch
- 4   cups broccoli flowerets
- 3   cups prepared white rice (optional)

① Combine chicken, vegetables, carrots, broth and 6 tablespoons of the teriyaki sauce in slow cooker. Cover; cook on HIGH for 2½ hours or on LOW for 5 hours.

② Stir together remaining 2 tablespoons teriyaki sauce with cornstarch. Stir teriyaki mixture into slow cooker along with broccoli and cook an additional 30 minutes or until sauce has thickened. Serve over white rice, if desired.

PER SERVING 244 calories; 5 g fat (1 g sat.); 28 g protein; 19 g carbohydrate; 5 g fiber; 545 mg sodium; 95 mg cholesterol

A SUPER-SIMPLE HOLIDAY MENU GIVES YOU LOTS OF EXTRA TIME TO BAKE A BEVY OF GOODIES, INCLUDING GINGERBREAD CAKES, PEPPERMINT ICE CREAM CAKE, A CLASSIC BÛCHE DE NOËL AND MORE.

PEPPERMINT ICE CREAM CAKE, PAGE 309

DECEMBER

311

315

316

Sugar and Spice

...and everything nice to make your holiday extra sweet.

**GINGERBREAD CAKES,
PAGE 309**

**CHOCOLATE COCONUT
CAKE, PAGE 311**

BÛCHE DE NOËL

MAKES 12 servings **PREP** 15 minutes **BAKE** at 375° for 15 minutes

CAKE

½ cup all-purpose flour
⅛ teaspoon ground nutmeg
Pinch of salt
6 egg whites
¼ teaspoon cream of tartar
¼ cup plus ⅓ cup granulated sugar
4 egg yolks
½ teaspoon almond extract
Confectioners' sugar

FILLING AND FROSTING

1 cup milk
1 cup heavy cream
1 box (1 ounce) sugar-free white chocolate-flavored instant pudding mix
Cocoa powder, for dusting (optional)

① Heat oven to 375°. Coat a 15 x 10 x 1-inch baking pan with nonstick spray. Line with waxed paper. Coat paper.

② **Cake.** Sift flour, nutmeg and salt.

③ Beat egg whites and cream of tartar in large bowl until frothy. Gradually beat in ¼ cup granulated sugar; beat until stiff peaks form. Set aside.

④ With mixer on high, beat yolks in second bowl with ⅓ cup sugar until thick and lemon-colored, 5 minutes. Beat in extract. Fold flour mixture into yolks. Fold yolk mixture into whites. Spread evenly into pan.

⑤ Bake at 375° for 14 to 15 minutes, until center springs back when gently pressed. Sift confectioners' sugar over kitchen towel. Invert cake onto towel; remove pan and paper. Starting from long side, roll cake up inside towel. Cool, seam side down, on wire rack.

⑥ Prepare **Filling and Frosting.** Combine milk, heavy cream and instant pudding mix. Beat on high speed for 2 minutes, until thickened.

⑥ Unroll cake. Spread with half of the frosting. Reroll cake without towel. Cut ends off cake, using parallel diagonal cuts. Reserve ends to use as "knots." Place cake, seam side down, on serving plate. Place "knot" on each side of log. Spread remaining frosting over log and "knots," leaving all ends exposed. Dust with a little cocoa powder so log resembles a birch tree, if desired.

PER SERVING 179 calories; 11 g fat (5 g sat.); 4 g protein; 16 g carbohydrate; 0 g fiber; 133 mg sodium; 95 mg cholesterol

GINGERBREAD CAKES

MAKES 6 mini cakes **PREP** 20 minutes
BAKE at 350° for 25 minutes

CAKE

¼ cup molasses
½ cup boiling water
¾ teaspoon baking soda
1½ cups all-purpose flour
1 teaspoon baking powder
1 teaspoon ground ginger
1 teaspoon cinnamon
¼ teaspoon ground cloves
¼ teaspoon salt
6 tablespoons (¾ stick) unsalted butter, softened
⅔ cup sugar
2 eggs

ICING

2 cups confectioners' sugar

① Heat oven to 350°. Coat indents of a cakelet pan (see Note) or a jumbo muffin pan with nonstick cooking spray.

② **Cake.** Blend molasses, water and baking soda in small bowl; this will bubble. Mix flour, baking powder, ginger, cinnamon, cloves and salt in another bowl.

③ Beat butter and sugar in large bowl, 2 minutes. Beat in eggs. Stir in flour mixture and molasses mixture, beginning and ending with flour. Pour into prepared pan.

④ Bake at 350° for 25 minutes. Cool in pan on wire rack 10 minutes. Invert cakes from pan to rack.

⑤ Trim cakes level. Make **Icing.** Blend confectioners' sugar and 3 tablespoons water. Pipe outlines of bows; fill in with icing.

PER CAKE 521 calories; 13 g fat (8 g sat.); 5 g protein; 96 g carbohydrate; 1 g fiber; 354 mg sodium; 101 mg cholesterol

PEPPERMINT ICE CREAM CAKE

MAKES 16 servings **PREP** 15 minutes **FREEZE** 4 hours and overnight
MICROWAVE 2 minutes **LET STAND** 5 minutes

1 frozen pound cake (16 ounces), thawed
¾ cup starlight mints, plus a few more to garnish (optional)
12 mint chocolate cookies, plus more to garnish (optional)
1½ quarts (6 cups) vanilla ice cream
1 teaspoon mint extract
1 cup heavy cream
8 squares (1 ounce each) semisweet chocolate, chopped

① Line a 9 x 9 x 2-inch baking pan with nonstick foil. Trim browned edges from pound cake. Balance cake on one long side, and slice loaf lengthwise into 4 equal pieces (each about 9 x 3½ x ½ inches).

② Unwrap mints. Place in food processor. Pulse to crush. Transfer crushed candies to a large bowl, chopping pieces that seem too large. Place cookies in food processor and pulse to make into coarse crumbs.

③ Place 2 cake slices in bottom of foil-lined pan, trimming length if needed. Add ice cream to mints in bowl. Working quickly, blend ice cream, crushed mints and mint extract until smooth. Spread half of the ice cream into pan, spreading all the way to pan edges and completely covering cake. Top with remaining 2 cake slices, and then remaining ice cream, spreading smooth. Sprinkle crushed cookies over ice cream, and gently press to adhere. Cover with a sheet of foil and freeze for 2 hours.

④ Remove cake from freezer and use foil to lift from pan to a cutting board. Working quickly, slice cake in half. Use a spatula to stack one half on top of second half. Use foil to transfer back to pan. Re-cover with foil and freeze overnight.

⑤ Microwave heavy cream for 1 to 2 minutes or until it just begins to bubble. Pour over chopped chocolate in small bowl. Let stand 5 minutes. Whisk until smooth.

⑥ Remove cake from freezer. Remove foil and invert cake onto a small cookie sheet lined with nonstick foil. Trim off any bumpy sides with a sharp knife. Pour chocolate mixture over cake in batches, using a large spatula to spread down the sides. Top with extra chopped cookies and candies, if desired. Return to freezer until serving (at least 2 hours). Transfer to serving platter before slicing.

PER SERVING 391 calories; 23 g fat (13 g sat.); 4 g protein; 44 g carbohydrate; 2 g fiber; 166 mg sodium; 74 mg cholesterol

HOT CHOCOLATE CUPCAKES

MAKES 12 cupcakes **PREP** 20 minutes **BAKE** at 350° for 25 minutes

CUPCAKES

1	cup all-purpose flour
¼	cup unsweetened cocoa powder
½	teaspoon baking soda
¼	teaspoon salt
6	tablespoons unsalted butter, softened
½	cup granulated sugar
2	large eggs
1	teaspoon vanilla extract
½	cup milk

TOPPING

2	cups confectioners' sugar
¼	cup solid vegetable shortening
2	tablespoons plus 2 teaspoons milk or water
1¼	cups mini marshmallows
3	candy canes

① Heat oven to 350°. Line indents of a standard-size 12-cup muffin pan with cupcake liners.

② **Cupcakes.** In medium-size bowl, combine flour, cocoa powder, baking soda and salt.

③ In large bowl, with mixer on medium-high speed, beat butter and sugar until smooth and creamy, 2 minutes. Beat in eggs and vanilla until fluffy, 1 minute. On low speed, beat in flour mixture alternately with milk, beginning and ending with flour mixture. Fill each cupcake liner two-thirds full (about 3 tablespoons of batter per liner).

④ Bake at 350° for 25 minutes or until toothpick inserted in centers comes out clean. Remove cupcakes from pan to wire rack; let cool.

⑤ **Topping.** In medium-size bowl, with mixer on low speed, beat confectioners' sugar, shortening and milk or water until smooth. Spread over cupcakes, about 2 tablespoons for each. Top each cupcake with 8 or 9 mini marshmallows. With a serrated knife, cut wrapped candy canes into 2-inch pieces. Unwrap and tuck a piece into each cupcake.

PER CUPCAKE 291 calories; 11 g fat (5 g sat.); 3 g protein; 46 g carbohydrate; 1 g fiber; 124 mg sodium; 52 mg cholesterol

CHOCOLATE PEANUT BUTTER BITES

MAKES 15 mini cakes **PREP** 20 minutes
MICROWAVE 1½ minutes **BAKE** at 350° for
15 minutes **LET STAND** 5 minutes

CAKES

2	squares (1 ounce each) semisweet chocolate, chopped
⅔	cup all-purpose flour
½	teaspoon baking powder Pinch of salt
3	tablespoons unsalted butter, softened
¼	cup sugar
1	large egg
2	tablespoons milk

FILLING

3	tablespoons heavy cream
2	tablespoons creamy peanut butter
1	teaspoon sugar

TOPPING

¼	cup heavy cream
2	squares (1 ounce each) semisweet chocolate, chopped
2	tablespoons peanuts, finely chopped

① Heat oven to 350°. Coat a 15-indent mini cake pan or 15 indents in two mini muffin pans with nonstick cooking spray.

② **Cakes.** Microwave chocolate in glass bowl for 30 seconds. Stir. Microwave another 30 seconds. Stir until smooth. Set aside.

③ In small bowl, whisk flour, baking powder and salt. In medium bowl, beat butter until smooth. Beat in sugar until

blended, then beat in egg. Beat in slightly cooled melted chocolate. On low speed, beat in flour mixture and then milk. Transfer batter to a resealable plastic bag. Snip off corner and pipe batter into prepared pan(s). Bake at 350° for 14 to 15 minutes.

④ Remove cakes from pan(s) directly to rack to cool. Trim rounded tops level; return to pan. Make **Filling.** Beat heavy cream, peanut butter and sugar in a small bowl until smooth. Transfer to a disposable plastic pastry bag. Snip off point about ½ inch from tip. Poke a hole in cakes with a chopstick. Insert pastry bag into holes and gently squeeze to fill.

⑤ Invert cakes onto a serving platter. Prepare **Topping.** Heat cream in microwave for 30 seconds or until just bubbly. Pour over chocolate in small bowl and let stand 5 minutes. Stir until smooth. Spoon about 2 teaspoons chocolate mixture over each cake, allowing topping to drip over sides. Sprinkle with chopped nuts. Refrigerate until serving.

PER MINI CAKE 141 calories; 9 g fat (5 g sat.); 2 g protein; 13 g carbohydrate; 1 g fiber; 32 mg sodium; 30 mg cholesterol

CHOCOLATE COCONUT CAKE

MAKES 16 servings **PREP** 15 minutes **BAKE** at 350° for 30 minutes **REFRIGERATE** 1 hour

CAKE

2	cups all-purpose flour
½	cup unsweetened cocoa powder
1	teaspoon baking soda
½	teaspoon salt
1½	sticks unsalted butter, softened
1½	cups packed light-brown sugar
2	eggs
1	teaspoon vanilla extract
1	cup low-fat buttermilk

FROSTING

1	box (16 ounces) confectioners' sugar
¼	cup boiling water
1½	sticks unsalted butter, cut up
4	ounces reduced-fat cream cheese, cut into pieces
¼	teaspoon coconut extract
3	cups sweetened flake coconut Raspberries and mint to garnish (optional)

① Heat oven to 350°. Coat two 9-inch round cake pans with nonstick spray.

② **Cake.** In bowl, whisk flour, cocoa, baking soda and salt. In large bowl, beat butter until smooth. Add brown sugar; beat until blended. Beat in eggs, one at a time, and vanilla. On low, alternately beat in flour mixture and buttermilk, beginning and ending with flour. Spread into prepared pans.

③ Bake at 350° for 30 minutes or until toothpick inserted in centers comes out clean. Cool in pans on wire rack for 10 minutes. Invert cakes directly onto racks; cool completely.

④ While cakes cool, make **Frosting.** Place confectioners' sugar in a large bowl. Beat in boiling water. Add butter and cream cheese, beating well on medium-high speed after adding each piece. Beat in extract. Refrigerate until firmer consistency, 30 minutes to 1 hour.

⑤ Place one cake layer on pedestal. Spread top with 1 cup frosting and ½ cup coconut. Add second layer. Spread frosting on top and side of cake. Press remaining 2½ cups coconut into frosting. Garnish with raspberries and mint, if desired.

PER SERVING 499 calories; 24 g fat (16 g sat.); 5 g protein; 70 g carbohydrate; 3 g fiber; 257 mg sodium; 77 mg cholesterol

Help Yourself!

This do-it-ahead holiday spread lets you kick back and celebrate.

PORK & CHERRY-ANCHO SAUCE

MAKES 12 servings **PREP** 20 minutes **ROAST** at 400° for 65 minutes **COOK** 3½ minutes **LET STAND** 15 minutes

2   tablespoons olive oil
1   tablespoon grainy mustard
3   large cloves garlic, finely chopped
     Juice and zest of 1 lime
1   center-cut pork roast, about
     4 pounds
¼   teaspoon salt
¼   teaspoon black pepper
½   cup chopped red onion
1½   teaspoons ancho chile powder
1   cup cherry preserves
1   tablespoon rice vinegar
1   tablespoon chopped mint, plus
     more mint leaves to garnish

① Heat oven to 400°. Coat bottom of roasting pan with nonstick cooking spray.

② In a small bowl, stir together 1 tablespoon of the olive oil, mustard, garlic, lime juice and zest. Place pork roast in prepared roasting pan and rub mustard mixture over top and sides. Season with salt and pepper. Roast at 400° for 60 to 65 minutes or until internal temperature registers 150° on an instant-read thermometer.

③ In a small nonstick skillet, heat remaining tablespoon olive oil over medium heat. Add onion and cook 3 minutes; stir in chile powder and cook 30 seconds. Add preserves

and simmer until melted, stirring occasionally. Add vinegar and remove from heat. Stir in mint. Set aside.

④ Remove pork from oven; let stand 15 minutes before thinly slicing.

⑤ Serve sliced pork with cherry sauce at room temperature. Garnish with additional mint.

PER SERVING 307 calories; 10 g fat (3 g sat.); 33 g protein; 19 g carbohydrate; 0 g fiber; 150 mg sodium; 83 mg cholesterol

SNAP PEA SALAD

MAKES 12 servings **PREP** 15 minutes
COOK 4 minutes

¼   cup white balsamic vinegar

2   teaspoons Dijon mustard

⅛   teaspoon salt

⅛   teaspoon black pepper

¾   cup extra-virgin olive oil

2   teaspoons chopped fresh oregano

1½   pounds sugar snap peas, strings removed

2   cups grape tomatoes, halved

8   ounces bocconcini (small mozzarella nuggets), drained

1   cup slivered baby carrots

½   cup pitted kalamata olives, coarsely chopped

⅓   cup slivered red onion

① In a small bowl, whisk together vinegar, mustard, salt and pepper. Drizzle in olive oil, whisking constantly. Stir in oregano. Cover and set aside.

① Bring a large pot of lightly salted water to a boil over high heat. Add snap peas and simmer 4 minutes, until crisp-tender. Drain and rinse under cold water.

① Place snap peas in a large bowl. Add tomatoes, bocconcini, carrots, olives and red onion. Toss with ⅓ cup of the dressing. Serve additional dressing on the side or reserve for Red Rice & Lentils, page 317.

PER SERVING 189 calories; 14 g fat (4 g sat.); 6 g protein; 8 g carbohydrate; 2 g fiber; 310 mg sodium; 15 mg cholesterol

So much holiday food is rich and indulgent—and that has its place—but this feast offers a nice change of pace. Fresh and light, it features lean meat, lots of crisp and fresh vegetables, and hearty grains and legumes.

SHRIMP WITH TWO SAUCES

MAKES 12 servings **PREP** 15 minutes **REFRIGERATE** at least 1 hour

CREAMY MANGO SAUCE

½   cup prepared mango chutney

1   cup plain Greek yogurt

2   tablespoons lime juice

2   tablespoons chopped cilantro

HORSERADISH SAUCE

¾   cup light mayonnaise

¼   cup ketchup

1   tablespoon prepared horseradish
Snipped chives (optional)

2   pounds cooked cold shrimp
Lemon wedges, to garnish

① **Creamy Mango Sauce.** Place chutney in a small bowl; chop any large pieces. Add yogurt, lime juice and cilantro. Cover and refrigerate at least 1 hour. Makes 1½ cups.

② **Horseradish Sauce.** In a small bowl, whisk together mayonnaise, ketchup, horseradish and chives, if desired. Cover and refrigerate at least 1 hour. Makes 1 cup.

③ Spread half the shrimp on a platter with 2 sauces separated into 2 bowls. Garnish with lemon; refresh shrimp as needed.

PER SERVING 152 calories; 7 g fat (1 g sat.); 14 g protein; 8 g carbohydrate; 0 g fiber; 425 mg sodium; 118 mg cholesterol

POPPY-SESAME PARTY LOAVES

MAKES 4 small loaves, 24 servings
PREP 20 minutes **RISE** 2½ hours
BAKE at 350° for 30 to 35 minutes

¼	cup warm water (105° to 115°)
1	package active dry yeast
3	teaspoons sugar
3	cups all-purpose flour
2	cups semolina flour
2	teaspoons salt
1½	cups warm water (105° to 115°)
1	egg white, lightly beaten
2	teaspoons poppy seeds
2	teaspoons sesame seeds

① Place ¼ cup of the warm water in a small measuring cup. Stir in the yeast and sugar. Allow to stand 5 minutes, until foamy.

② In a large bowl, whisk together both flours and salt. Make a well in the center and stir in yeast mixture and remaining 1½ cups water. Stir until dough forms. Turn out onto lightly floured work surface and knead dough until smooth and elastic, 6 to 8 minutes. Form into a ball.

③ Place the dough in a greased bowl; turn to coat evenly. Cover with plastic wrap and a clean towel. Let dough rise in a warm place 1¼ to 1½ hours until almost doubled. Punch dough down; divide into 4 equal parts.

④ Grease four 3 x 5½-inch mini loaf pans. Roll 1 portion dough into a 6-inch square. Roll up jelly-roll style and place into a loaf pan seam side down. Repeat with remaining dough and pans. Brush tops of loaves with egg white and sprinkle with the seeds. Cover and allow to rise 45 to 60 minutes or until almost doubled.

⑤ Heat oven to 350°. Bake loaves at 350° for 30 to 35 minutes, until lightly browned and the bread sounds hollow when tapped. Remove from pans to wire rack and allow to cool completely.

PER SERVING 113 calories; 0 g fat (0 g sat.); 4 g protein; 23 g carbohydrate; 1 g fiber; 197 mg sodium; 0 mg cholesterol

RED RICE & LENTILS

MAKES 12 servings **PREP** 10 minutes
COOK 15 minutes

- 3½ **cups reduced-sodium chicken broth**
- 2 **cups red rice and lentil blend (such as Rice Select)**
- 1 **cup (4 ounces) chopped mixed dried fruit**
- ½ **cup toasted hazelnuts, chopped**

① Place broth and rice in a medium-size saucepan and bring to a boil over high heat. Cover and simmer on low 10 minutes. Stir in fruit and cook another 5 minutes or until rice is tender.

② Place rice on a platter; sprinkle with hazelnuts. Serve with extra dressing from Snap Pea Salad, page 315, if desired.

PER SERVING 186 calories; 4 g fat (0 g sat.); 4 g protein; 34 g carbohydrate; 3 g fiber; 155 mg sodium; 0 mg cholesterol

SAY CHEESE

Complement our party-perfect selections with figs, nuts, honey, crackers or our Poppy-Sesame Party Loaves.

Cabot Private Stock Cheddar Extra-sharp, smooth, clean-flavored cheddar. Aged 16 months.

Moody Blue (Emmi-Roth Kase) Creamy blue from Wisconsin. Subtle smoky undertones, reminiscent of roasted nuts and coffee.

Garcia Baquero's Gran Maestre Manchego Hard-pressed sheep's milk cheese from La Mancha region of Spain. Distinctive piquant-nutty flavor with just a hint of salt.

Purple Haze (Cypress Grove Chévre) Award-winning goat cheese from California. Sweetness of lavender and fennel are good counterpoints to the natural acidity.

Jarlsberg Semisoft cow's milk cheese that has a mild, nutty taste and creamy texture.

Woolwich Dairy's Triple Cream Goat Brie Luscious and buttery with a delicate earthy flavor (think mushrooms).

Index

C

Pinch Substitutions

It can happen to the best of us: Halfway through a recipe,
you find you're completely out of a key ingredient. Here's what to do:

Recipe Calls For:	You May Substitute:
1 square unsweetened chocolate	3 tbsp. unsweetened cocoa powder + 1 tbsp. butter/margarine
1 cup cake flour	1 cup less 2 tbsp. all-purpose flour
2 tbsp. flour (for thickening)	1 tbsp. cornstarch
1 tsp. baking powder	¼ tsp. baking soda + ½ tsp. cream of tartar + ¼ tsp. cornstarch
1 cup corn syrup	1 cup sugar + ¼ cup additional liquid used in recipe
1 cup milk	½ cup evaporated milk + ½ cup water
1 cup buttermilk or sour milk	1 tbsp. vinegar or lemon juice + enough milk to make 1 cup
1 cup sour cream (for baking)	1 cup plain yogurt
1 cup firmly packed brown sugar	1 cup sugar + 2 tbsp. molasses
1 tsp. lemon juice	¼ tsp. vinegar (not balsamic)
¼ cup chopped onion	1 tbsp. instant minced
1 clove garlic	¼ tsp. garlic powder
2 cups tomato sauce	¾ cup tomato paste + 1 cup water
1 tbsp. prepared mustard	1 tsp. dry mustard + 1 tbsp. water

How to Know What You Need

Making a shopping list based on a recipe can be tricky if you don't know
how many tomatoes yields 3 cups chopped. Our handy translations:

When the Recipe Calls For:	You Need:
4 cups shredded cabbage	1 small cabbage
1 cup grated raw carrot	1 large carrot
2½ cups sliced carrots	1 pound raw carrots
4 cups cooked cut fresh green beans	1 pound beans
1 cup chopped onion	1 large onion
4 cups sliced raw potatoes	4 medium-size potatoes
1 cup chopped sweet pepper	1 large pepper
1 cup chopped tomato	1 large tomato
2 cups canned tomatoes	16 oz. can
4 cups sliced apples	4 medium-size apples
1 cup mashed banana	3 medium-size bananas
1 tsp. grated lemon rind	1 medium-size lemon
2 tbsp. lemon juice	1 medium-size lemon
4 tsp. grated orange rind	1 medium-size orange
1 cup orange juice	3 medium-size oranges
4 cups sliced peaches	8 medium-size peaches
2 cups sliced strawberries	1 pint
1 cup soft bread crumbs	2 slices fresh bread
1 cup bread cubes	2 slices fresh bread
2 cups shredded Swiss or cheddar cheese	8 oz. cheese
1 cup egg whites	6 or 7 large eggs
1 egg white	2 tsp. egg white powder + 2 tbsp. water
4 cups chopped walnuts or pecans	1 pound shelled